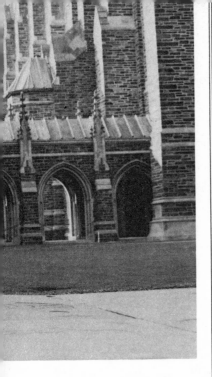

THE

ACADEMIC'S

HANDBOOK

Edited by

A. LEIGH DENEEF,

CRAUFURD D. GOODWIN,

ELLEN STERN MCCRATE

© 1988 Duke University Press
All rights reserved
Printed in the United States of America
on acid-free paper ∞
Photographs by Joan Milligan
Library of Congress Cataloging in Publication Data
appear on the last printed page of this book

Contents

Preface

The impetus for the present volume of essays grew out of three incidents that occurred during one week in March 1984. The first involved an article submitted to a journal. Just before going to press with the spring issue, it was discovered that the manuscript in question had already been published. The authors, when contacted, responded that they had no idea such a republication was improper professionally and that they were merely trying to reach a wider audience.

Later that week the chancellor happened to be speaking at a meeting of one of our departments. At the end of his talk one young assistant professor rose to say, "I have no idea what a chancellor is. Can you tell me what you do and what your position is in the administrative structure of this university?" The chancellor responded by taking out his diary and describing his activities to a rapt audience!

Finally, still in the same week, one of our teaching assistants complained about how his training for the classroom had been focused exclusively on the subject matter of his discipline, with no attention to the more general dynamics of the kinds of relations one might establish, or have to establish, with a class; the different ways of testing and evaluating; or ways of stimulating or even curtailing discussion. He was professionally depressed by his unpreparedness.

The cumulative effect of these and similar incidents raised for us a significant question: has the American academy of graduate education failed, in the 1980s, to arrange for the acculturation of its new entrants? Maybe it has never performed this task very well. The implicit assumption on which many academics have always operated is that the budding professional will pick up the lore of the tribe, its unwritten codes and rules of behavior and academic etiquette, at the knees of the old crones. Could it be, however, that today's crones either don't themselves know that lore or don't know how to impart it to those they are ostensibly training to replace them? Or is it that the young don't want to listen in the old and still venerable ways?

Reflection on these questions and on the broader issue of academic acculturation led us to propose a colloquium series for graduate students at Duke. We decided to select a group of about twenty-five students who were in the final stages of completing their dissertations and about to enter the academic job market and to invite a number of prominent scholars to prepare papers for this group. Our original plan called for three kinds of presentations: factual descriptions of the academic profession that could initiate the new academic into such mysteries as university governance; consciousness-raising papers on such issues as plagiarism and conflicts of interest; and how-to-do-it papers on getting research funding or preparing a manuscript for publication. We asked each scholar not only to prepare an essay to be circulated among our group of students, but also to meet with those students in order to pursue in active discussion the topics raised in the essay.

Our initial plan proved considerably more exciting than we had imagined. With the generous support of a grant from the Andrew W. Mellon Foundation, we were able to conduct a two-year colloquium series. We discovered very quickly that our own colleagues were extremely eager to try to impart their own views of the modern academy to prospective new members and that our students were equally eager to learn as much as they could about the profession they were about to enter. Discussions, as a consequence, were lively, challenging, and informative; and the authors of the original papers welcomed the opportunity to revise their initial thoughts on the basis of these discussions so as to reach a wider audience.

The present volume, then, represents the collective effort of professors and students coming together over some of the essential issues of modern academic life. Its intent is to provide the budding academic with a fuller and more realistic sense of the profession he or she is about to enter and thus to help in the general task of academic acculturation. We are more convinced than ever that traditional graduate programs have not adequately assumed this task or this responsibility, but we are also certain that it is a serious and necessary one. Our own students need to know there is considerably more to being a successful academic than becoming a successful chemist or mathematician or literary critic. Individual disciplinary subject matters and research methods aside, those of us who claim to be or hope to become academics share a common ground and operate under a common order. The essays that follow attempt to define that commonality and thereby to assist in the broader acculturation of those who would join it.

As editors of the present volume we have probably been the least essential of the colloquium participants. We would like, therefore, to register formally our gratitude to the Andrew W. Mellon Foundation, and especially to John Sawyer and James Morris, for supporting our efforts, and to each of our student and faculty participants, without whom this collection would not have been possible.

Presenters

Robert Gleckner, Professor of English and Director of Graduate Studies, Duke University

Stanley Hauerwas, Professor of Theological Ethics, Duke University

Frank Lentricchia, Professor of English and Literature, Duke University

Emily Toth, Professor of English and American Studies, Pennsylvania State University

Nellie McKay, Professor of Afro-American Studies, University of Wisconsin

Bernice Sandler, Executive Director, Project on the Status and Education of Women, Association of American Colleges

Henry Wilbur, Professor of Zoology, Duke University

Sudhir Shetty, Assistant Professor of Public Policy Studies and Economics, Duke University

Matthew W. Finkin, Professor of Law, University of Illinois

Craufurd Goodwin, James B. Duke Professor of Economics, Duke University

Ellen McCrate, Assistant to the Dean of Arts and Sciences, Northwestern University

A. Leigh DeNeef, Professor of English; Associate Dean of the Graduate School, Duke University

Norman Christensen, Associate Professor of Botany and Forestry, Duke University

Anne Firor Scott, William K. Boyd Professor of History, Duke University

Elizabeth Studley Nathans, Assistant Dean of Trinity College, Duke University

Christopher Kennedy, Director of Academic Support, Duke University

Ronald Butters, Associate Professor of English, Duke University

Thomas Greene, Professor of Education and Philosophy, Syracuse University

Louise W. Knight, Director of Foundation and Corporate Relations, Wheaton College

Fred Crossland, Program Officer for Higher Education and Research (retired),

Ford Foundation
Boyd Strain, Professor of Botany, Duke University
Louis Budd, James B. Duke Professor of English, Duke University
Richard Rowson, Director, Duke University Press
Joel Colton, Professor of History, Duke University
A. Kenneth Pye, President, Southern Methodist University

Discussants

Jeffrey Biddle, Department of Economics
Lawrence Bohs, Department of Biomedical Engineering
John Carr, Department of History
Kimberly Flint, Department of Classical Studies
Robert Frank, Department of Biomedical Engineering
Douglas Gilmour, Department of Philosophy
Dan Harkins, Department of Political Science
Matt Hearn, Department of Literature
Susan Hirsch, Department of Anthropology
David Hoaas, Department of Economics
Sheila Hobbs, Department of Chemistry
Stephen Houseworth, Department of Psychology
Greg Jones, Department of Civil and Environmental Engineering
Greg Jones, Department of Religion
Kevin Keller, Fuqua School of Business
Raymond Knapp, Department of Music
Doug Lanier, Department of English
Harold Layton, Department of Mathematics
Kate Loudon, Department of Zoology
Elizabeth Lyons, Department of Botany/Genetics
David Mutchler, Department of Computer Science
David Newman, Department of Forestry
Bruce Pittman, Department of Mathematics
Robert Eric Ruiz, Department of Anthropology
Beth Rushing, Department of Sociology
Cliff Sachs, Department of Pathology
Wanda Wallace, Department of Psychology
Mary K. Weaver, Department of Mechanical Engineering
Gary Wessels, Department of Anatomy
John Wibel, Department of Anatomy

ONE

The Academy and the Academic

All new Ph.D.s share at least one important characteristic: if asked who they are and what they do, all respond with some version of an *ist* or an *ian*. Biologist, sociologist, political scientist, historian, theologian —the suffixes all announce formal entry into a disciplinary guild. It is likely that new Ph.D.s have been thinking of themselves in such guild, if not gilded, terms for some time, certainly for as long as they have been in graduate school. With the first job, however, the terms of self-definition suddenly change: now one is a college or university professor, an academic, in addition to a guildsman. What exactly does that addition mean and what obligations or responsibilities accrue to one because of it?

In the essays that follow these two questions are taken very seriously. In fact, it might be said that our authors argue that unless these questions are faced squarely and openly no sense of a university community would develop and no sense of the self as a responsible academic could arise. To all authors, academics share more crucial obligations than sometimes acknowledged. To be an academic, they insist, is not to withdraw from the more active and pragmatic arenas of social existence but to enter more meaningfully and responsibly into them. To be an academic is to be an intellectual; to be an intellectual is to be committed to the knowledge that academic life is not only educational, but also moral and political to its core. Failure to act upon that knowledge is both an abnegation of professional responsibility and a culpable denial of the very mission of the university itself.

A hasty glance at the present chapter might suggest that it is more idealistic than practical, more philosophical than useful. Our authors, however, would object to such distinctions: all would insist, in fact, that the new academic must accept from the start the intrinsically moral and political dimensions of the community he or she is about to enter. Without that commitment, every aspect of his or her university life would inevitably be seriously diminished and ultimately unrewarding.

The individual essays to follow raise this challenge to rethink the role and function of the academy and hence of the academician from various perspectives. Professor Gleckner's taxonomy of the range of institutions comprising the academy tries to direct attention to how the new Ph.D.'s conception of professional and personal goals will determine the kind of institution within which employment is sought. Professor Hauerwas argues that the moral activity of teaching is the center and ground of the entire academic enterprise. Professor Lentricchia, whose paper was initially presented orally as a challenge to scholars at the National Humanities Center, would certainly agree with Professor Hauerwas's position, but he would resituate that moral imperative within broader sociocultural obligations to make an intellectual and political difference, to be a force for positive social change. Professors Toth and McKay focus on more specific problems: of women in academia, of minority faculty in academia. As a whole, then, the chapter may suggest that the development of the budding biologist, sociologist, historian, and so forth both within and without academia itself involves, or should involve, an ongoing confrontation with a variety of *isms*: an amoral objectivism, an apolitical intellectualism, overt or covert forms of sexism, racism, classism. Although none of the essays state this explicitly, the implication is clear enough that all our authors are concerned to emphasize that the academic community you are about to join is as fraught with pressures and demands as society at large. How each of us remains attentive to and acts upon those pressures will define both our own success and the success of the institution as a whole.

Robert F. Gleckner is Professor of English and Director of Graduate Studies in English at Duke University, but his long experience with a number of different kinds of colleges and universities affords him a unique perspective from which to survey the academic landscape in America. Williams College, Johns Hopkins, the University of Wisconsin, Wayne State, and the University of California-Riverside have all been significant stops in Professor Gleckner's career. His scholarly field is English Romanticism, on which he has written four books.

Stanley Martin Hauerwas is Professor of Theological Ethics in the Duke Divinity School, as well as Director of Graduate Studies in Religion. Professor Hauerwas's many publications include *Vision and Virtue* (1974), *Character and Christian Life* (1975), *The Peaceable Kingdom* (1983), and *Suffering Presence* (1986). Given this scholarly interest, it is not surprising that Professor Hauerwas would be concerned with the relationship between the discipline of ethics and the profession of teaching.

Frank Lentricchia is Professor of English and Literature at Duke University and a specialist in American literature and critical theory. His several books, particularly *After the New Criticism* (1980) and *Criticism and Social Change* (1983), have received wide attention for the political and social challenges they issue to academic intellectuals in America today.

Emily Toth's commitment to various issues of women in modern society is evident in her own scholarly studies (which include five books—a cultural history, a biography, a civil war novel, and two casebooks), in her position as Director of the Graduate Program in Women's Studies at Pennsylvania State University, and in her experience as President of the Women's Caucus for Popular Culture. She is currently Professor of English and American Studies at Penn State.

Nellie Yvonne McKay is Associate Professor of American and Afro-American Literatures at the University of Wisconsin-Madison. She has served on a number of advisory boards and commissions studying both the status of women in the academy and the status of black women in the modern university. Among her numerous publications is an essay on "Black Woman-White University" (in *Women in Academe*, ed. Resa L. Dudovitz) that bears particular relevance to her topic here.

1   A Taxonomy of Colleges and Universities

Robert F. Gleckner

Over one hundred and fifty years ago William Blake, that extraordinary artistic/poetic genius of the late eighteenth and early nineteenth centuries, wrote in an angry moment:

> I turn my eyes to the Schools & Universities of Europe
> And there behold the Loom . . . [and] woof . . . whose
> . . . black . . . cloth
> In heavy wreathes folds over every Nation; cruel Works
> Of many Wheels I view, wheel within wheel, with cogs
> tyrannic moving by compulsion each other . . .

The severity of this criticism, of course, needs to be referred to the sociopolitical and religious milieu of the period, within which Blake pursued a lonely enterprise dedicated to undermining, if not annihilating, virtually all aspects of the regnant "establishment."

The wheels-within-wheels metaphor, however, purged of some of its Blakean vitriol, is not entirely an inapt characterization of the complexities and intricacies inhabiting the landscape of higher education—that world out there into which the new Ph.D. enters largely unarmed if duly cloaked with the knowledge, skills, and other academic accoutrements commonly thought to be sufficient preparation for such entrance. That is to say, although we may be exceedingly well prepared to teach and do research in our "fields," maybe even to have some impact on the worlds of our scholarly specialties, in fact we are ill prepared for, not to say vulnerable to, the implications for our career of the kinds, structures, and workings of those colleges and universities in which we plan to invest our talents, hopes, and ambitions once those institutions (or at least one of them) have expressed interest in investing in us.

Distinguishing Kinds of Schools

Since in this brief space an exhaustive and minutely detailed taxonomy of colleges and universities — and, more importantly, all the implications of such institutional variousness for the new (or recent) Ph.D. job-seeker — is impossible, it is best to regard my generic differentiations as a more personal than impersonal survey, bred in large part of my own experience (as student and teacher) at a small private men's college, two medium-sized private research universities, a medium-sized city university, a large midwestern state university, a large urban but state-supported university, and a small public university that is part of a nine-university state system. As my adjectives here suggest, one simple (even simplistic) mode of carving up this landscape is <u>differentiation of size</u>, only mildly complicated by the distinction between <u>publicly and privately</u> supported: (1) small private colleges, some with a few M.A. programs but most without graduate programs; (2) medium-sized or larger private universities; and (3) large municipal or state universities, the former now few in number, both now frequently "flagship" campuses of far-flung state systems.

As is obvious, one does not get very far with such a generic scheme. If, however, we superimpose on this basic size pattern some more fundamental and precise discriminations, we not only can see something of the complexity of the academic landscape but can at least glimpse the difficulties in constructing neat differentiae. Most of the surveys of higher-education models I have seen, for example, resolve themselves into something like the following list of kinds, though with little indication of the potential impact of these kinds upon the job-seeker: land-grant universities; denominational colleges and universities; universities and colleges with seminarian origins though currently with but nominal (if any) church or other religious orientation or affiliation; urban universities, either municipally supported (in part or *in toto*) or merely located in urban areas; military institutions (other than the four major academies), which, as in the case of Louisiana State University, have developed toward more broadly based curricula or have otherwise outgrown their military-school origins; technical and/or agricultural colleges and institutes, which, like those with military-school backgrounds, have developed into full-fledged universities (e.g., Pennsylvania State, Iowa State, VPI, Michigan State, and other erstwhile "A & M" institutions); technical schools, some of which have developed in ways analogous to the A & M colleges and some of which have retained much of their "technical" orientation (e.g., M.I.T. and Cal Tech); colleges (and, more recently, even universities) that have emerged out of humble normal-school beginnings and now have moved beyond their intermediate state-teachers-college designations; ex-women's and ex-men's colleges, virtually all of which in recent years have become coeducational but may still tend to exist in the public (and even professional) mind as men's or women's institutions with whatever advantages or disadvantages are perceived to be inherent in such educational policy; junior (or more often now, community) colleges, which came into being about 1902, proliferated in the next decade, and now exist in huge numbers everywhere. These offer, in addition to two-year terminal degrees in various vocational and other skills areas, articulated two-year academic programs geared to students intending to transfer to (usually) a state university for their junior and senior years.

I'll come back to these in a moment with comments on some of their differences that are pertinent to the new Ph.D.'s process of choosing a first job. But first let me complicate the confusion a bit more with two other kinds of taxonomies that one tends to find in those books (or articles) that advance theories of the *idea* (or the ideal) of the university. In some sense the modern polarizations evident in all such attempts stem from Cardinal Newman's extraordinarily influential *The Idea of the University* at one end of the spectrum and Clark Kerr's *The Uses of the University* at the other, not the least indication of the yawning chasm between their positions being inherent in their titles. Somewhere in the middle, I suppose, is Abraham Flexner's "The Idea of a Modern University," circa 1930, included in his still useful book *Universities: American, English, German.*

For my purposes here, however, Robert Paul Wolff's anatomizing of universities seems more apropos, even if one does not subscribe to the guiding thesis announced in his book's title, *The Ideal of the University.* Basically Wolff describes paradigmatically four functions of the university—though he seems not to realize that his taxonomy is appropriate to a wide array of colleges as well: (1) the university as a sanctuary of scholarship; (2) the university as a training camp for the professions; (3) the university as a social service station; (4) the university as an assembly line for the production (or reproduction) of establishment men and women. Wolff, of course, is aware of the more-usual-than-not overlap of his categories in speaking about any given university, but it is clear from his characterizing labels that his own sense of the fundamental differences in institutions of "higher learning" derives from his categorization of colleges as either an extension of high school or the opening stage of professional training. What they too often are not is what he wishes they were, genuine intellectual, cultural, and emotional experiences that serve as a crucial transitional stage in life, not merely as career-oriented knowledge factories or, more denigratively, as obligatory rites of passage or passport-to-the-world way stations.

Small Private College

Given the plethora of institutional distinctions I have been summarizing (all of them, I hasten to add, further particularizable if one had world enough and time), let me return to my initial simplistic size paradigm—with now a complicating interpolation of at least some elements drawn from the more elaborate taxonomy found in many published guides to higher education.

My first category is the small private college with little or no graduate study in its curriculum. By and large these are not, nor do they pretend or aspire to be, research institutions, mini-universities as it were. Although research and publication by their faculty is not frowned upon (it is increasingly encouraged in the best of such places), teaching students, in and out of class, formally and informally, is clearly the prime desideratum. More broadly, one is usually given to understand that one's role in the small private college is that of not merely participant in but responsible shaper and modifier of the academic community of teachers and students that sustains the fundamental idea of collegiality. What most universities call "service" (to the college, the community, and to a moderate extent the profession) thus looms far larger in considerations for advancement and promotion than research and steady publication.

Part of this orientation stems from the origin of many of these small colleges in denominational schools, established basically to train students for the ever-increasing demand (particularly in the era of westward expansion) for ministers and potential leaders of the civil state. Such origins account in large measure for the small-town (later small-city) locations of these institutions, originally deliberately remote from the potentially corrupting influence of the metropolis, places where (more or less according to the American agrarian myth) life was sounder, more moral, more character-building, more (to use an Enlightenment term) according to nature.

Needless to say, some of these idyllic locales have been swallowed up by urban expansion, but clearly the effort remains within these ivy-clad walls to *think* of themselves and their enterprise as in some manner continuing to reinvigorate the British collegiate ideal without the protective or sustaining umbrella of university status and obligation. Classes are small and the interrelationship between students and teachers often close (sometimes, perhaps, uncomfortably so). Research support is rarely munificent, libraries equally rarely supportive of advanced research, but in many of these colleges the students are a joy as well as a challenge. Concomitantly, the faculty at such colleges is small so that the opportunity of teaching in one's specialty immediately and regularly is a strong one, and the sense of a rather close-knit faculty community is potentially both comfortable as well as intellectually stimulating.

On the other hand, it is often the case that in the small private college you will have more obligations to "serve" in a wide variety of extracurricular activities—including perhaps the faculty softball team, the annual picnic and beer-bust, and the like—in addition to routine committee service. If the college is in a small town, as many are, the social circle may be more or less restricted and, as in any small town, the individual's eccentricities, not to say peccadillos, sweep through the village as well as the college telegraph system with predictable rapidity and vividness. If you regard such impingements on your privacy as less than comfortable, even threatening, that risk, depending on how you handle it, may be a price worth paying in order to teach superb students. Or, of course, precisely that closeness and camaraderie among faculty members, and between faculty and students, may (upon self-examination) be precisely how you see your own future career prospering.

It is perhaps clear by now that I am speaking about the Williamses, Amhersts, Swarthmores, Oberlins, Reeds, and others of that commonly acknowledged caliber. There is obviously an enormous range of private colleges of (in one way or another) less prestigious standing or reputation, including as well some relatively unsung emulators of the group mentioned above. While in general you can expect from these much the same experience I have outlined in the previous paragraph, it is probably fair to say that the issue of intellectually stimulating collegiality may be at least a bit more problematical even as there usually is a greater democratization among the several professional ranks. Similarly, one could probably expect at those "lesser" places inadequate research support, less than satisfying libraries and laboratory facilities, perhaps even heavier teaching loads. At the same time, it is often the case that the pressure-factor is reduced to a minimum at such schools, certainly with respect to research and publication as well as to the expectations of major problems attendant upon one's rising through the ranks. Such a diminishment is in part counterbalanced by a fairly heavy investment of patience in the teaching of less well-prepared (and perhaps less motivated) students, who may be drawn from a relatively restricted geographical area or region.

Complicating the neatness of the above scheme are those small colleges that are known for innovative or otherwise unconventional curricula and that therefore may offer unusually exciting teaching possibilities. These would include such places as Antioch, Hiram, Wells, Bennington, Sarah Lawrence, Rollins, and Evergreen State; and there are others, of course, less well known. Different sorts of variations obtain in the considerable number of small sectarian colleges where the presence, influence, and even governing power of a particular church or religion are steadily evident, as distinct from the nominal relationships that subsist between church and school in other institutions. Though I can speak but hesitantly of these, having no direct knowledge or experience of them myself, my hearsay evidence suggests that in general such schools have quite heavy teaching loads (up to five courses per semester), plus an obligatory commitment to be available to students on all matters curricular and extracurricular, academic and personal. Your own research and writing, implicitly at least, is to be accomplished on your own time and may not even be rewarded significantly if you can steal such time. Dedicated teaching will. Again, since the vast majority of these schools are located in small towns or villages, your social and public lives may be scrutinized (even restricted) in ways that may prove to be stultifying to a free spirit.

If I seem to paint here a rather bleak (or at least not particularly inviting) academic landscape of what we often call at the secondary-school level parochial institutions, there are clearly a number of such schools that rival in quality, intellectual excitement, and challenge some of the best nonsectarian (or merely nominally sectarian) small colleges. One needs to remember that such institutions as Princeton, Vanderbilt, Yale, Dartmouth, Williams, Amherst, Oberlin, Bowdoin, Middlebury—not to mention Miami of Ohio, Wheaton, Knox, Centre, Lafayette, Dickinson, Denison, Randolph-Macon, Wake Forest, Wofford, and Wabash—all emerged out of what was often a petty sectarianism early in their histories.

Medium-sized Private and Public Universities

Let me turn now to my second size-category, medium-sized (or larger) private colleges or universities. My adjectives, of course, are impossibly fuzzy, a matter often of one's present perceptive stance. To the faculty member of Williams, say, with about 1,200 students (or Mt. Vernon College for women at 500), Duke is large at about 9,000 students, but from the angle of vision of a Harvard or Cornell or Chicago, Duke is at best of moderate size. And Rice is less than half that moderate size, William and Mary in between at about 6,600.

Distinctions in size in this category, then, tend to matter proportionately less to the individual faculty member than the differences in kinds of small private colleges—or, as will be seen shortly, the differences in size among gigantic, large, medium-sized, and small public or state institutions. For example, one determinant of size among "large" private universities is the number of professional schools. The University of Southern California has over two thousand graduate students in its School of Public Administration alone, whereas Princeton has but a little over one hundred in its Woodrow Wilson School of Public and International Affairs. Harvard's School of Education normally enrolls over one thousand graduate students, as does Syracuse's. The degree to which this aspect of size impinges on one's teaching and research in such larger private universities obviously varies according to the subject or discipline the new faculty member professes. In certain areas, let's say political science, the proximity of and interaction with a Woodrow Wilson-type professional school can be a boon. To the professor in Romance languages and literatures its presence, perhaps even the presence of a college of education, is of less consequence (if any) than the availability of stimulating colleagues in history or even art history, not to say the non-Romance languages and literature.

The other major determinant of size is the number and range of undergraduate departments and programs. In addition to teaching all of the more familiar modern and classical languages and literature, Harvard has programs (in many of which one can major) in Arabic, Burmese, Chinese, Hebrew, Hindi, Indonesian, Japanese, Kashmiri, Korean, Marathi, Pali, Persian, Sanskrit, Shan, Tai, Tibetan, Turkish, not to mention those languages, literatures, and "area studies" that fall under the rubrics "Russian and East European Center" (e.g., Old Church Slavonic), "Latin-American Studies" (e.g., Quechua), "African Studies" (e.g., Amharic and Chi Bemba in addition to the more familiar Swahili), and the like. Mt. Holyoke, on the other hand, offers the usual minimum: French, Spanish, Italian, German, Russian, Latin, and Greek. Comparable, if not so extensive, subdivisions into subdisciplines obtain in the social sciences and the sciences.

Paralleling this sort of diversity of programs and majors is the wide range of course offerings within each department in these larger private universities, a range that enables each faculty member to pursue in class, as well as in his research, a greater range of narrower specialties within his discipline. In contrast, at least some departments at relatively smaller universities such as Princeton and Johns Hopkins (not to say the Mt. Holyokes) are commonly staffed by a small number of faculty, distributed generally one or two to a conventional academic subsection of the department's "field." In my discipline, for example, there might be in such universities one medievalist, two Renaissance and seventeenth-century specialists, one professor in the eighteenth century, one each in the Romantic and Victorian periods, two in modern literature, two in American literature, perhaps one in literary criticism. One of the potential consequences of such smallness, however, may be illustrated by my undergraduate education at Williams College, where I was taught Shakespeare by an assistant professor in American literature, modern poetry by a Renaissance professor, and James Joyce by a Keats scholar. In schools with graduate programs, such crossings at the graduate level of conventional historical and national fields or specialties are far rarer.

How do prestigious (and something less than prestigious) medium and large private universities differ experientially from the small colleges dealt with earlier — aside, that is, from the basic structure of all universities as a cluster of colleges or schools? I have sketched some of the obvious differentiae, but it is far more difficult to codify precisely what it is that attracts some Ph.D.s to these larger schools, assuming a rough equivalence in the prestige factor. One major distinction, of course, is the availability of graduate teaching, of directing dissertations (or at least master's theses), of producing thereby *your* students — and, in turn, being the recipient of that kind of intellectual and pedagogical challenge dedicated (and even those less dedicated) graduate students implicitly, and even explicitly, present you.

But along with this "advantage" (depending on your own point of view and sense of your own calling) go some at least initial disadvantages — especially in private universities of some size, not to say stature. The larger the institution, the greater the number of courses offered in any given department. Moreover, and seemingly paradoxically, the more courses there are, the larger the number of professors who teach regularly in this, that, or the other discipline, historical period, subdiscipline, or other specializations. And since the graduate student component of the department is considerably smaller than the undergraduate, the likelihood of being able to teach one's specialty at either level (but especially the graduate) in one's first few years is small. In fact, especially at larger private universities, recruiting may not be geared to fields or specialties at all, but rather to quality regardless of field — an indication in itself that one's early years at one of these institutions are years of a kind of curious apprenticeship — less to the senior professors in your discipline or subdiscipline than to the general-education and premajor business of the department (survey courses, introductory courses, perhaps even semiremedial courses).

At the same time, one is usually given to understand in crystal-clear terms that he or she is expected to demonstrate significant ongoing research and at least the substantial beginnings of a publishing career—a scholarly apprenticeship, then, without always a mentor present for special guidance. It is a nice point to try to discriminate the relative weight any given university department places on one's early teaching and early publication—as the basis for awarding more advanced teaching in the undergraduate program, perhaps even a course in the graduate program as well. Spectacular achievement in both almost always bears such fruit as one might expect, but my guess is that fine teaching may elevate one's status somewhat faster than publications—unless one quickly makes a major or substantial breakthrough in the discipline or writes one of those rare "landmark" articles that may even outdistance a book in ultimate and enduring value.

Perhaps I can illustrate these several points anecdotally from my own career, though admittedly my experience is probably more relevant to the job-seeker in the humanities and social sciences than to the science Ph.D. With my degree in late eighteenth- and early nineteenth-century English literature, my first full-time teaching job was at a medium-sized midwestern university, not of the first rank, jointly supported by city and state funds. I taught freshman composition, introductions to literature for non-English majors, and a survey of American literature. When, two years later, I managed, with considerable help from my dissertation director, to secure what we now call a non-tenure-track instructorship at the University of Wisconsin, I began to discover what one had to do to advance (if not prosper) in the profession. Although I got a $300 raise in salary with the Wisconsin job, it was made immediately clear to the rather large corps of instructors of which I became low man on the totem pole that, despite the many of us who were "called" to Wisconsin, few of us indeed would be chosen for advancement beyond the instructorship.

With guidance and encouragement from several senior faculty members, some from fields other than mine, I began to produce articles and, perhaps of equal importance, said "yes" to any and all teaching assignments, whether I had been "trained" for the specific course or not. In my three years at Wisconsin, I taught eleven different courses, only two of which were in my specialty. It was the greatest education of my life. While that old system of three or four years, up or out instructorships has gone by the boards, blessedly, the present situation parallels it rather remarkably, for we now have many non-tenure-track beginning assistant professorships in the annual job lists in addition to those that are tenure track. And there are some universities that even have non-tenure-track associate professorships for a fixed number of years (then "out," not "up"), and a few that don't even grant tenure until one is promoted to the full professorship. It is well to find out these things, obviously, as soon as one can—though it must be admitted that it is extremely rare, unfortunately, to be told, orally or in writing, precisely what it takes to be advanced through the ranks or to tenure. Perhaps in the very nature of things, strict codifications of "requirements" in teaching, research and publication, and service are finally impossible.

From Wisconsin I then moved to a large urban university, also state supported, that was clearly not in Wisconsin's league but promised me steady teaching in my field at both the undergraduate and graduate levels —something virtually impossible at Wisconsin unless several people higher on the totem pole than I retired or died. Since Wisconsin was Wisconsin and had offered me an assistant professorship, my decision to leave "to teach in my field" was greeted with some scorn on the part of my dissertation director—not to mention my colleagues, junior and senior, at Wisconsin. But that move did get me into the scholarly world of my field, did spur me to publish more steadily, did afford me the chance of directing graduate students, and so on. If my colleagues were, in general, not of the caliber or reputation of the Wisconsin faculty, there was no lack of encouragement from those senior to me in or near my field. As a result, my research and publication career essentially got launched.

By now it may be apparent to you that while ostensibly speaking of colleges and universities of different sizes and reputations, I have also been speaking about the crucial matter of collegiality. By that I mean interrelationships with fellow faculty members in the same department who are not necessarily social pals but colleagues with whom you can talk about your work, their work, developments in your field, half-baked ideas you think you may be able to bake fully, and so on. "Shop" in the best and most exciting sense of the word. Without *that* sort of collegiality, any department, in my judgment, is a sort of intellectual desert. Paradoxically, what led me to the advantages of my post-Wisconsin career was my interaction with several bright fellow instructors at Wisconsin, my being able there to rub shoulders with a distinguished senior faculty, and the generosity of several of those in reading my work when asked, advising me where to publish (or to junk the essay and start again), and generally guiding me through some of the mysteries of departmental and university operation. All in all, if you are fortunate to be hired in such a department, only your own inaction and shortcomings will stand in the way of beginning your climb up the somewhat dizzying academic ladder.

Perhaps it has become reasonably clear by now that I do not think there is any essential difference between large, medium-sized, and small private colleges and universities, and large, medium-sized, and small state-supported colleges and universities. Or if there is a fundamental difference, it is in the stretched spectrum of size of the latter, which really range from gigantic to small (though there are rather few that are really small).

Large State and Private Universities

What I have to say about public institutions, then, is largely applicable as well to my earlier taxonomy of private ones. As with them, the larger the state university, the greater number of courses (or sections of the same course) there are and the greater number of professors there are to teach those courses. The competition to teach squarely in one's field, then, is considerable for a junior faculty member. It is also true that the larger institutions, public and private, frequently hire new Ph.D.s regardless of their fields, so long as their credentials are attractive and promising in general. Under such circumstances, the junior faculty member may be assigned little more than the required elementary courses that are prerequisite to advanced study in the departmental major. On the other hand, senior faculty in one's field do take sabbatical leaves, especially distinguished faculty members often teach but few courses, some regularly visit at other universities or run institutes or work mainly on grant projects, and a few generous ones invite junior faculty to assist them in their courses in one capacity or another, invite them to join their research groups, or otherwise pave the way to more advanced teaching.

Aside from such opportunities, which are more or less infrequent university to university, my sense is that high quality teaching in whatever courses one is assigned is the prime way to earn the "right" to teach the more advanced courses when they come available—that and a good deal of patience, as distinct from lobbying one's department chairman. Though in such circumstances one may recall, unhappily, Milton's moving lament

> How soon hath time the subtle thief of youth,
> Stoln on his wing my three and twentieth year!
> My hasting dayes fly on with full career,
> But my late spring no bud or blossom shew'th

one should also remember his more famous line from another sonnet, "They also serve who only stand and wait." Or rather, stand and *work*, not only at one's teaching but at developing at least the beginnings of a research and publishing career. Meantime, given the right university, partly *because* of its very size, one may well be enjoying the most exciting part of his academic career — something like my before-described experience at Wisconsin long ago.

Despite these aspects of sameness, however, there is one fundamental difference between large public universities and large private universities, one that is due largely to their quite different origins. Shortly before the Civil War, agitation had already begun for federal grants of lands for the establishment of "agricultural colleges," "people's colleges," or "industrial universities" (all three of these terms used synonymously). In 1862 the first Morrill Act was passed granting to each state thirty thousand acres for each senator and representative to which it was entitled. Proceeds from the sales of these lands by the state were to be dedicated to

> the endowment and maintenance of at least one college where the leading object shall be, without excluding other scientific and classical studies, and including military tactics, to teach such branches of learning as are related to agriculture and the mechanic arts, in such manner as the legislatures of the states may respectively prescribe, in order to promote the liberal and practical education of the industrial classes in the several pursuits and professions in life.

Confluent with this indigenously American idea of public education, liberal and practical, was the inception of The Johns Hopkins University in 1876 on the pattern of the German medieval universities — that is, an institution dedicated first and foremost to graduate education and an emphasis on research, with undergraduate liberal arts instruction as, to put it crudely, a base of support for the grander research and preprofessional enterprise.

Among other things that ensued from this extraordinary confluence was the *idea* of a graduate school with very high academic standards; the renovation of earlier modes of professional education, particularly (but not exclusively) in medicine; the growing preeminence (and power) of departmental infrastructures; the creation of research institutes and centers, of university presses and learned journals; the regularizing, as it were, of the academic ladder of instructorships through the three ranks of the professorship; and, needless to say, the proliferation of courses focused more and more on segmentalized aspects of the broader, more general "disciplines."

It is this confluence that, as Clark Kerr and others have argued with various emphases, ultimately produced *the* American university as a collocation of colleges, departments, programs, research units, and professional schools. Such a university, it has been said with tongue not entirely in cheek, would be as British as possible for the sake of the undergraduate students, as German as possible for the sake of the graduate students and research personnel, and as American as possible for the sake of the democratic public at large, the farmers and workers as well as the middle and upper classes. To return to my elongated size spectrum, however, I think it worth repeating that, perhaps predictably given the above mini-history, there are few (if any) state institutions that can properly be called small. The former come generally in the large economy size or not at all. While there is an Evergreen State (in Washington) of about 2,800 students and a Jersey City State of 4,500, Arizona State, Michigan State, and Wisconsin-Madison are at about 40,000, Florida at 36,000, Cincinnati at 35,000, California-Berkeley and UCLA at about 30,000, Georgia at 25,000, Northern Illinois at 24,000, Cleveland State and Delaware at 18,000, University of Missouri at Kansas City at 12,000, Wyoming and South Alabama at 10,000, Northern Michigan at 6,500, and the University of Wisconsin at River Falls at 5,200.

What one can observe here is that the "smaller" state institutions tend to be branches of a statewide university or college system, similar to the one pioneered many years ago by the State of California Master-Plan for Higher Education. According to that plan higher education in the state was divided hierarchically into the University of California "system" (comprising now nine campuses: Berkeley, Los Angeles, San Francisco, Santa Barbara, San Diego, Davis, Irvine, Santa Cruz, and Riverside), the California State college system (e.g., San Francisco State, Los Angeles State, San Diego State, et al.), and the community (or junior) college system of two-year institutions (some sixty to seventy at last count). The top 12½ percent of the state of California high school graduates were eligible to enter the university system, and the top 50 percent were eligible to enter the state-college system, or were obligated to enter the community college system to earn their way into either of the four-year systems.

Most states now have in place some version of this overall structure. Needless to say, there are significant differences of various kinds, quantitatively and qualitatively, between *the* university system and the "state-college" system. But there are, as well, differences less easy to specify (and even harder to learn) among the "branches" of both of these systems—not to say among the far-flung community colleges. Teaching loads tend to be heavier, even considerably heavier, in the two lower "tiers" than in *the* university; students obviously vary in quality and, moreover, tend to be more local in origin at the state college and community college levels; pay scales differ from top to bottom of the three tiers; availability of graduate work decreases as well, and even varies a good deal with the size of the individual state colleges from full graduate programs to none; requirements for faculty research and publication vary not only from university system to state-college system but even within the latter as well as between one state's university system and another's.

Some Conclusions

It is, to be honest, a mind-boggling, probably even impossible, task to try to distinguish among the myriad institutions that fall somewhere in the scale of state and community systems of higher education. Upward mobility in the three tiers, however, can be confidently said to depend upon one's research and publication achievements—albeit achievements that must be made in a milieu generally unconducive to such achievement. Not impossible, mind you, but surely unfavorable. But it is simply a fact of life that few new Ph.D.s can afford to apply only to institutions in the university system and ignore what well may be major opportunities in the state-college system.

Also pertinent to such decisions is the crucial question the new Ph.D. must ask him or herself: what *kind* of academic career do I envision for myself? That is to say, if you want mainly to teach, with research and publication as decidedly secondary, that desire points you in certain directions for possible jobs and points you away from others—whether in private *or* public institutions. Contrariwise, for those who conceive of themselves as future publishing scholars, dedicated to making contributions to knowledge (as we say), and who prefer a good share of their students to be graduate students, those desiderata will lead them to seek positions in Ph.D. granting institutions. But if perchance the "plum job" does not come along at the outset of your search, you *must* convince yourself of a fundamental truth of academe: no matter how "bad" the place may be (or seem), there are worse; but even from the worst it is possible to graduate via dedicated and vigorous teaching, and/or the establishment of a research and publication record of substance and quality, and (it should not be ignored) steady and valuable service to your department, your college, your university, and your profession. Standing and waiting, *pace* Milton, is never enough.

One last note, the bottom-line question: Suppose I grant you all of the above, you will say, how can *I* know the good place from the bad; the collegial department from the snake pit; the benevolent chairman from the used-car salesman (or worse); the attractive sectarian school from the straight-jacketed one; the tolerable Podunk from the morass of less tolerable, even impossible ones; the odds of my teaching squarely in my field early in my career at *any* of these schools; when to say "No, I'd rather not" or "Yes, I'd be delighted"; when to leave one place and try another; when to *ask* to teach something (and when to decline); how to become indispensable; how to get promoted; how to get tenure; whether to fraternize with the students or not; whether to invite the dean to dinner; how (exactly) even to survive in these places of many wheels, "wheel within wheel with cogs tryannic [or even with cogs not tyrannic], moving by [at least seeming] compulsion"?

My answer to all of these questions smacks of the placebo, the predictable response of the jaded and grizzled veteran of foreign wars. But I'll give it to you anyway: *ASK*! Ask everyone you know, teachers, fellow students, friends, acquaintances, chairmen, deans, faculty advisers, et al. — at your school and elsewhere. Check your graduate school bulletin's faculty roster for the name of the university from which your teachers received their doctorates — and ask the ones who studied where you might like to go. If you have a friend who has a friend who taught at the place you've an eye on, call up the friend of your friend and ask him or her. The academic grapevine is a wonderful instrument, remarkably fine-tuned even given its distortions. You may not find a new Jerusalem in your first job, but after all, you all know what was not built in a day. Despite his melancholy lines, with which I began this essay, Blake also said, "Blessed are those who are found studious of Literature & Humane & polite accomplishments" — and he looked forward to that time he steadily envisioned as the "reign of Sweet Science." Even if one's early or middle journey through the academic landscape seems less steadily blessed than one would like — possibly less than one passionately believes he or she has deserved — one must sustain that vision, or else surrender to the grinding of those wheels and a tacit commitment to a perfunctory career. "The true American University," David Starr Jordan (a distinguished past president of Stanford) once said, "lies in the future." It still does. Nothing endures, after all, but change.

2 The Morality of Teaching

Stanley M. Hauerwas

A few months ago I was asked to write an essay on ministerial ethics which, I think, would strike many as a bit unusual. If you cannot trust ministers, who can you trust? That we have to think about the kind of ethic that ought to characterize ministers seems to support those who claim we live in a morally confused, if not corrupt, age.

No less odd, I think, is to be asked to write an essay to help "enculturate" those planning to become university teachers. After all, those who become professors have been around universities for years, and you would think there is nothing they do not know. Just as city kids become "streetwise," graduate students become "university wise"—it is a survival strategy. Being asked to write a manual on how to be an academic, therefore, seems analogous to being asked to write a sex manual. What has happened that we now do not seem to know how to do what everyone thought was a matter of nature and/or a fairly simple learning procedure?

It is not accidental that these concerns are currently being raised, for it seems we have simply lost some of the skills that in the past have sustained the professions and, in particular, academic work. For example, consider the incident reported in the 13 September 1984 issue of the *New York Times* concerning a book written by Timothy Cooney on moral philosophy. Mr. Cooney, in *Telling Right from Wrong*, asserts that while there is such a thing as morality, it is a highly restricted category. Using the refined skills of contemporary philosophy, Cooney argues that morality applies only to those issues that threaten to destroy society. Everything else is simply a matter of taste and/or manners.

Mr. Cooney, who is not a professional philosopher, submitted his book to Random House accompanied by a letter from Professor Nozick of Harvard University urging its publication. Jason Epstein, the editorial director of

Random House, was not only extremely impressed with the book but also that it was recommended by a philosopher as distinguished and as professionally competent as Dr. Nozick. The publishers therefore accepted the book and started the process of publication. Since Mr. Cooney was not well known, Mr. Epstein thought it would help to ask Dr. Nozick to draft an advertisement commending the book and made such a request. He was shocked to receive a letter from Dr. Nozick saying that he had never read the book.

On investigation the publishers discovered that the letter from Dr. Nozick had been written by Mr. Cooney and that he was not the least bit apologetic about having forged it. After all, he had done nothing wrong since his act did not threaten to destroy society. Mr. Cooney contended that his writing the letter raised no ethical problem but was simply an example of "vigorous game play." Since he was unknown, his book would have been ignored unless it had been accompanied by the bogus letter. Rather than being ashamed of his behavior, in fact, he claimed to be extremely proud of what he had done. The publishers, obviously embarrassed, are not sure whether they will publish the book or not. They have suggested that they will do so only if Mr. Cooney writes an afterword justifying on grounds of the argument of the book why he could write the kind of letter he did in the name of Dr. Nozick.

Such an incident would be merely humorous were it not so relevant to our current concerns. Mr. Cooney's attempt to justify his action by appeal to the standards of contemporary moral philosophy, which may be a mistaken view of that discipline, is a haunting reminder of a general unease about the intellectual and moral nature of the contemporary university. Too often the training associated with graduate work in the many disciplines in the university provides no rationale to sustain, and may even undercut, the ethos necessary to maintain the university as an intellectual and moral community dedicated to a common task. What we seem to have lost is any sense that the university is or should be a community that places intellectual and moral demands on those who would be part of that community. Yet I do not believe the university is in so hopeless a condition. Substantial and profound moral commitments continue to shape university life. We may fail at times to acknowledge, articulate, or act on those commitments but yet they remain embodied in our most basic activity—teaching. By focusing on that activity I hope to elicit the sense of common endeavor that continues to inform those who work in the university and that should shape the lives of those attracted to service in the university.

I must admit there are also autobiographical reasons that I take this tack.

My own experience has been that I began to appreciate what the university was about only as I came to the realization that my vocation in life was to teach. This came as a bit of a surprise to me for during my graduate work—a professional degree in ministry and a Ph.D. in theology—it never occurred to me that I was training to be a teacher. I was being trained as a theologian who could further the discipline. It was an unpleasant shock for me to be asked in my first interview: "What courses do you plan to teach?" For at that time I began to realize that I was going to earn my living by being a teacher. Nothing in graduate school had prepared me for my beginning awareness that most of my life would be consumed by the effort to learn to teach.

While I in no way want to dismiss the possibility that my naiveté was unique, I think that my surprise on discovering that I was to teach is not all that uncommon today for young graduate students. Of course, graduate students have often assisted in courses and know that it will probably be necessary for them to teach in order to further their research. But the fact that they will spend most of their time and life teaching is seldom fully acknowledged. After all, graduate training is meant largely to initiate us into a discipline and to teach us that that is where most of our future rewards are to be found. Few people do Ph.D.s today in any discipline in preparation to teach. People do not enter Ph.D. programs in order to teach; they see the Ph.D. as the only way to become a sociologist, a botanist, or a classicist. Our primary hope, even if we teach predominantly at the undergraduate level, is to find a few undergraduates who may become interested enough in our discipline so we can send them off to do Ph.D.s in what we have been trained to do.

The idea that we have a responsibility to train students to embody the skills necessary to make the general life of our societies more civil—that is, more peaceful through reasoned discourse—never occurs to us. Not only do we not think of the university as a community that places demands on us, we fail to see that the university is responsible to other communities in order to sustain its activity, responsible not just materially but for sustaining the moral purpose that legitimates freeing many from labor in order to be scholars. Having been given the privilege to spend most of our lives reading books is a reminder that our task as teachers is to ensure the wisdom of our civilization by instilling in our students a passion for the examined life.

Commitment to a discipline, of course, is often justified on intellectual grounds. After all, is that not what knowledge is about, extending the boundaries of a field? If this were not the case, then teachers would have nothing to teach. We rightly distrust colleagues who seem more interested in teaching than research, suspecting they are no longer "keeping up" in the field. Good teachers are not those who know how to interest students, but those who teach what is interesting because it is crucial to their disciplines. Such arguments are not to be taken lightly as they are also moral claims about the task of the university.

In more realistic terms, however, we also know that loyalty to a discipline is keyed to the ways we will be rewarded as members of a university. Indeed, if we are to be respected at our university, we must first of all acquire reputations in our discipline. For those who are so unfortunate as to be stuck in a first teaching job in a college or university that does not live up to personal ambitions, then acquiring a reputation in your field is the only hope of moving. The more we think about the profession in these terms the more likely it is that we will assume that the university exists to serve our discipline, not vice versa.

As a result, most of us seldom feel members of a university faculty. Instead we are members of departments—those people who come the closest to understanding what we are about. After all, what do we have in common with someone in sociology, biochemistry, or theology? This feeling may well lead us to believe we have no responsibility to serve, for example, on university committees, except as such service is necessary either for tenure or the goodwill of our chairman (which may be the same thing). Any sense that we are members of a community dedicated to the exploring and passing on of the wisdom of our culture seems to have been lost. What I am suggesting is that such a sense of community will not be regained unless we are able to recover the obvious, but no less important, realization that our first vocation as university people is to teach. That is what we share in common and what makes us part of a cooperative endeavor.

I am aware that to emphasize the importance of teaching will not make the life of the young academic any easier, for those who are beginning their teaching careers often find they are caught in not easily reconciled tensions. The tensions begin as early as the first job interview. We approach that interview thinking the interviewer will be concerned about our views on Rawls's account of the original position, and we discover that she could care less about such matters. She cares only about whether we will be able to teach a course that can attract undergraduates in areas that are not required by the curriculum. Without students the department has no case to make clear to a dean or provost why it should have that faculty slot rather than sociology or microbiology. Confronted by this degradation of the academic enterprise, many despair at the thought that they must now try to please a bunch of eighteen- to twenty-two-year-olds rather than being concerned about their disciplines. How will we ever get time to do the kind of research we need to further "knowledge," not to mention "our careers," if we have to be worried about whether undergraduates are actually interested in the courses we teach?

This kind of tension tends to create a good deal of cynicism on the part of young instructors. They know their careers depend upon being able to publish beyond the confines of the university, and yet the very demands that they should be popular and interesting local teachers tend to undercut that ambition. Indeed, it might be argued that the fundamental task of the young instructor is to negotiate this tension—at once teaching just well enough to get by, but primarily working in the disciplinary field.

This tension, of course, can easily be overdrawn. I am not suggesting that we become so concerned with teaching that we let our own work languish. No one can or should teach teaching. We teach about this or that; or rather, we initiate students into skills necessary for them to be continual learners. Put concretely, if you have to choose between reworking a lecture for class or reading an important book just published, read the book. Read the book because the enthusiasm that it generates in you will infect your students. The first rule for being a good teacher is to teach only what (and in a way that) sustains your interest and enthusiasm. That is as true of the most introductory course as of the most advanced, for if the teacher does not believe in what he or she is doing, we can hardly expect students to take it seriously.

Yet I want to make a more substantive claim about the importance of teaching for sustaining intellectual growth. Teaching is not just the way we get paid in order to sustain our research, but our most important intellectual resource to challenge the current captivity of the university to the "disciplines." Graduate school, after all, is an extended initiation into a guild through which one is taught to think the way the masters of that guild would have us think. In the process we often fail to notice the limits of the craft, either in our particular school or in general. We know that what it means to be a literary critic is different from one school to another, but we are sure that the way we are being trained is right and feel a bit sorry for those people at other schools who are wasting their time learning faddish Marxist criticism, etc. As a result we do not notice, indeed we are trained not to notice, the limitations of our own graduate training and/or discipline. We assume that we really do not need to know much about other "disciplines" as long as we are good sociobiologists, psychologists, physicists, and so on—at most, we ought to subscribe to the *New York Review of Books*.

Teaching, however, can be a rich resource to challenge the limits of our discipline. Through teaching we discover that there are other people in the university who can enrich our work—that is, we discover those most blessed of people, colleagues. Even students bring with them what they have learned elsewhere in the university, and other universities, and through them we learn new perspectives and interests that can throw new light on what we are about. We can learn through our teaching, that is, if we can restrain our temptation to intimidate students with our "expert knowledge." Our task is to give students the confidence, to empower them to take themselves seriously as people who would rather know than not know. In this way we free them not simply to give back what they have learned from us but to refract their work with us through what they have learned elsewhere.

This understanding of our task is but a reminder that teaching at every level is a profession—that is, teachers are joined in the common endeavor to respond to a basic human need. Just as medicine and the law are ideally attempts to meet the needs of health and justice, so teaching is a way to enhance our society through knowledge and wisdom. The moral authority of the teacher derives from this commitment and is the reason why the society as a whole feels betrayed when it is not honored.

In this respect, it is interesting that many professors in universities no longer think of themselves as intellectuals. Rather, they think of themselves as academics, as people who have become technically proficient in a subject. Academics are those who have learned the ins and outs of university life and who know how to negotiate those in order to secure a place within the university for themselves and others loyal to them. It is generally a compliment when we refer to someone as a "real academic," for we usually mean such a person is a "professional." By "professional," however, we do not mean one who has committed his or her life to pursuing tasks for a good commonly held; rather, we mean someone who has become an exhort whose expertise gives power over others. When teaching becomes solely a matter of expertise, the very nature of scholarship is perverted or our specialization or discipline legitimates what might be inconvenient to know.

Too often today teachers do not think our task is to entice our students to be intellectuals because we do not think of ourselves in that way. We do not hold ourselves accountable to have intelligent views on a wide range of subjects and to be able to defend those views among equally thoughtful people. Even when we are intellectuals, we do not understand ourselves as such, preferring to take refuge in our disciplines. Thus we say "speaking as a sociologist" or "from the perspective of my discipline," as if we do not exist at all as thinkers. Such formulas are well known and may voice appropriate intellectual humility, but too often they reflect a defensive, if not cowardly, attitude that is the death of the academic enterprise. Moreover, when we use such formulas, we are tempted to abdicate our responsibility to serve our social order through sustaining the discussion of the true, the good, and the beautiful the university is pledged to sustain.

Nowhere is this ambivalence about our roles as teachers and intellectuals more powerfully displayed than in our self-defensive denial of our task as moral educators. The modern university, uncertain of its mission, claims moral neutrality and professes no or at least very limited interest in any substantive attempt to shape the moral life of students. We lay out information for our students, and they can use it in whatever way they wish. By common testimony, undergraduates have taken a wide range of courses, all of which have introduced them into a remarkable range of views about this or that, from which they learn they should never be dogmatic about anything. In other words, contemporary university education is an extended training in cynicism. We teach students never to care about anything too strongly, as otherwise they may not have treated the subject fairly. We call this "objectivity." We ignore the fact that our mission is a moral one or self-deceptively hide that fact from ourselves by openly denying it.

I am aware many will resist this point because they fear they lack the resources to be moral educators, or some may see this as an attempt to sustain the importance of my own "discipline" of ethics. In spite of that danger, I maintain that there is no way for those who teach in the university to avoid morality. To teach Shakespeare or to insist that economic majors learn the history of economic thought is a moral endeavor, for it says to the student that this is not only worth knowing but that by knowing it you will be a better person. The failure of the modern university is not that those teaching in it fail to shape students morally, but that we fail to take responsibility for doing so. As a result our students mimic our fears rather than what we care about—that is, those convictions that have led us to spend our lives believing it is better to know than not know.

There is no way as teachers we can or should avoid being moral examples for our students. We often ignore or dismiss the fact that students often choose courses more by who is teaching than by what is being taught. There is no doubt that students do so at times and that can be a mistake when they are attracted to the "flashy" rather than to the patient and disciplined scholar.

Yet on the whole I think students are right to want to learn from those who manifest in their lives the lessons they have learned from their scholarship.

I think such issues, moreover, are not unrelated to the more mundane and concrete matters that confront new teachers. For example, one of the shocking discoveries many of us made when we began to teach was that there is no such thing as a university qua university. Universities come in many different shapes and sizes, largely determined by their past histories — for example, that the college was founded by Swedish Lutherans and now serves upper-middle-class students from north Chicago. One of the challenges for those beginning teaching is how seriously they will let both the limits and possibilities of that particularity shape their intellectual agenda. Will they, for example, try to come to terms with the fact that they are teaching students from either rural or urban backgrounds and what that means for the presentation of their subject matter? Such matters may appear trivial, but they are at the heart of what it means to become a teacher. For if the university is doing what it is meant to do, there is no way to avoid critically confronting both positively and negatively the morality of our society that comes embodied in our student's lives.

I cannot pretend, of course, that a recovery of our vocation as teachers will not cause problems. It certainly can cause a tension in how we have been formed by our Ph.D. work. A Ph.D. too often is the way that we make sure that our knowledge of the past is appropriately fossilized in living representatives who continue to underwrite that knowledge by passing it on through the contemporary university. We thus are hesitant to challenge assumptions about where things are in our disciplines. Nowhere does that become more clear than when we look at undergraduate curricula that are oftentimes relics of the past. What is required is an ongoing attempt to make our curricula live up to the best that we currently know. Otherwise we end up continuing to teach the errors of the past as the truths of the day because we simply lack the ability to think of any alternative.

One of the implications of this is that intellectual life often has as much to do with courage as with being smart. It means we must be willing to act on what we know in a way that will have an effect on other people's lives. We cannot rely on the achievements of the past to avoid making decisions about how a curriculum should be organized and what ought to be read that once was ignored. No issue is more central to the university than whether faculties will find the courage to determine the "classics" that make any curriculum intelligible.

An appreciation of the university as a moral community requires a return to politics as essential to the university's intellectual mission, for the politics of the university must be governed and shaped by the common purpose to educate and form students to know and desire the right things rightly. Put simply, it is our moral task to help students love to read on the slim but real hope that by being serious readers they will be better persons. Politics is not the unseemly side of the university, but the essential conversation that must go on about what it is students should read and how they are best taught to read. Whether to hire someone in American rather than Asian history can and should provoke the kind of discussion necessary for the university to be an institution that stands for something.

One oftentimes gets the impression that many in the modern university fear acknowledging the moral significance of such decisions. We know that such matters are seldom black and white but involve judgments about which we are less than certain; still, they must be made. Because we tend to fear the necessity of having to make and defend our judgments, there is a tendency in the university to rely on authority. Nowhere is this better seen than in the continuing temptation of many universities to assume whatever is done at Yale or Harvard is the standard for everyone. We thus fail to notice that often Yale, Harvard, or Stanford know no better than we what they are doing. What we must acknowledge is that there is simply no ideal of a university that currently exists or ever has existed. As a result we must, as faculties of universities, trust our own judgments, and working with our colleagues try to do the best we know how to further our task as teachers.

It may be objected that I have presented a far too idealistic prescription of the modern university. In fact, the university is not the kind of community I have described. Rather, it is a loose confederation of departments that jealously protect their turf against one another. They cooperate only in the face of the common enemy—the administration—but even then their cooperation is more a matter of self-interest than genuine concern about the purpose of the university. The modern university, in other words, has tended to look more and more like a modern corporation, the only difference being that the university lacks the clear purpose of a business since we are sellers of that most ambiguous of products, education.

I have no reason to deny such an account of the university has descriptive power. I have tried, however, to suggest that if we allow our lives as teachers to be shaped by such forces, we will fail to live up to the purpose of our calling as members of the university community. Moreover, to the extent that that happens, we cannot help but produce more people like Mr. Cooney who cannot recognize the difference between being smart and being wise. If we acknowledge, however, that first and foremost, we are at the university because we are committed to teaching, we may well discover that there is a richer and more sustaining community present there than we had thought possible.

3 The "Life" of a Humanist Intellectual

Frank Lentricchia

About a week ago a nonacademic friend of mine, his name is Nick, upon overhearing me tell someone the title of my talk tonight, asked me what my *real* subject would be. I told him, "The humanist intellectual as corpse." Nick replied, "I hope you'll speak after the dinner." I said, "Yeah—maybe for dessert." He came back with, "Maybe they'll refuse it." I said, "No, I don't think so. We humanists, you know, we're half in love with speculations about our spiritual death." Then Nick said, "The mid-life crisis is making you depressed." "I'm not depressed," I said, "because this obsession we have with our lifelessness, in a way, it makes me hopeful—it may turn out to be our last vital sign of life." "So your corpses aren't dead?" Nick asked. "Not quite," I told him.

The contemporary humanist of my title is defined by his or her residence in academic departments of history, philosophy, and literature—especially philosophy and literature, and those of you in such departments understand why I say "especially"—and by virtue of the fact that this kind of intellectual is almost never called upon by government or by business for consultation: almost never asked to apply his or her particular expertise as humanist intellectual to particular material problems that concern us *now*. Such neglect is not necessarily evidence of intellectual sterility. It is a potential badge of honor. No one with any sense confuses the humanist intellectual who might wear such a badge with what are called "hard" or "social" scientists. The popular conception of the humanist—here, I believe, is the unhappy evidence—is that *he* is the sort of male who is not now, nor ever will be, in danger of penetrating the social texture of his time. His ideas are not now, nor ever will be, in danger of inseminating everyday life.

It was T. S. Eliot who saw the humanist first, and with unforgivable, prophetic clarity, when he spotted him in *The Waste Land*:

> Unreal City
> Under the brown fog of a winter dawn,
> A crowd flowed over London Bridge, so many,
> I had not thought death had undone so many.
> Sighs, short and infrequent, were exhaled,
> And each man fixed his eyes before his feet.

These walkers in the city are connected (a delusive word in this context) only by physical proximity: at best they are a crowd, never a community. Locked in the prison house of their self-absorption, they are typically located by Eliot in the great modern city called London. But spiritually they are in Hell. In the passage I have just quoted, Eliot happens to be thinking about that special spiritual site reserved by Dante for the living dead, who are not encountered way down in Hell, where the powerfully malevolent reside, but up toward the very top—just barely in Hell (being just barely in Hell, of course, is like being just a little bit pregnant). Eliot insists that we understand why we have not achieved, yet, the honor of condemnation that comes from doing evil with a capital letter, why *we* will make it only into the vestibule of Hell, where we will meet our original ancestors: those angels who refused to take part in the rebellion in Heaven, who could not make up their minds, who refused to take sides, who said, in effect, "Both Lucifer and God have much to commend them. Reality is complex. One cannot be too careful."

   In a later reflection on this problem in an essay on Baudelaire, Eliot wrote, "So far as we are human, what we do must be either evil or good; so far as we do evil or good, we are human; and it is better, in a paradoxical way, to do evil than to do nothing: at least, we exist. It is true to say that the glory of man is his capacity for salvation; it is also true to say that his glory is his capacity for damnation. The worst that can be said of most of our malefactors, from statesmen to thieves, is that they are not men enough to be damned." The living dead, the barely human: those who do nothing. If it is really the case, however, that the living dead do neither good nor evil, why is it, we have to ask, that Dante and Eliot condemn them to everlasting Hell? The luminous contradiction in Eliot's meditation on the great sin of the modern world—moral paralysis—is that *doing nothing is a doing* nevertheless, a special kind of deed which connects us with thieves, statesmen, and other robbers, for how else are we to understand Eliot's cold rage, directed at those who in their so-called nonaction are yet said to be "our malefactors"? Wherein lies their evil-doing? My central proposition is this: that the "waste land" of T. S. Eliot is really an uncanny forecast of the modern university—particularly of its humanities wing; that the true hollow men and women of our time are humanist intellectuals; that far from being ineffectual angels beating our wings in the speculative empyrean of human values—far from doing nothing—we have in fact, all along, been among the leading, if somewhat surreptitious and somewhat un-self-conscious, malefactors of each other, of ourselves, and of our youth.

I had better say at this point that though Dante and Eliot rank high on my list of significant writers, I do not assent to the sacred referent of their Christian interests. My interests are only temporal and secular. Dante and Eliot give me metaphors for ourselves, not a basis for a New Christian Right (or Left, for that matter) of humanist intellectuals. And by way of further definition of both my perspective and its would-be critical object, let me say what ought to go without saying: that there is no need for us to be concerned about the vitality of the new intellectual Right—the New Right is vigorously alive and at work at all sorts of sensitive points of human interaction in the university, at intellectual think-tanks like the Heritage Foundation, from which the current administration draws frequently for advice, and in places like Orange County, North Carolina, where I live, where parents know how to act on their beliefs, where parents know that education is always and necessarily a form of moral and political action that gets manifested in and as *teaching*: they know that teaching is always an act of giving counsel; they know not only that books like *The Origin of Species* and *Huckleberry Finn* carry much ideological weight, but also that the interpreting perspective of the teacher is value-laden. *They* know, in short, what too many of us have forgotten—that the teaching and the reading that go on in our schools have serious impact on how we conduct our lives.

I know of no easier target available to university humanists, especially those who think of themselves as liberal-minded and pluralistic, than that provided by the New Right. I admit to feeling repulsion for the New Right, because it often seems to me to represent totalitarianism with a Christian face, but my admiration is almost equal to my repulsion. Emerson once said that the one thing in the world of value is the active soul. If that is the case, then the New Right stands fully in the world, actively taking sides, working its beliefs into the social fabric and in the process putting itself at risk in more ways than I care to stipulate. Suffice it to say that such risks always accompany those who understand the key insight of Marx: that it is not enough to interpret the world—one must try to change it as well. Of course, the clever New Right intellectual will quickly point out that the *New Testament* is an authority for that view, too.

Marxism as such has never gone down very well in the United States, but a historically independent version of its central activist conception of the intellectual has always been the mark of the American idea of the intellectual, from Emerson to William James and beyond. When the humanist intellectual, on the liberal side, finds himself in the waste land of his own intellectual torpor, it is because he has lost (if he ever possessed) all conviction in the social efficacy of his intellectual activity. It is not that he is insufficiently Marxist, but that he is insufficiently pragmatist, insufficiently American. He can see no connection between what he does when he teaches his course in, say, Milton—what he believes as philosopher, literary critic, or historian —and what goes on, and goes down, in places like Raleigh, Washington, D.C., El Salvador, or the Philippines. And put that way, there is no connection—no quick political validation of the cultural work of interpreting a master poet of the seventeenth century, no immediate evidence that what we do day in and day out in the classroom involves us in an authentic and integral relationship to the so-called outside world. Unlike our counterparts in Chile, the Philippines, Guatemala, and El Salvador, apparently nothing we do as intellectuals seems likely to get us assassinated. That, of course, is what makes us, or should make us, glad to be alive and teaching in this country rather than in Guatemala, where college professors are frequent targets of death squads. But also it makes us, or should make us, feel just a little guilt. Is there anything we can do as intellectuals to make the "outside world" angry with us—real angry? Is there anything we *should* be doing to irritate the status quo? If the answer to both of these questions is "no," then might that be an unrefusable sign of our living death? A sign that says: what we do has merely a decorative function, useful only for those hours of the weekend (for arts, entertainment, leisure, amusement) when one is not seriously involved, as one is on Monday through Friday, with matters of social, political, and economic import?

The problem is that humanist intellectuals typically find themselves preoccupied seven days a week with what our culture defines as leisure-time pursuits. This problem forces upon the self-conscious humanist two basic questions: (1) Can he take himself seriously? (2) Does anyone "out there" take him seriously? I want to offer two pieces of evidence: the first will encourage a depressing *no* in response to the question as to whether we take ourselves seriously; the second will indicate that we might feel some grim gratitude for the fact that some of the politically powerful in our country take us seriously indeed.

First the depressing news. It has to do with two South American writers of the highest international stature, Jorge Luis Borges of Argentina and Gabriel García Márquez of Colombia. García Márquez is a winner of the Nobel Prize for Literature; Borges has not yet been awarded that prize, but he should be. Both have publicly declared their respect and love for the literature of the United States; neither has been shy about admitting the shaping impact of our literature upon his writings. Borges has written a book about our literature, and García Márquez suggests that William Faulkner is his literary father—and many who have read *One Hundred Years of Solitude*, a book commonly rated among the two or three best novels written in any language in this century, will instantly recognize Faulkner's paternity. On numerous occasions Borges has called himself and his writings "apolitical"; García Márquez, on the other hand, has openly linked himself (though not explicitly in his writings) with the Left—curious son of Faulkner. Not too long ago, Borges accepted a literary medal from the government of Chile —that is, from the regime of Augusto Pinochet, who, we will remember, has won acclaim worldwide for being one of the singular monsters of twentieth-century political history, a man who honors human rights as the butcher honors the throat of the lamb. It is a fact that Borges regularly visits this country: he is invited to our colleges and universities, even, once, was invited to the grand annual meeting of the Modern Language Association. García Márquez, on the other hand, if he enters this country now, will have to enter it illegally: his requests for a visa (unlike the requests of Roberto D'Aubuisson) have been regularly denied by the Reagan administration. García Márquez cannot speak here.

About the situation I have just sketched for you—which has so many intimate connections to the American scene—what has our humanist intelligentsia had to say? With a couple of rare exceptions, they have said, they say, nothing. A nonact, which is an act for which (as Eliot reminds us) we can go to Hell. It seems reasonable, though, that a living, engaged humanist might want to ask what it means for a writer (in this case, Borges) to call himself and his writings "apolitical," on the one hand, and on the other for that same writer to accept a literary medal and a hug from Pinochet? It is a legitimate concern of the university humanist to ask what connection, if any, exists between Borges's fiction and the official approval of Pinochet. And what can it mean for a Marxist and novelist from Colombia to say that Faulkner is his literary father? What might that say not only (this is the obvious question) about the writings of García Márquez, but what provocatively might it say about Faulkner and American culture? Why doesn't Borges stand in silent exclusion and solidarity with García Márquez? What sort of political act does the self-described "apolitical" Borges perform when he implicitly endorses censorship in the United States? Working from these examples, it is legitimate for us to ask: how does the United States differ from the parody of society and justice called the Soviet Union when it silences voices it does not wish to hear? It won't do at all for us to congratulate ourselves (defensively, pitifully) for the fact that our CIA, as far as we know, unlike their KGB, has not yet, in the pursuit of liberty, murdered a novelist. American literary critics have traditionally shown little interest in matters political, but the Reagan administration has shown much interest in matters literary. Two cheers for the Reagan administration: it, at least, has no trouble integrating "high" culture, politics, and society.

Now for the good news, which I'll grant may sound like the worst news. It has to do with a keynote address delivered at the College English Association Conference in Asheville, North Carolina, in April 1983, by Richard Ekman, current director of education programs for the National Endowment for the Humanities. Mr. Ekman appears to have had two purposes in his speech: first to exhort college English teachers to recommit themselves to what he calls the "tradition of truly great works of literature"—to preserve and protect this tradition, to encourage their students to study it as a container of eternal human truths and values, while at the same time doing all in their power to resist the ideas of contemporary critical theory and method that Mr. Ekman aligns, in error, with the quasi-scientific modes of reasoning that he finds in the social sciences, which for him reek of politics. His second purpose is to tell us—and he does so with candor—what *he* is willing to do, as director of the Division of Education Programs, on behalf of a cause, "the great tradition," which he believes to be beyond political or social purposes. The division will put forward new programs, he says, and under the guidelines of these programs grants will be awarded. Let me quote Mr. Ekman: "I will not regale you with the details of the guidelines of all these grant categories, but I do want to make plain that the thrust of these changes is to undergird the main structures of American education, not to set up competing structures that detract precious resources and faculty imagination from the strengthening of the already fragile and endangered institutions." For the teachers of English and American literature in his audience, Mr. Ekman's rhetoric is only faintly coded: what he means is that the NEH will take a position with the traditional literary establishment against any positions that challenge the idea that the great tradition (as Mr. Ekman understands it) is above political purposes. The NEH, he is saying, will come out against feminist, structuralist, deconstructionist, Marxist, and other nontraditional efforts to question the "main structures of American education" and their supposed apolitical status. And it will do so not just rhetorically, but economically. It will deny grants in the name of strengthening our fragile and endangered institutions: *already* fragile, even Mr. Ekman concedes this—in "danger" *before* the invasion of foreign ideas. In the name of American education, the NEH will endorse only those projects that are safe for democracy. In the name of American education it will endeavor to enforce politically and economically a literary vision that Mr. Ekman says is beyond politics. I won't tease out Mr. Ekman's bad faith any further. Even he knows that education in America has been killing itself for a long time. My point is a semihappy one: somebody out there is taking some humanist intellectuals with complete seriousness. Two cheers for some humanist intellectuals.

There was more to my conversation with my friend Nick. He asked me if he could read this address. I was glad for his interest. By day, Nick is a carpenter and a housepainter; by night, a reader, especially of Emerson. Emerson, he once told me, doesn't make any sense, except in sentences here and there that are hard to forget—no big theories, no explanations, just little things that are good in an emergency. Late Thanksgiving Day, after a long walk through the deserted streets of Hillsborough, Nick read the manuscript. When he finished, he said to me, out of the blue, " 'Your goodness must have an edge to it—else it is none.' That's from Emerson. The 'American Scholar' essay." I came back with "That's my field, remember? Emerson also said that 'words are deeds.' I forget where that's from." Nick ignored the lapse in my expertise. "An edge," he told me, "that's my putty knife, my chisel, what I work with, how I make houses look better. It's how I change things." Myself, I'm pretty much worthless with chisels and putty knives. But that wasn't Nick's point.

4   Women In Academia

Emily Toth

We like to think that women who choose academia tend to be among the best, the brightest, and the most idealistic. They believe in the life of the intellect; they want to be mentors and molders of young minds; they want to make genuinely original contributions to knowledge.

Often they've made their vocation in their twenties, choosing academia over a traditional personal life. They've resisted the push to marry (only half of female Ph.D.s are married), and they've consciously *chosen*, rather than fallen into, their careers—unlike many Vietnam-era men, who entered graduate school as a way to stay out of the draft.

Long before graduate school, academic women were resisting social pressures to lower their aspirations: most girls' grades still suddenly sink in seventh grade, when they get the message that boys don't like "brains." Most academic women will have avoided the football-fraternity scene in college: two-thirds of achieving women attended women's colleges. If they're in psychology, at least 20 percent of academic women have endured sexual harassment in graduate school; if they're in technical fields, academic women have refused all their lives to believe that "girls can't do math."

They come into their first academic jobs believing that things will be different now—that they will pursue knowledge for its own sake and be rewarded with acclaim from their colleagues. And in academia the new faculty with the stunning academic records (national grants and prizes, book contracts, novels already in print) are frequently women—who expect their profession to be a citadel for souls devoted to the pursuit of truth and learning.

Of course I'm writing about myself, a decade ago when I finished grad school, as well as about younger women. Yet all of us have been trained to refer to women as "they," as if to distance ourselves from other women. We've been trained to think of ourselves as unique individuals—not as women. That is a useless and deadly tactic.

Among academic men, women are still regarded as outsiders—or interlopers. The messages are more subtle than they were a decade ago, when the men in one academic department crowed that they'd hired "two chicks from Berkeley." But there's still the assumption that real professors are male (and white): just a few months ago, an assistant dean at my university suggested establishing a library school, "so professors' wives will have something to do." Universities are still turtle-slow in creating child-care facilities. And women entering all-male departments are still apt to be told the story of the last token woman in that department: "We used to have Z——, but she didn't work out." Z——is usually a woman who couldn't or wouldn't play the academic game. Often she was a woman of great integrity and brilliant promise—but she didn't get tenure. What went wrong?

The standards by which academic women are judged are not the same ones applied to academic men.

The overt criteria—university tenure and promotion policies—are usually written down, and ideally, all new faculty are told what's expected of them from the start. Will research or teaching be more important? How much service (committee work, advising, community speaking engagements) will they be expected to do? How will their teaching and research and service be evaluated, and by whom? The last question is a critical one —because academic women are also judged by criteria that are not openly acknowledged. An academic woman has to be aware of hidden agendas —and that task can be difficult, painful, and infuriating.

Unless she's had an extraordinarily candid mentor in graduate school (and it's more difficult for women than men to find such mentors), the new assistant professor is not apt to know much about academic politics—and, after all, she entered academia believing that it was above sordid power plays. Some fledgling faculty members will find it consoling to recall George Santayana's famous comment that in academia the fights are so fierce because the stakes are so small. But for the untenured woman the stakes are not really small—for she's often staked much more than her male counterpart has on her choice of the academic profession. And to stay in her chosen profession, she needs political savvy.

Information is power, and so is collegiality—and a new assistant professor should immediately get to know all the faculty in her department. Over lunch with tenured professors, a new faculty member can get tips on research funding, publications, and conference opportunities—but she must also learn about department workings, lore, and feuds (every department has them). She can get advice about teaching, and she can (and should) discuss her research agenda. Self-promotion is a vital component of an academic career, and something many women find difficult to do, because we've been socialized to depreciate our own achievements.

Dinner parties are also opportunities for collegiality, although for women professors they can be (as one of my colleagues says) "fraught." If the new faculty woman is an excellent cook, her male colleagues may think of her as fitting more appropriately in a kitchen than in a classroom; if she's a poor cook, she'll offend everyone with her food. (If her husband happens to be a good cook, though, everyone will be delighted.) But a single woman inviting a male colleague to dinner at her home will be sending a mixed message (is it academic? is it socio-sexual?)—and that may complicate her life. (Erica Jong has written, in "The Bait," about a one-time lover who "attacked / my poems & cooking— / which he'd got confused.") Lunch is easier.

And, in fact, lunch is politically essential for women, who are excluded from most of the channels of male communication. Drinking parties, sports talk, squash games, and poker clubs are all opportunities for academic male bonding—including cementing friendships and sharing vital information. Some department heads, among them a man chairing a communications department on the West Coast, have tried to get their colleagues to abolish poker clubs, as discrimination against women—but few other administrators acknowledge that such groups are not just boys' clubs, but power centers. Men become allies through their informal networks, but academic women are often both alone and in a fish bowl.

Academic women have to learn to walk on eggshells, playing two contradictory roles: the woman and the professor. Female assistant professors must present themselves as neutral professionals—wear the success outfit, discuss the latest scholarly discoveries—while still being faced with demeaning or peculiar requests. They may be asked to pour the tea at a faculty reception, to do the xeroxing for the department head whose secretary is away, to bake cookies for a departmental gathering. They may be asked for advice about sewing, interior decoration, and gift giving; if they're short, they may be called "our little assistant professor" and even be patted on the head.

And except for nuns, no academic woman ever has quite the right marital status. If she's single, her colleagues will either expect her to decamp for better romantic opportunities or assume that she's somehow shriveled (and perhaps deserving of sexual overtures from married men). If she's married, she'll be asked constantly (chronically) what her husband does and whether he's happy at it—with the apparent assumption that if he's not, she'll decamp. If she becomes pregnant, everyone's embarrassed (she's a woman after all), and if she has children, her male colleagues may imply, or even say, that she should be at home taking care of them.

The traditional academic career expectations do not, of course, take into account reentry women or people without wives to do their entertaining and errands or people who have responsibility for children. In two decades in academia, I've seen countless forms asking for faculty members' scheduling preferences (courses, times), but only one form has ever offered to accommodate child-care schedules. That form was created by a woman department head.

A woman who is an assistant professor has high visibility (even more so if she's black). Her presence or absence is always noted. Especially in her first year, she should regard departmental colloquia, visiting speakers, teas, and receptions as unbreakable obligations. They are her chances to meet people and to shine. Women have been taught to handle small talk and social graces, but rare is the academic male who was not a nerd in high school. Academic men, left to their own conversational devices, may awkwardly take turns, one lecturing while the other waits. But women are assumed to be good listeners, and men love to perform and orate in front of women, so it's easy to make oneself popular by smiling and saying very little—although a woman also has to insist, firmly, that her ideas be heard.

Ideally, of course, one would rather be respected than be popular, but popularity may do at least as much to get a woman tenure. She must let her colleagues know what she's published and presented at conferences, and she must tell them personally: department newsletters are not enough. But unless her colleagues also find her personable, they will not want to keep her.

A tenure decision is senior academics' way of answering the question, "Do we want this person to be around for the next thirty years or more?" They are most apt to want someone like themselves: a white male squash or poker player. Most academic men are still not very comfortable with women as colleagues.

And so every academic woman also needs at least one mentor. The best mentor will be a full professor with a national reputation who's been in the department for years, has the respect of department members, and is in the would-be mentee/protégée's field. From her mentor, a protégée can find out how the department really runs, how decisions are really made, and who makes them. And since her mentor is apt to be on committees that judge her, he can help her negotiate many treacherous slopes, if he likes her and admires her work.

But finding a mentor can be tricky for a woman. Most often a new faculty woman's chosen mentor will be male, and he may misconstrue her friendly overtures. Also, he'll usually be sympathetic, in the abstract, to the cause of women's equality. But he's not apt to be very knowledgeable. He may overestimate—wildly—the number of women in the university and their power; he may think—in spite of the statistical evidence and the evidence before his eyes—that affirmative action is overturning university merit policies and that unqualified women are everywhere being given preference over white males. (In fact, academic women tend to have considerably better records than their male counterparts.) A senior faculty male may also think women are being paid the same, or even more, than comparable men (in fact, academic women earn 85 percent of what comparable men earn, with the same rank and qualifications). In short, a male mentor can help a new faculty member as a colleague but not as a woman.

And so a new woman faculty member should also find herself a female mentor. If there are no senior women in her department, she should look around the university administration for a senior woman. (Usually there's one token.) Often there's a commission on the status of women; usually the affirmative action officer is a woman; and sometimes a dean's administrative assistant will welcome the opportunity to advise women. A new woman faculty member should join whatever women's faculty groups exist: whatever her field, she'll almost certainly need them. She needs a support system: women who'll tell her honestly what goes on at the university, for women.

But to remain in academia, an academic woman also has to be able to say no.

New women faculty tend to be overwhelmed with service work: one young assistant professor dreamed that her whole body was covered with nibbles. New assistant professors are put on committees as the token women —and if they're black, their committee burden is doubled. (A white woman I know was put on seven committees during her first year; a black woman was put on *eighteen*). A new woman must decline to be on committees not involved in useful work (e.g., committees setting up procedures for other committees; committees devising endless variations on degree requirements; committees ratifying decisions already made about the campus radio station or the newspaper or the student union). She should restrict herself to committees that make her academically visible or put her in touch with powerful people; she should serve on committees controlling personnel or money only if her votes can't be used against her when she comes up for tenure. This is ruthless—but it is also survival.

Early in her career an academic woman should, tactfully, enlist her department chair to help her distinguish among service requests: which ones are really important to her career? which ones should she neglect or decline in order to concentrate on teaching and publishing? One of my department chairs once, kindly, withdrew my name from the department's most controversial committee—and probably saved my tenure in the process.

An academic woman must also resist the compassion trap: being always available to everyone. Universities are full of needy students, and we do what we can for them, but no one person can be the adviser for all the women students. We must close our office doors and do our research. Otherwise, we won't be around to open the doors for other women to share our responsibilities.

Sometimes academic women have to be silent, for survival. Most educational systems, in fact, actively discourage girls and women from speaking. As Bernice Sandler's "Chilly Classroom Climate" essay later in this volume shows, many kinds of classroom behaviors keep women down. Professors call on male students much more frequently. Professors ask women students simple, recall questions but ask male students critical ones—and give the male students more time to answer. Professors and fellow students are much more apt to interrupt women (some 80 percent of interruptions are men interrupting women); professors still use sexist jokes to "spice up" their lectures, especially in technical and business fields; academic men even make more eye contact with men than with women.

Many of these sexist classroom behaviors—including judging women by looks and men by ability—spill over into the professoriat. An untenured woman sometimes has to swallow insults to preserve her energies. Occasionally, she may also have to stifle laughter about the posturings around her: new academic women are often bewildered or astonished by the academic male's preoccupation with what other men think of him.

Questions of "reputation" surface in particular among men in the liberal arts, whose sense of their own masculinity is often a little bit uneasy. ("Real men" go into science or business.) Men in literature give enormous attention to deciding who is a "major" or "minor" author; they continually discuss how writers measure up against one another—comparing the "thrust" of one versus the "seminal" and "penetrating" qualities of another. Scientists, whose sense of worth comes through the size of their grants, seem to be less prey to playing this grown-up version of "Whose is bigger?" (Kenneth Burke has called this preoccupation "The Little Man Afraid for His Widdler.") Women can't play this game and ought not to try.

In graduate school an academic woman is often faced with a political choice her male counterpart hasn't had to make: whether to do her research on women. In most fields in the humanities and social sciences, the excitement is in feminist research. In American literature the ferment over who belongs in the literary canon—and whether there should even be a ranking of "major" and "minor"—comes from feminists and black scholars. In history, "history from the bottom up" is being written by women and a few male allies—and more than half of the most prestigious national fellowships are going to women (including women of color) who are writing women's history.

In political science feminist scholars have spent more than a decade challenging the definition of what is "political"; in art history feminist art historians have pointed out gaps, errors, and distortions in the historical record, so that few surveys of art history would, today, leave out women entirely. In psychology feminists have taken on Freud and his biases; in communications they've shown how women's speech is different—less pompous, more engaging; in religious studies they've analyzed matriarchies and madonnas.

In the "real world" two thirds of the employees in publishing are women. Up to 40 percent of law and medical school students are women. Women buy 70 percent of the books sold in this country and write more than half of them. At university presses virtually all the copy editors are women—so that academic books now published display much more awareness of sexist language than do academics as a whole. The University of Tennessee Press, as of 1986, was staffed wholly by women.

Still, the picture of the world given in graduate school is, with rare exceptions, white and male and phallocentric. (Of the over 30,000 courses offered on women in the United States, only a handful are at the graduate level). And the impact of feminist research has not been translated into greater career opportunities for women: the professoriat remains largely male and white. Only some 10 percent of full professors nationally are women, a figure that hasn't changed in fifteen years.

Women in academia are more and more clustered in the low-paying, temporary, academic-gypsy end of the profession. Of the women receiving Ph.D.s in English in 1983–84, only 31.8 percent were hired for tenure-track positions; 48 percent were hired for temporary academic jobs, while the rest were either outside academia or unemployed (9.9 percent). The academic temps are most likely to be women teaching freshman composition—a field now called "the kitchen." Nor are women on the tenure track faring as well as their male counterparts, despite better publication records: men are judged on "promise," but women are expected to have books already in print.

When productive, publishing women faculty are turned down for tenure, often their work turns out to be highly original feminist research—although it's also possible that feminist scholars are most apt to know their rights and insist on getting them. Most feminists, for instance, follow the recommendation of Committee W of the American Association of University Professors: they keep tenure diaries, documenting what they've been told about expectations and evaluations, and jotting down any comments that do not seem to derive from professional expectations (e.g., a chair's repeated discussion of a candidate's clothes instead of her research agenda). So far, feminist researchers may be the most vocal and best prepared to file complaints if they are denied tenure or promotion. They also have the most commitment to staying in college and university teaching: it's what they want to do with their lives.

Some women graduate students believe that working in "mainstream areas" (i.e., working on white men) will benefit their careers more than working on women. That may be true for some entry-level jobs, and it *is* valuable for a job candidate to have another field besides Women's Studies: I have American literature and nonfiction writing, for instance. But a woman who decides to write on, say, Herman Melville rather than Margaret Fuller is putting her energies where they don't matter: she's digging out minutiae and chewing old cud, instead of discovering something new. "I spent eight years of my youth on one dead general," says one well-known feminist historian who wishes she'd pursued Susan B. Anthony instead.

For studying women there are archives never opened, papers never read, manuscripts never discovered, oral histories never recorded. As social historians have noted, one can't simply "add women and stir" in the historical record: putting women into the scene changes the scene. American history, in fact, looks better with women in it: it's about making homes and raising families and working for social betterment, not simply about wars and violence, genocide and slavery.

Doing feminist research means studying genuinely original materials—a dancing through the mine field, a diving into the unknown that too many young women are told they shouldn't do.

Some young women are advised to postpone childbearing and feminist research until after they have tenure. They're told to write on subjects to which they're not committed, to wait in silence and cunning until the tenure decision is made. And then, somehow, everything will flower: the academic woman's life will become her own.

But she may not have a soul left. She's apt to be in her thirties, with an ingrained habit of deference and fear. Whenever I do something outspoken —such as writing this article—someone warns: "You're going to do damage to yourself." That may be true—I may get eight o'clock classes or a distant parking space—but I went into academia for academic freedom, not to sell my soul for tiny payoffs.

A woman who waits until after tenure to write on women has given up a decade or more of intellectual life. She won't have done the years of feminist reading and writing one needs to be knowledgeable in the field; she'll be taking baby steps, when she should be making adult strides. A woman who sacrifices her intellectual integrity throughout her twenties won't suddenly get it back in her thirties. No one demands that kind of sacrifice from men and no one should.

Still, I'm a survivor, one of a handful of tenured women who've always been out-front feminists doing feminist research: my first book, *The Curse: A Cultural History of Menstruation*, both embarrassed and intrigued job interviewers—and I still have colleagues who can't mention it without blushing. I've since published a biography of a popular woman writer (*Inside Peyton Place: The Life of Grace Metalious*) and a Civil War novel (*Daughters of New Orleans*), along with two edited academic books (*A Kate Chopin Miscellany* and *Regionalism and the Female Imagination*). My current project is the first new feminist biography of Kate Chopin, a nineteenth-century novelist rediscovered by the women's movement—and my book's been pursued by eight eager publishers.

Still, all of us academic women make sacrifices and compromises: we're forced to. We have to pick our battles and (before tenure) try to avoid public ones, such as those at department meetings. We have to conform in dress and behavior and speech—but we should not compromise on our research interests or in our treatment of our students, who deserve the best. The women students, in particular, will rarely get to see a woman intellectual in action. Anne Firor Scott, the only woman professor I saw in graduate school, showed me how to teach as a woman: not as a tweedy, pipe-smoking, elbow-patched lecturer, but as the leader of a community of fascinated, engaged scholars and critical spirits. I'm grateful to her every day when I step into the classroom.

To most of our male coworkers, we are women first and scholars second. That will happen no matter how "mainstream" our research may be. And so it behooves women to make alliances with each other. Academic women should create departmental caucuses that include women faculty, graduate students, and secretaries—who have access to valuable information and can use our help in their own job struggles. (I know many things my male colleagues will never know simply because I share the bathroom with the secretaries.) We should be sharing each other's successes, fighting together against the same obstacles, and making sure that hiring committees include women and hire women.

Outside our own universities, we should be active in women's caucuses in our fields, we should join the National Women's Studies Association, and we should help one another. Just last year a literary scholar was denied tenure on the grounds that her work—on women—was not "substantial." But she had published in nationally known women's studies periodicals and had made contacts through women's caucuses and NWSA. Some fifty letters of support flooded her university, attesting to her national reputation—and she has her tenure.

The myth of meritocracy still pervades academia: the belief that the smart and the hardworking will always be rewarded. With women in particular, that's often not the case: what is forthright and bold in men is considered aggressive and bitchy—and noncollegial—in women. In academia, the myth of individualism is still strong: the belief that we're judged solely on our individual merits and that our sex or our race has no relevance.

Women must see through the myths but retain our integrity; we must work hard and be smart, but the smartest thing we can do is to reach out to other women, both in our research and in our professional lives. Even in the individualistic halls of academe, sisterhood is the most powerful weapon we have.

5 Minority Faculty in [Mainstream White] Academia

Nellie Y. McKay

The problem of the twentieth century is the problem of the color-line, —the relation of the darker to the lighter races of men [*sic*] in Asia and Africa, in America and the islands of the sea. —W. E. B. DuBois, *The Soul of Black Folk.*

Thus intoned the famous W. E. B. DuBois in 1903 as he looked out across the unknown years of an infant century with hopeful dreams for the future of his race. More than sixty years later, Martin Luther King, Jr., expressed DuBois's understood wish in his own vision of an America in which all people would be judged by their characters and not by the color of their skins or their national origins.[1] And while DuBois (as did King) spoke as a black man for black people, he knew that the problem—racism—pervaded every aspect of American life and conduct, extending far beyond his country's complex relationship to the children of its ex-slaves. If its harshest manifestations were more easily discernable in black/white relations, nevertheless, it had equally wide implications for relations between Anglo-Europeans and the vast "majority" of non-Anglo-European peoples around the globe.[2] Today, DuBois's sentiments still find echoes in the cries of peoples of many colors, races, and cultures in many places, who, ironically, although far outnumbering the dominant white group, have come to be known as "minorities." We know too, that the Anglo-American academy has been a stronghold for this intellectual, cultural, and social problem, which remains the most serious issue affecting the lives of minority faculty in the white mainstream academy.

In 1903, when he published *The Souls of Black Folk*, DuBois was a young black intellectual with a lifetime of struggle for human rights ahead of him. Educated at Harvard University at the feet of men like William James and Josiah Royce, who respected and praised his mind. (He earned his undergraduate degree there and later became the first black to receive a Ph.D. from that institution.) He also studied sociology, history, and economics at the University of Berlin before he completed his doctoral dissertation. In spite of his superb Western training and brilliant promise, he had no opportunity to join the faculty of any white college or university in America. Although, in his day, few Americans of any color were more qualified than he for such positions, because of his race such an offer never came to him. What might he not have contributed to the intellectual coffers of Western civilization had he not been forced to concentrate his brilliance and energies on problems of race and human rights? Still, this inequity did not cause him undue concern for his own sake. He saw his life's mission as a much larger commitment to the future welfare of all black people, not only as the need to fulfill his personal ambitions. The battle for black faculty access to the white academy fell to others who followed him. Instead, he hoped and worked for basic solutions to the problem of the color-line, those that might have dissolved the duality of identity that he and all black people felt. His hopes were never realized. In 1963, when he died, disillusioned and in self-exile in Ghana, black and white Americans were engaged in the most widespread violent racial confrontations in the country's history, and black intellectualism was in a struggle for recognition as an aspect of American culture. DuBois's life remains a poignant symbol of the infamy of Western racism and the concomitant waste of black (minority group) intellectual power.

Now in the late 1980s, with the problems still occupying enormous dimensions in our national life, I focus my contribution on minority faculty to *The Academic's Handbook* specifically on "Minority Faculty in [Mainstream White] Academia." I begin with the recognition that in addition to having the difficulties of faculty of Anglo-European racial and cultural heritage (hereafter called mainstream faculty for conciseness), minority group faculty members in dominant white colleges and universities encounter others caused by racism and classism, and for women in this group, sexism that is different from that which white mainstream women experience. I note, too, that the term "minority" has internal problems for me. As used by the dominant culture, it embraces and erases, simultaneously, any distinctiveness between people of different races and cultures, with different lengths of stays in the country, or reasons for coming, and who had different receptions on arrival. Thus it subsumes all who appear to be outsiders in the eyes of the dominant white American culture. As a result, any discussion of problems of "minorities" in the academy, especially by a black woman who feels the tensions between race and gender oppression, cannot accurately represent the concerns of the multiple groups included in the term. At best, I address the subject broadly as the interrelations between white male dominant (privilege) versus the "other" (powerlessness) in the mainstream Anglo-American academy. My essay on black women in the mainstream academy would be significantly different.

The special problems that confront minority group faculty in mainstream white colleges and universities are rooted in the premises that informed Western culture's white, male-dominated, closed intellectual system for hundreds of years. This system originated in the self-serving dictates of race, class, and gender. Its perpetuators, a small group of privileged men, claimed exclusive right to define accepted knowledge based on their opinions as exclusive knowers. So closed, exclusive, and elite was this system that for centuries it excluded everyone outside of its designated knowers, including Anglo-European women. Clearly, it had no place for other races and cultures. In America, in regard to black people, racism, which spawned classism, and as Maya Angelou once noted, erased black female experience,[3] was so deeply embedded in the system that after the abolition of slavery, the intellectual tradition continued to reinforce the economic framework in dehumanizing people of African descent. Segregated inferior education, the denial of social and economic access, and the refusal to acknowledge the existence of the black intellectual tradition that developed outside of the dominant tradition were means to this end. Before the 1860s literacy was largely forbidden to blacks; in the 1860s two separate educational systems came about on all levels: one white, the other black, separate, and deliberately instituted to offer unequal training and fewer opportunities for social and economic advancement to the descendants of the slaves. In addition, the scholarship of whites overwhelmingly produced only ancillary and negative images of Afro-Americans until beyond the middle of the twentieth century.[4] For all of this, much was achieved by blacks, and an Afro-American intellectual tradition emerged.

Pressure by blacks to end this intellectual oppression by whites culminated in the 1950s and 1960s in the struggle to integrate white educational facilities. First, there was the *Brown* v. *Board* 1954 Supreme Court decision that overturned the hypocritical doctrine of separate but equal in public education and, later, black political confrontations for civil rights. But legal mandates have not improved the attitudes of many white Americans toward the "others," and, since the 1960s, issues that once affected only blacks in their relationship to the dominant educational system have extended to other groups of minorities as they have come into the mainstream academy.

My assignment implies both the positive and negative realities of life for minority faculty in the white academy. On the positive side, for all of the peculiar problems they face on the inside, there are now blacks and other minorities in the white academy where almost none existed twenty-five years ago. Their presence has changed the face of American education and revised the premises of accepted knowledge in material content, philosophical approaches, and interactions with and between students and faculty. On the negative side, the lingering problems associated with race, class, and ethnicity, which minorities in the academy experience, denote the tenacity of the "problem" and the distance we have yet to go. The mistakes of history, like a recurring nightmare, haunt us even in the daylight of our best intentions to dispose of them forever.

For the remainder of this essay, I will attempt to delineate some attitudes that black and other minority group faculty can take toward some of the difficulties they will encounter, as "other," in the mainstream academy. I have no definitive answers to any of the problems and only suggest that as a black woman survivor my observations and my own strategies over time may be helpful to others. My approach is philosophical and reflective, and I look at broad, generally observable phenomena especially associated with blacks in the academy over the past twenty years.

In launching efforts to integrate the white mainstream academy in the 1960s and 1970s, black students and faculty, as "others," were violently opposed to the system that denied their human and intellectual worth. They determined to change the demography of the institution with their presence and to alter the premises of previously perceived knowledge to take cognizance of their racial and cultural experiences. Predictably, the system responded by resisting changes to its long-held authority. But the outsiders fought well, and when the dust settled, around the middle of the 1970s, Afro-American Studies, as a field of inquiry, had taken firm hold in white colleges and universities across the country; a generation of black graduate students were completing their work in traditional disciplines in major universities; and for the first time in our history, there was a recognizable group of black faculty in a variety of fields (most in areas of Afro-American Studies in-the-making) entering white colleges and universities as peers of their white colleagues. They became the vanguard, and their successes paved the way for Women's Studies and other Ethnic Studies Programs that followed in the closing years of the 1970s. By then, too, the first group of black students and faculty on the front lines of the action, and the whites who had supported them in their struggle, had absorbed the worst of the system's resistance to change. It was time to look toward building a unified intellectual structure that was not a closed system of knowledge controlled by a privileged group of knowers.

In the first stages of the black struggle in the mainstream academy, political considerations were foremost for everyone. This was one avenue along which black students, and the black populace in general, were claiming their moral and legal rights to equal opportunities within a society they and their forebears had helped to build and for which many of them had given their lives. In their insistence on the recognition of the Afro-American experience as a subject for intellectual inquiry, not simply that black people should assimilate white Western culture inside of its academies, they publicly claimed the worth of their identity for themselves and all Americans. To the degree that blacks and other minority group people have moved into the mainstream academy within the last two decades, the early political pressures need no longer occupy all of our energies. We can now also consider our personal goals and ambitions as equal priorities with our political responsibilities. New minority group faculty should ask themselves why they chose to enter the mainstream academy in the first place, what they would like to achieve in the short-term, and, finally, how they perceive their long-term goals.[5] The opportunity to ask such questions in a serious manner represents a new dimension in our relationship to the mainstream academy. In spite of the history, such questions help us to maintain a posture of optimism, openness, and receptivity to others as we explore our possibilities in these places.

This does not suggest that full equality and respect for minority group differences are within our grasp. Racism, classism, sexism, and elitism are rampant in the mainstream academy, in spite of major changes in the makeup of student and faculty bodies, and drastic revisions of curriculums in most colleges and universities. But the game is different from what it had been a quarter of a century ago. Although some white mainstream scholars continue to resist the new trends, minority experiences are now valid areas of intellectual study in most institutions of higher education. Resistance remains because it is more difficult to change human attitudes, values, and irrational thinking than external elements like curriculum or faculty and student representation. To complicate matters, the negative behaviors have grown more sophisticated than they were before the system was disturbed. While we should not look for or borrow trouble, minority group faculty in the mainstream need to be aware that on a day-to-day basis they are likely to encounter insulting behavior in a variety of ways, including:

(a) Overt hostility on the part of individuals or groups of mainstream faculty members and students toward minority group faculty members and/or minority studies or minority group students.

(b) Subtle and less easily detected expressions of prejudices or biases than occur in (a), on the same issues.

(c) Unconscious racism, classism, and elitism toward minority group faculty colleagues or minority studies or students by otherwise well-intentioned mainstream faculty members.

At whatever level these are encountered, they are humiliating and difficult, and we do not always handle them with self-assuredness. Bigotry is unnerving and degrading to those to whom it is directed, although in actuality, it makes a greater comment on its perpetrators. We should keep in mind, however (as unfortunate as this is), that how the minority group faculty person deals with such situations often determines her/his future career in an institution. We fare best when our dignity appears untouched; otherwise, among colleagues, we are typed as overly sensitive, without a sense of humor, or uncollegial. Try to remain outwardly calm. Concentrating on one's personal and individual goals at these times can be a means of deflecting abuse and using time to devise strategies to cope with these negative behaviors. The offended person can see beyond the immediate affront to a larger plane of future action and find it easier to avoid internalizing the problem. Numbers of black and other minority group faculty, who would otherwise succeed, have failed inside of mainstream white colleges and universities because of the energy they expended on anger toward bigots and/or the dehumanization they experienced because of the repugnant behavior of their white colleagues. The more the minority group person is able to separate the self from immersion in self-consuming rage and a need for righteous vindication, the less is the personal distress and the greater the chances of self-defined success.

To the offenses in the first two categories named above, in dealing with obnoxious students, it behooves you to act firmly and to make it clear that you will not tolerate unbecoming behavior on their parts. Take whatever measures (short of physical ones) are necessary to establish this stance at the first sign of an offense. At times, I have invited students to drop my course or change their attitudes. Firmness and decisiveness in these situations are the only ways to retain both self-respect and the respect of the students. Do not permit yourself to be tested by them.

For colleagues who offend you deliberately, a useful ploy is to behave in a manner that the offender might not have expected. This involves the ability to think and act quickly.[6] In cases where the likely response is "sounding off," silence is golden. Whenever possible, walk away from situations that are actually or potentially explosive in their racial, class, gender, or ethnic properties. Avoid the company of those whom you know or suspect to hold antagonistic feelings toward you or the work you are doing. Aside from the waste of psychic energy these involve, in most instances, confrontation now proves unproductive. Choose open struggles carefully and selectively. It is wise to assume that we will encounter more battles than we can fight in public and emerge triumphant. It is wiser to enter no struggle without intending to win. Instead of frequent open challenges to others, discuss the circumstances that offend you with friends you can trust, in letters and on the telephone. The cost of long-distance telephoning (if necessary) is well worth it. For one thing, though sadly, you will discover that your minority group faculty friends in other institutions are having similar experiences. Writing is also an excellent way to get a manageable perspective on these situations. Make the time to write to the friends you trust.[7]

While overt hostility toward the minority group person is the easiest to detect and deal with, the subtler forms cause greater frustration. The minority person is often unable to be absolutely sure that offense is intended. It is easy to understand the prejudice behind the statement that labels black or other Third World literature as polemic and "not real literature"; more difficult to know how to respond to the sighted colleague who says to an Afro-American: "I never think of you as a black person." Sending him/her Pat Parker's "For the White Person Who Wants to Be My Friend" (which you might be inclined to do) is too obvious.[8] Even more difficult are the times when well-intentioned mainstream people, who are usually aware of the dangers of their unconscious negative biases toward others, are unknowingly guilty of speech or action that reflects the pervasiveness of the malady. For example, a popular black female instructor, under review for tenure in a major research university, had this experience with a young white woman professor friend. The latter, attempting to be supportive in a difficult period in the black woman's life, assured her that "the administration would not *dare* to deny your case." The black woman knew that support was intended. But more than once in recent history, that administration had denied tenure to worthy young professors. And the black woman also knew that, unconsciously, the implication was that because she was a popular *black* teacher/scholar, she would get preferential treatment, regardless of the merits of her case. Inwardly, she cringed at the remark but said nothing at the time. Several days later, at lunch with her friend, she calmly pointed out the offense in the remark—the hidden racist and sexist assumptions. By tact-fully handling the situation, the black woman saved a friendship and, hope-fully, increased the sensitivity of the white professor.

In the cases in which a minority group faculty member finds her/himself exposed to derogatory remarks *about* minority group students, similar treat-ment as above is the best strategy. Be prepared to defend students against racism in a rational way and, if appropriate, explain some minority group behaviors that might be unfamiliar to the nonminority faculty person. Be particularly alert to racism that emerges in preferential treatment and low expectations of minority group students. In your own classes make it clear that you have one set of standards for all students.

Understandably, minority group faculty often complain that they are the ones on whom the burdens of being tactful, of causing no offense, and of "educating" (sensitizing) their mainstream colleagues fall. When they do not accomplish this successfully, they are penalized, sometimes losing their positions. The situation is indelicately balanced, the unfairness of it indispu-table. Yet, the reality we face in attempting to gain our due still means we must often wrest it from those who hold it against our will. Malcolm X's adage, "by any means necessary," takes on new meaning in this struggle. The price of achieving long-term goals, for ourselves and our groups, means extra work and will. The difficulty is in knowing when to be calm and when to mount open challenge. There is no blueprint to guide us each time. As seventh sons and daughters of seventh sons and daughters, we must train our seventh senses toward this end.[9]

However, there are ways in which new minority group faculty members can take the offensive against prejudices or hostilities on the part of main-stream faculty. These approaches may be useful in other kinds of situations for all new faculty, but they are even more important for minority group faculty members. One is to avoid the "chip-on-the-shoulder" attitude. Enter-ing the mainstream white academy with an openness to both minority group and mainstream colleagues, and a genuine wish to become a member of the "team" without compromising the self, increase chances of finding support-ive relationships in a short time. It often takes a long time to develop close sustaining friendships in a new environment, but that need not preclude more casual relationships with different kinds of people in the beginning. The wise new faculty member listens attentively to everyone and everything, even (perhaps especially) gossip but repeats nothing. She/he should search out alliances with other minorities of the same and other groups, in the department and elsewhere in the institution, but do not expect close friendships to develop with all of these people. On the other hand, there are genuine friendships to be made with mainstream faculty, as well as with faculty from other groups, including one's own. Do not make hasty judgments about political power in your department. For instance, minority group individuals may seem less powerful and influential than others, yet many have been effective gatekeepers in mainstream colleges and universities. In short, during the first weeks and months of settling in, hold an open mind about everything and everyone in your department and beyond. Be the best student you can be of people and situations. Your professional life may depend on it.

One of the advantages of being open and receptive to many people in a new college or university is that one appears less emotionally needy and more socially attractive without giving the impression of a prima donna, a stance to avoid. Invitations to faculty social gatherings should not be ignored. These offer chances to discover what people are like when they are away from their classrooms and offices and give the new person useful information about the institution and his/her new colleagues. In a short time, the natural process by which friendships form will eliminate many early acquaintances from one's close circle, but not necessarily from one's support group. An open, confident demeanor goes a long way in diffusing ambivalences toward a new member of a department. Unless those who did not vote for the appointment of the new colleague (and you may never know who those were) are rigid in their opposition, they can usually be won over or at least softened up at this stage. The early months are the ones in which a new faculty member should aim to win friends and influence people into believing that she/he is someone everyone will want to have around for a long time. In the nebulous category called collegiality, one can never earn enough credit to ensure tenure or promotion, but many excellent young scholars and teachers have suspected that they failed to make the grade because members of their departments found them uncollegial. Aside from that, a sense of harmony with one's colleagues greatly reduces the inevitable stress that accompanies the first years of a new career. Ask other faculty members, seniors and juniors, about their work in a manner that expresses interest on your part; talk with recently tenured and/or promoted faculty about their experiences during the process; welcome advice from others; be enthusiastic but not effusive; show that you are pleased to be in the institution.

Committee assignments and formal and informal student advising are the bane of the minority faculty person's life in the mainstream academy. Every committee wants "one." Talk over the merits of committee assignments outside of your department with your chair before you accept them. Listen and learn to say "No." You do not want to appear unwilling to be a good team player, but no one was ever promoted or granted tenure on the volume of committee work she/he accepted and did well. Be protective of your time, especially if someone wants you to spend it in ways that will not have beneficial results for you. There is a thin line between selfishness and survival on this score. Formal student advising, if done in moderation, is the quickest and most efficient way to learn about the new institution and about some aspects of academia that one never hears in graduate school. If possible, accept all committee/formal advising appointments for a specified time. Indeterminate lengths of service can be dangerous for a new faculty member.

Minority students often automatically gravitate toward a minority group faculty member for informal advising and even for counseling on private matters. Take an interest in these students (few other faculty do) and in their group activities. Some may need extra academic help from you, but do not assume that without proof. Be alert lest the minority group student expect that your concern for him/her will translate into undeserved good grades. Set standards and offer help where necessary and when advisable. In every possible way, students will take as much as you will give to them and then some more. Set limits and insist that students respect them. It is advisable not to encourage them to call you at home; much easier on you to make an extra hour of office time than to be harassed by phone calls at midnight or on weekends. Our jobs depend on having students, and we owe it to minority group students to be even more available to them than others, but always within reason. As faculty, you are a role model for them in different kinds of ways. At the same time, you may be the only minority group authority figure that many Anglo-American students come into contact with at close range. You have a good deal to teach this group as well, and what they learn from you (consciously or unconsciously) will influence their future in ways neither you nor they can predict. A black woman friend of mine once discovered that a South African white student in her writing class was so profoundly affected by her handling of racial issues in discussions of literature that his attitudes toward the conflicts in his own country changed. By the end of the term he wanted to work toward a humanitarian resolution of the racial problems in his homeland. What astonished my friend most was that she had not consciously attempted to impose her political views on the class, it had just happened. We affect our students much more than we know.

If racism, sexism, and classism, for all of their devastating effects on minority group faculty, are almost always hard to prove and if in the final analysis collegiality is a matter of personality, teaching and scholarship can be documented. And on these hang the most important index of a junior faculty member's career. While all faculty need to be extremely aware of this, minority group faculty must do so even more. If the job is potentially permanent—one in which the new faculty person expects to earn tenure and promotion—it is absolutely necessary for him/her to understand clearly department and college or university expectations of him/her at specific times on a step-by-step basis. The faculty member needs to know exactly when she/he will be reviewed (as teacher and scholar), the nature of the review, and the value of each review in the total process. Also ascertain, if this was not done during the job interview, the role that teaching versus scholarship plays in promotion and/or tenure.

In the area of teaching, the dos and don'ts are fairly clear, and most graduate students know them well before the end of their degree work. I continue to be nervous (after sixteen years) whenever I meet a new class. Many of my friends report similar feelings each term. This is nothing to worry about and may well indicate how seriously we take our work and students. Minority group instructors, like all others, new ones or veterans, should aim to do their best in the classroom: they should always be organized, prepared, and meet classes on time; they must not condescend to students, but challenge them and entertain high expectations of them. Good teachers are firm but fair, do not require what the students cannot deliver, and do not play favorites among them. The best teachers gain the respect of their students; they are not in a popularity contest. New instructors can take heart in knowing that everyone, even the best teachers, has bad days. Expect them, and do not be too upset by them.

When scholarship is the most important criterion for advancement, obtaining information on how to proceed with a research agenda is crucial. Minority group faculty often feel tripped up by words like "standards" and "quality," which they often see as euphemisms trivializing them and their work, especially if the latter is in minority studies. On the other hand, "how much" is "enough," or "how good" is "good enough" are impossible to know. Still, one need not feel completely helpless. Aside from having a clear sense of the review timetable, new faculty need to understand, among other things, how an institution views the various stages through which a completed article or book manuscript goes: under review for publication; accepted for publication, no release date; in press; released but not reviewed. In some fields, especially in the social and natural sciences, articles and essays in prestigious journals receive high rewards; in others, especially in some humanities disciplines in some universities, one is judged on books. One needs to ask whether, for a new professor, edited volumes are worth the time and energy they require. To the great joy of many, new reprints of minority group texts, women's texts, and other long-neglected materials are making our teaching richer and easier. Some of us are involved in editing new collections, reprint series, and/or writing new introductions for reprint editions. A new faculty member must ask to what extent activities in editing count for or against her/him in quantity of work produced and which area of scholarship she/he should best focus on at this stage of the career. Ask about the value of book reviews among your publications, but do not review books you would not otherwise read in conjunction with your teaching or research. There are more profitable ways to spend your time. Whenever possible, the faculty member should secure all information on institutional expectations in writing from the department chair. Ask for it, do not expect that you will get it as a matter of course. It is also important to keep a personal record of all meetings with everyone involved in the evaluative process. Ask for feedback, preferably in writing, after each evaluation. If nothing else comes of it, such vigilance and care on your part will convince your colleagues that you are serious about the job and your future in the profession.

Whether a new minority faculty member is a scholar in a traditional field of inquiry or blazing trails in a new field, the first rule of the game is to take one's teaching and research seriously. We ought to enjoy what we do, but the importance of our work far exceeds our individual satisfactions. Institutional considerations prod us to do as well as we can for the rewards they offer (increased salaries, job security, released time to continue research). But beyond external validation, we owe our primary responsibilities for our work to ourselves. We are knowers, revising centuries of misperceptions of knowledge. As outsiders in traditional disciplines or insiders in our special cultural areas, we bring fresh perspectives to learning. The new areas we open up revise the entire structure of this civilization's knowledge base. Without us, this work would not get done. We are very important in our time and in the places in which we work.

Needless to say, the foregoing includes considerations of minority group women in the mainstream white academy. "Women in Academia" also addresses issues relating to minority group women. However, it bears repeating that this group, especially black and other Third World women, face unique difficulties in these institutions because of their race and gender. Their presence, as bearers of knowledge, is in direct contradiction to Western concepts of accepted knowledge. Of all groups, as bona fide intellectuals, they are the furthest removed from society's expectations of their "place," the least expected to succeed on merit, and the most vulnerable to insult. White male students are more likely to abuse verbally a minority group woman than her male counterpart; minority group male students expect her to be sympathetic to (excuse) their failings because she is aware of their previous depravation in the white male world (she represents mother, sister, and friend—Zora Neale Hurston's "mule" of the world; Toni Morrison's "hem" of Jude's garment—rolled into one);[10] she is constantly open to sexual and other kinds of harassment from male students and faculty of all groups; and Third World women faculty often find themselves faced with white female student and faculty hostility. It takes ever-new creative strategies to cope with and transcend each "assault" on the minority group female self. But unlike mainstream women scholars in today's academy, who are piercing the silences of their foremothers and giving them voice, black and Third World women especially, with a legacy of unheard (not silent) black women's voices, are making those voices audible in teaching and research. Their contributions to knowledge are among the most exciting of our times.

Achieving success in the competitive world of today's academy is difficult, and sometimes what seems like personal failure may be unrelated to the individual. Minority group faculty entered the profession at a time when most institutions had little room to expand their instructional staffs. Political pressures, Affirmative Action, and at times, moral conviction have made possible minority group representation in colleges and universities across the country. This has often created hostilities between mainstream and minority group younger faculty. White men, in particular, perceive themselves victims of reverse discrimination. This may improve as we enter the 1990s and more jobs become available. Still, many minority group faculty do not succeed in white mainstream colleges and universities no matter how hard they try. We need permanency for stability in our lives, institutions in which to work and grow, and colleagues with whom to interact and to support us. But our work and our worth transcend tenure and promotion decisions made on arbitrary and shifting rules. This makes it more crucial that we take what we do seriously, that we do the best we possibly can to meet the standards we set for ourselves, and that we understand the value of our contributions to knowledge. Minority group faculty have many hurdles to overcome in the mainstream white academy; the most effective way of dealing with them is to remain true to ourselves and to do our work to the best of our abilities.

Notes

1. Martin Luther King, Jr., "I Have A Dream," Speech at the Lincoln Memorial, Washington, D.C., August 1963.
2. Western civilization's negative attitudes to groups of people have not been confined only to "dark" races, but essentially include peoples whose cultural roots are other than those of the Anglo-European tradition.
3. Maya Angelou, *I Know Why the Caged Bird Sings* (New York: Random House, 1970), p. 151.
4. With few exceptions, studies by white Americans on black Americans from the eighteenth through the first half of the twentieth century revealed only negative characteristics about the group and completely ignored the role that racism played in the black experience. Exceptions to such racist materials include Gunnar Myrdal, *An American Dilemma* (New York: Harper and Brothers, 1944); Melvin Herskovich, *The Myth of the Negro Past* (New York: Harper and Brothers, 1958); and Lawrence Levine, *Black Culture and Black Consciousness* (New York: Oxford University Press, 1977).
5. These questions help us to better understand what we expect to achieve within the mainstream academy. We all need not have the same reasons for being there, but it helps to be clear on what we want as individuals.
6. Suppressing enormous rage, I once "swallowed" an insult directed at me through a black woman writer's work and almost immediately afterward wrote an essay incorporating the insult and my rage. A few months later I presented it at a professional meeting, to the applause of many of my colleagues. The essay found its way into a Women's Studies journal and was later reprinted in a collection of women's experiences in the academy. You can't help getting mad, but sometimes there are ways to get even as well.
7. Letter writing is especially useful, enjoyable, worthwhile, and sustaining, once the habit is formed. Since 1975 a black woman friend from graduate school and I, separated because of jobs in different places, have engaged in the kind of letter writing that astonishes most people. In fact, we have recreated the nineteenth-century tradition *à la* typewriter first and now computer. Writing an average of three or four letters each per week, we share much of each other's lives, including those things that cause us joy or anxieties in the academy. We seldom need to talk to each other on the telephone. This habit has taken us both through several rough times when we felt especially vulnerable as black women in a hostile white academy. In moments of great fantasy, we imagine graduate students in the twenty-first century reconstructing our lives through our letters. But we do not write for posterity—in our letters we share a sustaining and supportive meaningful friendship.
8. See Pat Parker, "For the White Person Who Wants to be My Friend," *Women Slaughter* (Oakland: Diana Press, 1978), p. 13.
9. As W. E. B. DuBois wrote: "The Negro is a sort of seventh son [*sic*], born with a veil, and gifted with second sight in this American world." *The Souls of Black Folk* (New York: New American Library, 1969), p. 45.
10. See Zora Neale Hurston, *Their Eyes Were Watching God* (Urbana: University of Illinois Press, 1965), p. 29. In Hurston's novel, the grandmother, who lived through the horrors of slavery, tells her granddaughter to accept, gratefully, her marriage to an older, financially secure man she does not love. Grandmother notes that this arrangement will make up for the years when black women, the "mules" of the world, were forced to bear the burdens

of life for everyone else. Janie, the granddaughter, rejects her grandmother's advice and goes on to become the first black female heroine in black women's fiction. Also see Toni Morrison, *Sula* (New York: New American Library, 1982), p. 83. Morrison approaches the theme from the perspective of the black man. When Jude, husband of Nel, a central character in this novel, contemplates marriage, he thinks of a wife as someone to give him the solace he needs to survive in a world that denigrates black men. She will be the "hem" of his coat, keeping him from raveling away. Black male students, especially, often see black women professors as their "safe harbor," to borrow another Morrison term, to protect them from the "burdens" of their "blackness" in the white college and university.

TWO

Academic Employment

In relation to the seemingly leisurely pace of the first three or four years, the final sprint to the Ph.D. is often hectic and harrowing. Not only must the "promising" research now bear tangible and readable results and the document itself be subjected to fearful professional evaluation, but the candidate must also find some way to metamorphose from learning pupil to learned professor. Neither dissertation nor defense could be as frightening as this last step. Horror stories abound: how the best student anyone can remember failed to get a single interview at the national convention; how Sarah Wells was forced to accept a job at South Central Tech and was never heard of again; how Joe Simmon's advisor sabotaged his dossier with a less than glowing recommendation; how Jill Adams got her dissertation published by Chicago but was still denied tenure. The entire ordeal is encompassed by two vast unknowns—one real obstacle called the job market and an even vaguer one called tenure. The essays that follow attempt at least to bring some light to these two dark threats. Professors Wilbur and Shetty offer practical advice on how to negotiate the dangerous currents of the market;

Professor Finkin explains the legal theory and the implications of tenure; Professor Goodwin outlines the three hurdles to achieving tenure; and Professor DeNeef summarizes the financial aspects of academic employment. The difference in approaches is itself a sign that the transition from Ph.D. to professor is neither a natural chronology nor an easy shifting of academic gears. Getting a job is one thing, but keeping it is many. As the stakes rise, so do the issues. The new academic will have to prepare as thoroughly as possible for the challenges ahead and a major part of that preparation is simply knowing in advance just what those challenges are about.

Henry M. Wilbur is Professor of Zoology at Duke University and a specialist in ecology and evolution, on which he has published extensively. Professor Wilbur also served for several years as Director of Graduate Studies in Zoology. In that capacity he developed extensive experience in guiding new Ph.D.s through the intricacies of preparing a vita, interviewing for academic and nonacademic jobs, and successfully negotiating a beginning contract.

Sudhir Shetty, who is currently an Assistant Professor of Public Policy Studies and Economics at Duke University, has more direct experience of the current job market than most of our contributors and thus can speak with considerable newness about this subject. Professor Shetty is a specialist in economic development, although he also works in the secondary fields of microeconomic theory and econometrics.

Matthew W. Finkin is Professor of Law at the University of Illinois. He served on the professional staff of the American Association of University Professors (AAUP) from 1967–72, and later as the Association's General Counsel. Throughout his distinguished career, Professor Finkin has written and taught about legal issues in higher education and can therefore speak with considerable authority on the topic of tenure.

Craufurd Goodwin is James B. Duke Professor of Economics at Duke University, but he has also served as Dean of the Graduate School and Vice Provost for Research. In the latter position, Professor Goodwin was for several years Chairman of the University Appointment, Promotion, and Tenure Committee; he writes, therefore, from considerable experience with how such committees arrive at their decisions. Professor Goodwin's scholarly field is the history of economic thought, on which he has written several books.

A. Leigh DeNeef is Professor of English and Associate Dean of the Graduate School at Duke University. His special fields of interest are Renaissance literature and critical theory, on which he has written four books.

6 On Getting A Job

Henry M. Wilbur

The first task of the new Ph.D. is to obtain an academic position. In the following pages I offer some tactics that may be helpful in locating suitable openings, submitting an application, surviving an interview, and negotiating an offer. My advice is admittedly personal and based upon my own limited experience, which includes successfully competing for positions that could fulfill my expectations and then serving on search committees as a faculty member during the past decade. On the basis of that experience, I immediately qualify my opening sentence: before you set out to obtain a job in a college or university, you should do some frank and honest soul-searching.

Preliminary Considerations

Not all graduate students are larval professors. Although this handbook is a guide to metamorphosis from graduate student life to professorhood, not all graduate students want to or should attempt this particular transition. There is life outside of the university—in industry, in government, and in private foundations—for students in all fields. Of course, the computer scientist or chemist probably has a broader range of options than the philosopher or classicist; nevertheless, it is important for graduate students continuously to question their career goals. Academics are generally not paid very well considering the length of time they have spent educating themselves. The hours are not very attractive, particularly in the first few years when you are expected to write three to six term papers (lectures) a week, establish yourself as a research scholar of national repute, and devote hours to committee work you are told is indispensable to the proper functioning of the department and the university. However, the rewards of academic life should be obvious to you by now. If you can't articulate them clearly, then you should investigate alternatives to an academic career. The choice *not* to become an academic is often difficult; it can seem an admission of failure at the very moment you have achieved significant graduate success. And yet a Ph.D. should never be viewed as a career answer, but rather as an opening of career options. College or university teaching is only one among many. For the remainder of this essay, however, I shall assume that you have decided to try your hand at professorhood.

There is a great deal that can be done as a graduate student to increase your chances of obtaining a satisfactory position in academia. The work ethic remains alive and there is always room at the top. A number of scholarly publications before the dissertation is submitted is becoming the norm, at least in the sciences. Attendance at meetings of scholarly societies and the presentations of talks or posters is not only good practice but good advertisement. A high level of intellectual interaction with fellow students and faculty throughout your graduate studies produces favorable letters of reference and propels you to the top of your advisor's list of "promising young scholars." Begin this behavior as soon as possible after entering graduate school. There is a high correlation between early publication and sustained publication. Graduate students who work hard their first year preparing their undergraduate research for publication seem to be the ones to get tenure ten years later. Too many students begin their publishing careers by pushing a series of potboilers off to journals six months before they intend to apply for positions. Today's competition demands that you prepare for an academic position as soon as you enter graduate school. I do not mean to imply here that scholarship should be motivated by employment prospects rather than intellectual curiosity, for without that curiosity all is already lost. There are, however, a number of practical strategies that can help your application rise to the surface of the sea of inquiries a search committee receives. This essay is about those tactics.

An early decision relates to the kind of position that you would accept. Your advisor and peers probably act as if you must get a position at a prestigious research university. Is that what *you* want? All students, to be sure, tend to get less selective the longer they go without interviews and offers, but you should anticipate this reaction from the start. You will quickly antagonize your referees (even if they have a word processor) if you ask for too many recommendations for positions for which you are not appropriate or which you would not accept if offered.

Schools vary considerably in the relative emphasis they give to undergraduate teaching versus externally sponsored research programs. A college that places a strong emphasis on undergraduate teaching may still expect you to have a research program, but one that involves undergraduates. Such a program may not require extramural funding to be successful. Some research universities may not expect you to teach undergraduates at all; rather, it is taken for granted that you will rapidly establish a nationally recognized research program that successfully obtains funds from the highly competitive panels of the National Science Foundation or National Institutes of Health. Graduate students may come later. Most universities have some intermediate expectation in which a balance between teaching and research is sought. Your task is to discover where on this continuum you would be most satisfied.

The decision of whether to apply for a particular job involves your personal as well as your career ambitions. You may be able to tolerate an urban (or isolated rural) campus for a one-year sabbatical replacement position, but would bypass it as a place to raise your family. A different decision is the one between a temporary position at a good school versus a potentially permanent position at a less desirable school. Temporary positions can vary from a postdoctoral research position that will almost certainly enhance your later opportunities to a teaching replacement that will help pay the bills but may impede progress toward your career goals. Temporary positions involving teaching of even a single course a semester are likely to stall your research progress.

Search committees at major universities are going to pay close attention to your scholarly productivity in the few years surrounding your doctorate. On the positive side, the responsibility for teaching a course may provide just the experience and letters of reference required to land a teaching position at a liberal arts college.

Finding Out about Positions

Different fields have different modes of advertising positions. Some scholarly societies have directories or newletters about openings and many journals accept advertisements for positions wanted or positions open in the field. In the sciences, especially the biological sciences, nearly all academic positions are advertised in the journal *Science*.

The "old boy network" is more alive in some fields than others. Many departments will circulate advertisement copy to colleagues throughout the country before it is submitted for publication. The rapid response by a candidate to such a notice assures some degree of attention because it demonstrates both that you are in contact with respected figures in your field and that you are eager. Some departments formally request nominations of promising scholars from established figures to fill open positions. A rapid and enthusiastic response by your advisor to such an invitation is essential. It is therefore imperative that you frankly discuss your aspirations and progress towards completing degree requirements with that advisor. The advisor should have at hand a current curriculum vitae and have read your statement of teaching and research interests (see below). He or she should not have to reach back to your oral preliminary examination for a recollection of your promise.

Submitting the Application

The materials you submit in response to an advertisement or nomination are going to determine whether or not you get an interview. Your application has to attract immediate, positive attention. It has to be brief enough to catch the eye of a search committee confronted with several hundred applications and yet must include detailed information to convince the specialist or skeptic. There is a wide variety of formats for presenting your credentials to a search committee, but the following suggestions would be appropriate for most university positions, at least in the sciences. It is important to tailor your application to both the type of school (major research university versus small teaching college) and the specific description of the position (don't dwell on your skill in introductory courses if the department seeks someone to strengthen its graduate program). Perhaps the most important thing to appreciate is that the search committee may be attempting to evaluate several hundred applications in a few weeks. Your application will probably be rejected or passed through the first filter based on one or two minutes of effort. You must present your credentials in a compact form that allows a reader quickly to appreciate your talents and then lures him or her to read the more detailed statements of your qualifications. Be sure your name is on every page of the application and staple each section separately!

Keep an organized checklist of where you have applied, when you sent the application, who you asked to write letters, and when you have received confirmation that materials have been received.

A. THE COVER LETTER

The cover letter should be a short formal statement of your interest in the position and a very brief list of the enclosed documents. If you were told of the opening by an advisor or have been contacted by a member of the search committee or department, this too should be mentioned. The cover letter is a good place to drop a name, if that can be done gracefully and with tact. The cover letter should also contain a clear statement of when you will complete your degree requirements, if you have not already done so. It may be important to have your advisor verify this expectation in a separate letter.

B. THE CURRICULUM VITAE

The curriculum vitae should be a *factual* outline of your life as a scholar. It will probably be the most carefully read and widely circulated document in your application. Letters of reference are generally considered confidential documents, but your vitae may be widely circulated to faculty, deans, and students. It tells who you are and is a very good indication of what you think of yourself. A suggested format follows.

Personal information: Name, birthplace and citizenship, university address and telephone, home address and telephone, social security number (these last two items may be needed for interview reimbursements). Some choose to include sex, birthdate, marital status, and number of offspring (these data may be considered irrelevant by some departments and very important by others).

Education: List the institution, department, degree, and date of all degrees earned.

Positions held: List employment that is not redundant with other categories. Casual summer jobs are not important but you should account for significant gaps between your degrees.

Awards: List honorary societies, scholarships, fellowships, and other recognition for academic achievement. For some positions it may be useful to list evidence of good citizenship outside of academics, but don't reach back to high school or scouts to find it.

Societies: List the scholarly societies to which you belong. Don't stretch this to include hobbies: an ornithologist should include the American Ornithologists Union (the publisher of a research journal) but not the Audubon Society (the publisher of a lay magazine). If membership is by election, list the date of election as evidence of sustained interest rather than a last minute membership to fortify your credentials.

Professional service: List journals or granting agencies for whom you have served as a reviewer and offices you have held in scholarly societies.

Teaching experience: List the courses by title that you have taught and include your responsibilities (lecturer, discussion section, laboratory section, etc.).

Papers delivered: If you have presented papers at meetings of scholarly societies or symposia it may be wise to list them by title, date, and meeting. This section should not be inflated by talks to the hometown crowd; it should definitely include presentations for which you were invited. The main purpose of this section is to establish your stature among the community of scholars outside your home institution.

Publications: This section presents some difficulties. Lists of publications can be seriously diluted by the inclusion of published abstracts, unrefereed publications, or publications in questionable journals. Established scholars vary considerably in what they include in their "publications." I personally prefer to see a list of publications in refereed journals (include publications in press) arranged by date, with titles, citations, and order of coauthorship clearly stated. A separate section can be established for published abstracts and technical reports. Titles "in preparation" should also be relegated to a separate section with a note explaining the status of each (e.g., in review, rough manuscript, research completed, a good dream).

C. STATEMENT OF RESEARCH INTERESTS

The curriculum vitae presents the facts of your research accomplishments. The statement of research interest is a concise presentation of what your research has been about and where you see it heading. This should be a statement that can be read quickly and appreciated by nonspecialists in your field. It may also serve as a sample of your writing skills. Since your success at obtaining an interview may depend on a vote of the entire department or the judgment of a dean trained in another field, you must avoid jargon without being condescending and you must be complete without belaboring the details. The statement should be a page or two.

The application packet should also contain reprints of publications or preprints of work in press. Some applicants include a paragraph or two describing the major results of each publication and each research project in progress. You should include an abstract of your dissertation or an outline of what you have completed. Very few members of the search committee will have time to read any of your publications but if you pass the first screening they may be read before you are invited for an interview. If, after the interview, there is still controversy about your suitability for the position, your publications may be read in detail.

D. STATEMENT OF TEACHING INTERESTS

This statement should be an honest evaluation of your qualifications to teach courses at the graduate and undergraduate levels. It is appropriate to include a statement of your personal approach to teaching. Short course descriptions are more useful than mere titles. It may be wise to include a detailed syllabus if you have designed a course or know what kind of course a prospective employer wants offered. Your interest in and approach to undergraduate independent research projects and graduate students can be described if you are familiar with how the department is structured.

E. LETTERS OF REFERENCE

Because many search committees are going to put great stock in letters of reference, your choice of who writes for you is significant. You need to pick professors who know you and your work well. Given a choice it is always better to have a letter written by someone known, and trusted, by members of the search committee. If you are known by someone outside your home department, he or she may add a useful dimension: a biologist with a minor in mathematics would profit from a letter from a mathematician. If you did collaborative work or took a course at another institution you may obtain a letter that places you in a national perspective. Respect your referees: they are busy and letters of reference soon become a great burden. The cost of an excessive number of requests is that you will get only a standard form letter. Personalized letters that address your suitability for a specific position are much more useful than the generic EGS (Excellent Graduate Student) letter of platitudes. If the referee knows a member of the department well, a photocopy of the letter sent directly to that contact may direct the attention of the search committee to your application. Give all your referees copies of your application so they have an updated curriculum vitae and are familiar with how you represent your teaching and research interests. Even more important, give them as much time as possible to write the letter and provide them with a return note to send you when they have written it.

The Interview

A completed application is an implicit statement that you are ready to interview on short notice. It is not at all unusual for the first response from a search committee to be a telephone call asking you to come for an interview the following week. A little preplanning can help both your mental health and your presentation. First, let your optimism prepare you for the telephone call; it will not help your case if you sound shocked and request additional time to get ready. Don't make it obvious that this is your first interview. On the telephone ask about the format of the interview: Will you have a chance to talk with students? Will you be able to see special facilities? Does the department expect a seminar? Who will attend and how long a presentation is expected?

Don't be shy about asking explicitly about reimbursement arrangements, but be prepared to pay for hotel accommodations and meals. You may have to tie up hundreds of dollars buying airline tickets and paying for living expenses, because reimbursements from some state universities require a month or even more. Now may be the time to get a credit card. Be sure to get directions as to whether you will be met at the airport or if you need to find your own way to a hotel.

Do your homework. Go to the library and get a *Bulletin* or *Peterson's Guide to Graduate Programs* and learn who the faculty are. Look them up in a biographical work such as *Who's Who* or *American Men and Women of Science*. If you review the names and have a bit of introductory information it will be much easier to carry on a personal or professional conversation. A bit of recognition will flatter your hosts, reveal your awareness of the profession at large, and demonstrate that you are serious about the position. A review of the department's course listings tells about the interests of the faculty and gives you a preview of the character and balance of the department. Such a preview may provide you with questions that you need to ask in order to evaluate the department as a potential home. Prior knowledge of the department demonstrates the sincerity and the depth of your interest.

Most departments will expect you to present a formal lecture on your research as a focal point for your visit. A department with an emphasis on undergraduate teaching may request that you give a lecture, perhaps on a topic of their choice, to an undergraduate class.

Your seminar should be expertly prepared within the format customary in your discipline. Science departments will expect a 45- to 50-minute paper with perhaps 15 to 20 minutes for informal questions followed by an open house or reception. The seminar gives faculty a chance to examine both the soundness of your research (few will have read any of your papers) and your skill as a lecturer. Your talk should be pitched at the general audience with a clear statement of how your own project contributes to the broader field of your interest. Very meticulously weed out lab-lore and jargon. Excellent slides and a well-practiced delivery are essential. Be sure that you have talked with the projectionist about how the lights and microphone work. Bringing a slide tray ready to go may ensure that your slides are projected correctly; there are seven wrong ways to load a slide and only one correct orientation. The more prepared you feel you are the lower the level of terror you will experience when you first stand up. Try not to read notes, but if you have a completely written script at hand you will have the assurance that there is a fall-back position that could save you. Remember, you may get less than a week's warning. Prepare your slides well in advance and practice your talk before the hometown crowd. Include a couple of nonspecialists in your audience and take their criticisms seriously. Coax them into listening to a revision.

Graduate students often seem very concerned about appropriate dress for interviews. The advice varies with both school and department. Urban campuses and humanities departments tend to be more formal than rural campuses and science departments. Note what the professors in your department wear when they lecture and dress at that level or slightly more formally. It is probably wise to be a bit more formal when you present a lecture and when you visit the dean than when you are making the rounds of the faculty. Personal appearance will be used to judge lifestyle. Some colleges are very concerned about the lifestyle of their faculty. If the department wants to know your marital status and number of offspring, it probably wants to see you in business clothes. Be sure you dress for the local climate; it is very important to feel comfortable.

Remember, they invited you; they are interested. But you should also interview them. The chair of the department should tell you about the position. Is it a new position or a replacement for a lost faculty member? What is the department's expectation with respect to teaching and research? You can respond with how you would meet these expectations. If you need research space, ask forcefully to see the space you would occupy. Talk about possible renovations. Ask to tour the facilities and try to find out to what extent equipment is shared. Ask about how the office works: is secretarial and other technical help available for research as well as teaching activities? Ask to see the teaching laboratories. Visit the library; does it have acceptable holdings in your area? Do they appear accessible? How are new acquisitions chosen? What are the computer facilities like? What is the nature of the research and grants office?

The chair should be willing to talk about how faculty is evaluated. When are appointments reviewed? Ask how the tenure system works without sounding accusatory. Ask why faculty have left the department. Now is probably not the time to talk salary or set-up money, but it is the time to talk about facilities and work conditions. Will you be a member of the graduate faculty right away or only after a separate election? Assert your concerns without dominating the interview or appearing too aggressive. Talk enough to demonstrate your intelligence, knowledge and tact, but don't become a bore or dominate conversations.

You will probably be circulated among the faculty for interviews of an hour or less. Now is when the homework pays off. If you know a little about someone before you are introduced, it may save insulting the National Academy member, and it will certainly flatter the assistant professor. Let them interview you, but ask them about their research and teaching roles in the department. Ask about department facilities and working conditions. Ask the young faculty about how they were received; ask the older faculty how they view the new appointment. Ask about plans for future appointments and try to learn about the age structure of the department. Is it likely that you can become a force in determining the future of the department? It is important to uncover schisms and to learn what the department prides itself on. Asking the same questions of several faculty members independently is a good way to find if there is a consensus on important issues. When you go to lunch and dinner with faculty try to gauge the familiarity among them as a way of predicting your own social and intellectual interactions.

You will probably be interviewed by a dean or two. This is often a courtesy interview that you need to get through with grace rather than aggression. Save your tough questions for the department head. The deans are probably looking at your professionalism rather than taking a hard look at your research or the details of the appointment. They may be interested to see if you can explain your scholarly interest to a lay person. It is probably appropriate to ask deans about promotion and tenure policies as they are applied to the school as a whole. It is also okay to ask how they view the future of the department, but this may be awkward if the department head is attending.

Try hard to get a chance to talk with students in the absence of faculty, especially if the department has a graduate program. Ask them about the strengths and weaknesses of the current program and how they view the new appointment. Graduate students are likely to be honest, but they too have axes to grind. Making a good impression with graduate students may exert a strong influence on the faculty. I think that the current intellectual vigor of a graduate department can be uncovered in an hour's conversation with a fair sample of students. Learn about how graduate students are supported with respect to both their stipends and their research needs. Ask about the fate of recent graduates. Are graduate students housed in faculty space or do they have their own offices?

The Offer

There may be a long wait between the interview and the next telephone call. Don't get pessimistic too early. Many search committees choose a slate of three to six candidates and interview them all before they make a decision. If you are pressed by another offer, it is entirely appropriate to call the department, tell them of your situation, and ask for advice. This game can get a bit complex. Do not let yourself be pressured into making a premature decision, but at the same time be honest with yourself and the departments involved. Never play games with potential employers. You may get caught.

Some schools will invite you for a second visit once you become their favored candidate, although this is more likely at senior rather than junior levels. In some circumstances it could be appropriate for you to request a second visit, even if you have to pay for it yourself. The tables are now turned and the department is courting you. On a second visit you should work very hard to gather the information you need to make the decision. This is the time to talk money, space, equipment, and teaching responsibilities. It is also appropriate to bring your spouse along and get a feel for his or her employment prospects, housing, and the community. It would not be ethical to accept an invitation for a second visit unless you are very serious about accepting the offer.

There is probably some negotiating room when considering an offer, although there is little latitude if the position is temporary or has only a very slight chance of resulting in tenure. There is much more room if you are being hired to strengthen a department or to expand its range of interests. Salary is probably predetermined, but it might be increased if you have more than the usual amount of postdoctoral experience or a firm, and higher, offer from another school. Salary can probably be negotiated every year and good work will be rewarded in time. Now is the time to negotiate space and initial equipment allowance, because once you arrive as an assistant professor it may be difficult to expand your research space and it may be impossible to buy that personal computer. Research grants will generally pay for the direct costs of doing research, but ordinarily they will not pay for renovations and office equipment. Get firm commitments for those file cabinets, bookshelves, blackboards, and word processors. The amount of set-up money that can be expected varies widely among schools and among fields. Talk to your friends and the junior faculty to help calibrate your negotiations.

As always try to get the results of your discussion in writing. Schools vary considerably in the formality of their offers. Some schools will present you with a formal contract; others will send only an informal letter from the department chairperson.

Thinking about changing positions

At the opposite end of academic employment is the question of moving from one school to another. Movement has always been common in academia and current trends in the market and in university tenure policies suggest that professors may become even more mobile. It is a fortunate group who landed the job of choice directly out of graduate school and have remained contentedly fulfilled ever since. It is far more common for academics to take a zigzag course toward the position that suits them best.

Your ability to obtain a position successfully certainly rises during graduate and postdoctoral studies. Some peak on the day of their dissertation defense and never fulfill the hopes of their advisors. A very high proportion of doctoral dissertations in all fields are never published. Only a few scholars continue to rise in stature until they are sought to fill endowed chairs at the most prestigious institutions. Most of us will fall in that vast middle group of promising young scholars who go on to timely promotion to full professors and then slowly burn out or go into real estate. The problem is to guess when you will peak as an academic commodity. I advise students to determine as soon as possible the kind of scholarly life they wish to lead and then to work hard to achieve it. Dedication to teaching and dedication to research are often in conflict, and it is important to realize your own goals as early as possible. When you obtain your first position, it is necessary to think about how you fit into a department and how you see your career developing. The first year or two of a position are intellectually, psychologically, and physically exhausting. Life may be very lonely, too. The graduate student's social life may be very different from the life of a single assistant professor in a department where everyone else is over thirty and has two kids and a house. But everything gets easier. In the second or third year you still have a good chance of moving up. Your doctoral research should be published or in press; you should have a new direction to your research independent of that of your old advisor; and, most important perhaps, you should have a realistic view of academic life and your own evaluation of the relative importance of teaching and research.

It is far easier to move up as an assistant professor than as a tenured professor. A change of positions as an associate or full professor may require paying the price of chairing a department for a few years. The decision to apply for another position has to be considered carefully. When to tell your present employer is a difficult decision. If your motivations are obvious, such as a change from a small college to a research university, or vice versa, there is little problem. But a move that appears to be a lateral one may antagonize the very people you have to live with. It is probably better to be frank up front than risk an awkward situation later. Using job offers to extort salary increases and more research space is an old tradition in academia, but it can be a dangerous game. In my opinion it is an unnecessary game: your needs will be met if you do well and can demonstrate that your case is valid. The time and energy involved in empty interviews will detract from your research and teaching productivity, and you certainly risk antagonizing your current colleagues. Academics are inveterate gossips: you may be able to play a few rounds of this game, but the offers will soon start to taper off. Remember also that a threat to resign unless an outside offer is met may be accepted.

What if you don't get tenure? The school owes you a full explanation of how the decision was made and why it was negative. You owe yourself a careful consideration of your performance and your aspirations. Do you want to try again at the same kind of school? Do you want to shift type of department? Or is now a good time to get out of academia? It is relatively easy to move from a prestigious university with a reputation for not granting tenure to another research university with a different policy. It is probably hard to move from a college position with an emphasis on teaching to a research-oriented university. It may be best to find a research position, probably on soft money, for a couple of years to help establish, or rejuvenate, your research credentials.

Conclusion

This essay may seem a bit commercial and crass. Is this the way a community of scholars should treat each other? Am I doing things for the right reason? Colleges and universities are increasingly run by hard-nosed administrators. They may come from academic backgrounds, but most of them have been faced with a decade of declining enrollments, declining government subsidies, rising costs, and a surplus of eager applicants for every position they offer. You have to apply some tactics of your own in order to obtain the freedom to set your own directions and standards. The best preparation for professorhood is rapid intellectual growth and productive scholarship. The best way to present yourself at an interview is as a dedicated scholar with fresh ideas and a willingness to work hard. The best way to negotiate in response to an offer is to consider your own needs as a scholar, teacher, and person. The best way to get tenure is to maintain the proper balance between those three. Once you have made it, your students will ask you how you did it. If they ask *why* you did it, the answer is far easier.

7   The Job Market—
An Overview

Sudhir Shetty

Perhaps the greatest remaining mystery for the newly minted Ph.D. is the actual working of the job "market." The description that follows is based entirely upon my experience of seeking a position in economics, but while the institutional details no doubt vary across disciplines, many of the general aspects noted below apply to the academic job market in other fields as well. My purpose, then, is to provide a look at this market from the perspective of the seller—the prospective Ph.D. The need for such a summary is inherent in my thesis: that success on the job market depends largely on preparation and awareness.

Although my emphasis is on the process of looking for a job within academia, there are sectors other than higher education (academics) that offer job opportunities for Ph.D.s in most fields. One of the first decisions you, as a job-seeker, must make, therefore, is whether to concentrate on only one of these areas or to look for both academic and nonacademic positions. My experience has convinced me that trying to appeal to two or more sets of employers, each of whom is looking for somewhat different qualities in their candidates, can present tricky problems in changing your hats to suit the occasion. If you prefer the simple life or are fairly sure where your future lies, it makes a lot of sense to concentrate on either the academic or nonacademic side of the market.

Almost all the initial interviewing for tenure-track positions in economics (and for the majority of the nonacademic positions) takes place in three hectic days at the annual American Economic Association meetings in late December. It is natural, then, to divide the present discussion into three parts, corresponding to the phases before, during, and after these meetings.

Before the Meetings

Prepare your vitae well before any application deadlines. Make it snappy—not much longer than a page. In particular do not exaggerate your qualifications or achievements, especially with regard to specialization and work in progress.

Also write it so that it appeals to the particular constituency you have in mind. If you are applying to different kinds of positions you should have more that one version of your vitae so that the most appropriate one can be sent out for each position.

In the semester before you plan to go on the market, you need to complete work on at least one paper that is worthy of being mailed out along with your applications and of being presented at job seminars. Usually, the paper represents the parts of your dissertation that have been written up for publication. It should follow the format of a journal article (even if somewhat lengthier), and particularly close attention should be paid to the Introduction, Conclusion, and the Abstract since these are usually the only parts that potential interviewers have a chance to read. If you have not made sufficient progress on your dissertation so as to be able to write a good paper from it, then postpone going on the market.

Circulate a draft of your job market paper(s) to departmental faculty members in your field and especially to your advisor(s). This not only attracts constructive comments that will help you in rewriting the paper, but also exposes you and your work to others in the department who might prove useful in either calling or receiving calls about positions in the field. Circulating papers in advance will also ensure that when you ask your faculty for recommendations they can speak directly and knowledgeably about the work you are doing rather than generally or vaguely about what a fine person you are.

By the middle of October start generating a first list of schools (or nonacademic jobs) to which you are interested in applying. In doing this, consult your department's job book and various issues of *Job Openings for Economists* (or the corresponding publication in your field). The latter is particularly important for academic jobs and might also include some listings for nonacademic positions.

In formulating this initial list, keep in mind the segment of the market you are aiming at: you should consider such things as the quality of schools, the types of positions, primary and secondary fields, and regional preferences. Use these questions as a basis for discussions with your advisor(s). Tell him or her what kinds of jobs you are particularly interested in. Talk to him about the positions on your list and others that he may know about. Find out at which schools your advisor has an inside connection or other links. Remember that the easiest way to get an interview with a school is for an advisor or faculty member to call a contact on the department's recruitment committee concerning your application. The most important consideration in deciding on this list of schools is position. Don't aim too high or too low. That decision is largely a judgment call, and the best guide for helping you determine is a frank and honest advisor.

Also, consider the placement record of past Ph.D.s from your department in estimating the appropriate quality range. Saturate this range with applications, but also apply to a few "insurance" schools (ranked lower) and some potential "miracles" (ranked higher). Apply to all schools within the range that you consider safe, irrespective of whether they have actually advertised any positions (unless of course, you are sure that the school is not hiring). This is a worthwhile strategy since job advertisements frequently appear later than you might anticipate.

By the end of October, you should have a tentative final list of schools and/or nonacademic positions to which you will be applying. It is also time to polish up the paper and vitae. The next step is to coordinate the mailings of your applications. Mailings should be completed before Thanksgiving—mid-November is best. Any delays beyond the end of November seriously jeopardize your chances of arranging interviews. Remember also that it is almost impossible to schedule interviews once you are at the annual meetings.

Apart from your vitae, the packet mailed to each school on your list contains the letters of reference. You have to ensure that all these materials get to whomever is coordinating the mailings so that you can meet your deadlines. This is hardest to ensure for the letters of reference. Therefore you should start reminding your referees about their obligations well before your deadline and continue doing so until these letters have been written.

For the top schools/jobs on your list and others that specifically require it, send a copy of your paper either with these materials or in a separate mailing after the applications have been sent. If you send the paper separately, explain in a very brief cover letter that this material is supplementary and that your other application materials should already have been received.

If your mailings were on schedule, replies from the schools should start trickling in by early to mid-December. Schools vary, however, in promptness: some departments wait as long as the week before the annual meetings to schedule interviews. Do not panic, therefore, if your calls are a little late in coming. If there are any schools in which you are especially interested and from which you have not heard by mid-December, get your advisor or another faculty member to check with someone in that department. You should do this only as a last resort and only if the department in question is among your very top choices.

Be organized in scheduling interviews. Each lasts between fifteen and thirty minutes, although some can be as long as forty-five minutes. Ask how long the interviews will last and be sure to find out the hotel and room in which each will be held. Find out what alternative times the school can offer you. Try to space interviews evenly between and within days. Even five interviews on any day are exhausting; six or more are dangerous. Since most interviews (at least for academic jobs) are held in the same hotels as sessions of the annual meeting, look at the architectural layout of the hotels (these are usually found in the program of the convention) so that you can schedule interviews without having to sprint between thirty-four floors. While scheduling the interviews, try to find out who will be interviewing (if this information is available). If possible, schedule important interviews on days two and three of the meetings; mornings and early afternoons are also preferable so that you are neither jaded nor quivering. Most of the time, however, the better schools on your list will leave you little choice on these matters.

Plan on spending almost all of the last three to four weeks before the meeting preparing for the interviews. Preparation with respect to the following is particularly critical:

(1) A five to ten minute "spiel" on your dissertation. This will be your response to the most common opening line at the interview—"tell us about your dissertation." Concentrate on defining the questions that are posed in your work, their importance and novelty, the link with existing work, and how your contribution adds to knowledge or fills in gaps. You might also want to mention how you got interested in the topic. Be specific about at least a couple of results and note how far along you are in the research and the actual writing. Expect some dumb questions and a few nasty ones. This preparation is by far the most important part of each interview and therefore spend a lot of time working on it. Practice your summary on friends and colleagues, especially those outside your major specialty (so they can tell whether you "make sense" to the *general* interviewer).

(2) Your research interests. This is another common question, particularly in interviews with research-oriented departments. You should have at least a couple of ideas ready. Even if these are not cut and dried, they should be conceived well enough to present to the interviewers an image of a serious and eager researcher who is prepared to set out independent of a graduate-school mentor.

(3) Courses you can teach. You must be prepared to be specific here, not only in terms of the courses but also their content, the texts you would use, your general preference for large or small classes, and so forth. Not all interviewers will ask you for such details, but one or two definitely will.

(4) Important ideas in your major field. This question is asked only by some of the better interviewers and is a test of whether you have kept abreast of developments in the field outside of your thesis topic.

(5) Your questions about the department. Always be prepared to ask a few of these, even if they sound trite. They indicate interest on your part, and they may elicit important information to help you make your final decision whether to accept a job or not. The usual questions concern the interests of the faculty, the nature of the undergraduate and graduate programs, the normal teaching load, computer facilities, summer support, etc. Do not ask about salary or the physical environment of the school. You will learn about these on a visit, if you are invited to make one.

(6) Special factors. If you are interested mainly in teaching schools or specific kinds of nonacademic jobs such as government agencies or consultancy organizations be prepared to explain the basis for that interest. If you can give good reason, your commitment will be established.

The Meetings

When you are on the job market, the meetings themselves are a sideshow. You will barely have the time and energy to get through your interviews. Most interviews are held in hotel rooms reserved for this purpose by the various schools and organizations. Since hotel switchboards do not give out room numbers of guests, you will have to get this information directly from interviewers. Therefore, when you schedule the interviews, always ask for the name in which the department will reserve its room.

During the meetings, the advantage of staying at one of the hotels that hosts sessions is the proximity of most of your interviews. The obvious problem is the cost relative to staying in cheaper hotels or with friends. In choosing your hotel, do not underestimate the convenience of being close to the action, and be sure that you make reservations early if you decide to stay at one of the main convention hotels.

The types of questions asked at the interviews are usually some subset of those mentioned above. Although the emphasis varies among interviews, your dissertation will almost always have pride of place in the questioning. Since the questions are so repetitive, you will often be saying the same things over and over, but sound fascinated with your work, react to questions enthusiastically, and do not get fazed by the responses or eccentricities of the interviewers. Apart from being tiring, it is also tiresome to go through this process more than five or six times each day of the meetings. This is another good reason for not scheduling too many interviews, especially if the schools do not interest you. The number of interviewers varies, but it is usually two or three. Most are friendly or at least amiable. Dispositions, however, also vary with time of day and quality of the department (the later in the day and the higher ranked the school, the more obnoxious the interviewers are likely to be).

Get to your interviews on time. Being punctual is not usually a problem, provided not too many of your interviews are scheduled back to back. Dress so that you convey a professional image: attempt to look presentable and well groomed, which does not mean that you need to wear a $500 suit! Do not give the impression of being overly chummy with the interviewer, but be sure to shake hands before and after the interview. Most important, try to relax. While this is usually easier said than done, draw comfort from the fact that most of your interviewers probably have not read your paper or any other work in your field. Therefore, if you have prepared well, it is very unlikely that you will face a question that you are unable to answer satisfactorily.

Keep your answers short and make your points without technical detail. Try to avoid responses that appear glib or cavalier. Be sure to stress the relevance of your dissertation research and if one or more of your interviewers has worked in the same area, note the relation of your research to his/her work. If you are interviewing at a teaching school, mention the importance you attach to teaching and the course material you intend to develop. Throughout these interviews and in preparing for them, remember that your ultimate objective is to portray yourself as bright, articulate, and congenial and to convince your interviewers that you will make a fine colleague.

After the Meetings

As with scheduling interviews, schools vary in the time it takes them to decide on which candidates to invite for campus visits. As a rule, higher ranked departments tend to make these decisions earlier but this varies also with the length of the Christmas vacations taken by members of the recruitment committee. If you plan to be out of town during the semester recess, leave a number where you can be contacted with the secretary in the department. Some early birds may call back as soon as ten days after the meetings.

After you receive a couple of callbacks, if you have not heard from some of the schools that interviewed you and in which you are still interested, call and tell them as modestly as possible that you are in demand. This helps them make up their minds more quickly. If you are invited to a school in a given region (e.g., California) and had interviews at the meeting with neighboring schools, call and tell them you will be in the area. If these schools were hesitant to pay the entire cost of your trip, such an offer often induces them to invite you to visit them as well.

If your interviews went exceptionally well, you may be flooded with calls from schools. Since each visit takes much energy, you may want to be choosy after a couple of visits. It is perfectly acceptable (even, perhaps, ethical) to turn down campus visits if you are not seriously interested in the school and think it likely that you will have offers elsewhere. Remember that the novelty of free rides vanishes quickly when a seminar awaits you at the end of each one. When you are contacted about the campus visit, you will also probably be informed about transportation from the airport and of the other arrangements for your visit. If such information is not volunteered, save yourself problems during the visit by asking for it at this stage.

In making your travel plans always use a travel agent (remember their service is free). You will find that the whole process requires substantial resources since you will be expected to incur most of the traveling expenses up front and will be reimbursed weeks or sometimes even months after your campus visit. The best preparation is to obtain a credit card or some other viable line of credit during the period.

Each campus visit is filled with a day of interviews and your seminar. The day usually begins at breakfast with a member of the department and ends only after dinner with a group of faculty. Each visit is exhausting, and you have to be prepared physically and mentally.

Apart from the sixty- to ninety-minute seminar in which you will be expected to present some of your work, the day will be filled with thirty- to forty-five-minute interviews with individual faculty members. These interviews with faculty are more informal than the interview at the meetings. The questions you will be asked during these can vary from technical ones concerning your current or future research to others about your graduate program or faculty advisors that are more mundane.

Your objectives during these interviews should be twofold. First, to present yourself in the best possible light, particularly as being stimulating and well informed. Second, you should get information about the department and the school so that you can judge how well you might fit in, if you are offered a position. Remember that most schools are selling themselves to you just as much as you are trying to impress them. So, they will be only too willing to talk to you about themselves. Relevant questions that you might ask include the research interests of faculty, the importance of teaching, relations between junior and senior faculty, research funding and summer support. You will definitely meet with the department chair and at least a couple of assistant professors—all of whom are good sources of information about the department.

The seminar is the most important part of the visit. Since it is on your performance here that your success usually hinges, work hard on preparing your presentation right after the meetings so that you are ready when the campus visits begin. Work especially on the introduction and conclusion. Give a practice seminar to friends or colleagues before you "take the show on the road." As you give seminars at different schools, pick up hints on substance and style and incorporate suggestions into your presentation at the next stop.

Don't count on being given time to prepare your talk right before every seminar. In your presentation, make your introduction and conclusion sufficiently general in tone and content so that you appeal to most of your audience rather than solely to those in your specific area. Try to keep calm even when some of the questioning turns pointed or critical. This will be easier if you can separate yourself from your work enough so as not to consider professional criticism a personal attack (obviously harder in practice than it sounds). It should help your nerves to remember that you know more about the material you are presenting than anyone else does and that you are the one in control during the seminar.

The key, then, to your campus visit is to relax and enjoy as much of it as you can. This is not easy since you will be the focus of attention, but concentrate on being alert, personable, and bright, and above all, don't worry about your competition.

It is excruciating to wait for offers after you conclude a set of campus visits. Even a day seems forever at this stage, but it often takes quite a while for schools to make final decisions. So you have to keep visiting other schools until something comes through. But remember that all you really need from all these visits is one acceptable offer! Once you have an offer, you can either accept or use it to pressure the other schools that you have visited into making a decision (if you think that you might prefer their offers).

Finally, it will all be over the day you sign on the dotted line, politely turn

What do I hope my students will know at the end that they
do not know now?

To actively involve students:

Assume they're anxious to learn

Small writing/research projects that are not overwhelming but
promote incremental growth in competence

Syllabus; clear + complete

Each day's responsibility should be spelled out along w/ questions to guide
students' reading? (what's the evidence? is evidence convincing?)

In list 8 logically articulated questions that will elicit principle ideas

Most questions = ask students to think + bring to bear what they have read, +
their kn of the wld on an issue at hand –

Begin w/ provocative & possible unexpected question

Shy students – assign specific questions for next class

Summarize frequently

Begin w/ summary of how course is progressing. Active learning changes
learning ≠ simply memorize. Memorize material is forgotten easy.
Student has spectrum → participate; one who is capable of learning whatever
out & the vast body & kn she needs to know for a particular purpose.

tchr must prove ...

tchr = help student learn how to come to UC & nurse...

nursing courses

— try to find out what students know

| learn names fast

— be willing to admit error

— be willing to experiment

— keep on being yourself all the time

— try to help students feel more more competent

— be accessible outside class

— keep thinking about the educational process — what it ought to accomplish, how one can make it work better

exams: set problems for students to tackle.

down any other offers you might have had, and celebrate your good fortune at not having to join the reserve army of the unemployed. After the partying is over, it will begin to sink in that the hardest part still lies ahead. You have to get back to the unfinished thesis that has almost been forgotten in all the excitement but that still lies between you and life after graduate school! After the ups and downs of the job market experience though, even the thesis may seem more appealing.

8 The Tenure System

Matthew W. Finkin

Most of the new Ph.D.s who obtain positions as an assistant professor at one of the three thousand colleges and universities in this country will serve under a system of faculty appointment and retention characterized by a relatively lengthy period of probationary service, at the close of which one is either given a terminal appointment or accorded academic tenure. Though the tenure system has always had its critics, and is being challenged today by devices that erode it indirectly, it continues to be an essential element of the academic enterprise. It is important, therefore, that the new assistant professor understand both the history and the nature of that system.

My purpose here is to explain the fundamental character of tenure, and I shall do so by reference to the 1940 *Statement of Principle on Academic Freedom and Tenure*. The 1940 *Statement* was drafted jointly by the American Association of University Professors (AAUP) and the Association of American Colleges (AAC) and is currently endorsed by over a hundred educational organizations and disciplinary societies. It represents a set of minimum standards of sound academic practice and has become widely accepted as the norm at the vast majority of four-year colleges and universities.

Academic Freedom

No discussion of the tenure system can begin without first exploring its reason for being: the protection of academic freedom.[1] The connection between the two may not be obvious to young academics who have not witnessed at first hand the intense academic freedom controversies of the past—over social and economic views in the early decades of the century, over political orthodoxy in the 1950s and early 1960s, and over the Vietnam

War in the 1970s. Indeed, one of the contemporary arguments made by those opposed to tenure is that because the first amendment of the United States Constitution has now come to protect the free speech of public employees—including professors employed in publicly operated systems of higher education—that direct protection, vindicated through the judicial system, obviates the need for tenure.

I refer to this argument at the outset not only because it allows me to talk about law, but more importantly, because a brief legal excursion will illuminate the distinctive meaning of academic freedom. Academic freedom has indeed been spoken of by the United States Supreme Court as a special concern of the first amendment, but that otherwise welcome expression is found only in cases of external political incursions upon the institution, by way of investigations into "subversive" teaching and mandatory disclaimers of "subversive" beliefs or advocacy.[2] The Court has not addressed the question of intramural regulation of professional speech or activity. Moreover, when the Court extended the first amendment to the public political utterances of public employees, in the *Pickering*[3] case in 1968, it did so by adopting a balancing test:

> [T]he State has interests as an employer in regulating the speech of its employees that differ significantly from those it possesses in connection with regulation of the speech of a citizenry in general. The problem in any case is to arrive at a balance between the interests of the teacher, as a citizen, in commenting upon matters of public concern and the interest of the State, as an employer, in promoting the efficiency of the public services it performs through its employees.[4]

Accordingly, among the factors permissible to be weighed in the balance are the employer's need to maintain discipline by superiors and harmony among coworkers. Thus, the Court stressed that the speech in the *Pickering* case, a teacher's published letter critical of the school board on a matter of public policy, did not interfere with close and harmonious relations with the teacher's immediate superiors or coworkers and did not make factual misrepresentations in an area in which the public might presume the teacher to have some special knowledge.

In contrast to a public employee's privilege to engage in political discourse, academic freedom rests squarely on the professor's special competence. The professor's claim to freedom to express, test, and extend knowledge rests upon long professional training, the development of specialized skills, and the mastery of a particular discipline. The claim is that one is exercising a professional prerogative not shared by the citizenry at large. In consequence, the academic is held to a standard of professional care. A university groundskeeper may publish a book arguing, on pseudo-scientific grounds, for the Ptolemaic conception of the solar system, but, depending upon the claims made, a professor of astronomy would do so at his peril.

The point is not the seemingly paradoxical one that as a matter of "free speech" a groundskeeper may write a bad book whereas a professor may not, but that academic freedom is at once more narrowly circumscribed and, within its confines, more protective than a public employee's exercise of political speech. Within the realm of professional utterance, so long as the professor has adhered to the canons of responsible scholarship—has not falsified evidence, knowingly misrepresented the evidence, or acted in wanton disregard of the evidence—he is not to be placed at risk because of the controversial nature of what he has to say. So long as the professor has adhered to a professional standard of care, his disciplinary discourse is not to be weighed against *any* consideration of collegial disharmony, hierarchical accountability, or extramural displeasure.

Academic freedom in teaching is less absolute, but not much. The freedom to select curricular materials may be constrained by a departmental prerogative to require a common syllabus and even a common text for multi-sectioned courses. The professor may be required adequately to cover the announced offering before addressing collateral, if seemingly more interesting, material. And the persistent interjection of controversial (or any other) matter not germane to the offering would not be protected. But, subject to a professional obligation to state opposing views fairly (analogous to the requirement in research that the evidence not be distorted) and to treat with respect students who disagree, the teacher is free passionately to espouse controversial views that are germane to the subject. I do not, therefore, understand freedom of teaching to be limited by any obligation of "balance" or "objectivity"; the freedom is accorded equally to dispassionate dissection and to committed partisanship.

The professor is not only a researcher and teacher, but, in a sense, a citizen of the academic community. Faculty members are expected to serve on a variety of committees and other agencies of academic government that decide or recommend institutional policy; they play a host of adjudicative and advisory roles. Accordingly, the profession has long understood the performance of these professional duties to be within the compass of academic freedom. A professor's appointment cannot be terminated because of displeasure with the views he or she advances on the content of the curriculum, admissions standards, grading practices, and the like. By extension, the professor is free to criticize institutional policies and practices with which he is in disagreement.

Here, the thinking of the United States Supreme Court is not merely off the point, as in *Pickering*, but fundamentally in error. In *NLRB* v. *Yeshiva University*[5] the Court held that faculty members in private universities who play an influential role in matters of educational policy are "managerial" employees exempted from coverage under the National Labor Relations Act. The Court recognized "that the professor performing governance functions is less 'accountable' for departures from institutional policy than a middle-level industrial manager whose discretion is more confined. Moreover, traditional systems of collegiality and tenure insulate the professor from some of the sanctions applied to an industrial manager who fails to adhere to company policy."[6] The Court concluded nevertheless that the extension of the right to engage in collective bargaining would produce the very result the managerial exemption was designed to preclude: "To ensure that employees who exercise discretionary authority on behalf of the employer will not divide their loyalty between employer and union."[7]

The essential point that eluded five of the Justices is that when a professor participates in policymaking, or criticizes that adopted policy, he is not doing so "on behalf of the employer" in the industrial sense, precisely because he is *not* subject to control or sanction on the basis of the position advanced. The theory of the *Yeshiva* decision, pressed to a logical conclusion, is inconsistent with the extension of academic freedom to faculty citizenship.

That extension, however, is not without recognized limits. As in the civil setting, the protection of speech on intramural affairs would not extend to incitement to riot, nor, on a very different level, would it extend to conduct (including speech) that is destructive of the department's or institution's very ability to function.

The last aspect of academic freedom that requires comment is the professor's speech and activity as a citizen. The 1940 *Statement*, promulgated almost thirty years before public employees were held to enjoy the protection of the first amendment, subsumed the professor's speech as a citizen under the rubric of academic freedom. That subsumption has been criticized because it necessarily assumes that the professor is to be held to a professional standard of care.[8]

The issue is illustrated rather nicely by President John Silber of Boston University, recounting a case that arose while he was a dean at the University of Texas. A nontenured professor of philosophy gave a political speech on the steps of the state capitol before a crowd composed of a large number of students and had "willingly and knowingly told a lie in order to make a rhetorical point"[9] by asserting the existence of concentration camps in the state. This, to Silber, was "a clear case of poisoning the well in the market-place of ideas, and a gross betrayal of academic freedom through gross academic irresponsibility."[10] On those grounds Dean Silber decided not to reappoint the instructor. "[T]he academic," Silber argued, "neither needs nor deserves greater protection for his political freedom than that afforded the ordinary citizen. There is (and in my opinion, should be) a price for glory."[11]

If misrepresentation in order to make a rhetorical point in a political speech is beyond the pale, American political discourse might be more accurate but it would also be a good deal less robust. Indeed, it is not all that clear that the young professor's speech would have been unprotected under *Pickering*. I do not think that anyone would understand a junior professor of philosophy, engaging in an obviously radical political harangue, to have made any tacit claim to specialized professional knowledge about the existence of concentration camps,[12] nor did his political speech bring him into irreconcil-able conflict with his immediate superiors. It did bring him into sharp conflict with Dean Silber, just as Marvin Pickering was brought into sharp conflict with his school superintendent, but neither the young instructor nor Picker-ing was in close day-to-day working contact with those superiors. Nor did the young philosopher's speech produce irremediable disharmony with cowork-ers, for his departmental colleagues ultimately voted to renew his appoint-ment, which recommendation Dean Silber rejected. It was Silber's extension of the claim of *academic* freedom to the young instructor's political speech that resulted in his having *less* political freedom than, say, a university grounds-keeper of a radical persuasion, had one such made the same assertion to the same crowd.

The AAUP has attempted more generously to accommodate the claim of political free speech even under the rubric of academic freedom. The 1940 *Statement* contains an elaborate admonition that the professor's "special position in the community imposes special obligations"—that as the public may judge the professor by his utterance he should "at all times be accurate, should exercise appropriate restraint, should show respect for the opinions of others." But these admonitions have not been understood as establishing rules of conduct. A failure to exercise "appropriate restraint" may, under certain circumstances, be a basis to inquire into a professor's fitness for office, but it cannot be a basis for dismissal. This distinction, drawn by the *Pickering* Court as well, is not without grounds for criticism.[13]

Let me add two additional points to this overview of academic freedom that bear upon its relationship to tenure: first, as the *Yeshiva* decision illustrates, the courts cannot be trusted routinely to vindicate academic values,[14] and, second, even if they could, that vindication would arrive only after the professor had been dismissed and pursued years of pretrial discovery, litigation, and appeal. What is needed, in order to protect the exercise of academic freedom, is the insulation of the individual from that risk as well: whence tenure. As William Van Alstyne put it:

> The function of tenure is not only to encourage the development of specialized learning and professional expertise by providing a reasonable assurance against the dispiriting risk of summary termination; it is to maximize the freedom of the professional scholar and teacher to benefit society through the innovation and dissemination of perspectives and discoveries aided by his investigations, without fear that he must accommodate his honest perspectives to the conventional wisdom. The point is as old as Galileo and, indeed, as new as Arthur Jensen.[15]

This function of tenure has been challenged, in President Silber's words, as "absolutizing" academic freedom: "[T]enure can never protect or guarantee academic freedom. . . . Academic freedom is protected and guaranteed by the *courage* of individual professors, and by individual administrators who protect individual members of the faculty, and by students. If they express their freedom responsibly, they will not expect immunity from criticism or public dissaproval; they will recognize these risks as one of the essential conditions of responsibility."[16] That argument was dispatched over thirty years ago by the economist Fritz Machlup:

> Great scholars, great discoverers, great inventors, great teachers, great philosophers may be timid men, or they may not care enough to face vilification, or they may be too "realistic" to invite trouble. A society that wishes to avail itself of the fruits of their intellectual enterprise must give them as much immunity as possible. Assuming as a fact that scholars may be timid or too "realistic," society has developed the institution of academic freedom in order to reduce the penalties on unpopular unorthodoxy or on unfashionable orthodoxy and to encourage scholars to say whatever they feel that they have to say.[17]

Tenure

Irrespective of individual disciplines, all new academics are one in their hope to achieve tenure. They are also probably one in their misconceptions about what tenure really means. I shall try, therefore, to clear the doubts somewhat by dealing first with what tenure is and then with what it is not. A good general explanation of tenure has been supplied, again, by Van Alstyne:

> The conferral of tenure means that the institution, after utilizing a probationary period of as long as six years in which it has had ample opportunity to determine the professional competence and responsibility of its appointees, has rendered a favorable judgment establishing a rebuttable presumption of the individual's professional excellence. As the lengthy term of probationary service will have provided the institution with sufficient experience to determine whether the faculty member is worthy of a presumption of professional fitness, it has not seemed unreasonable to shift to the individual the benefit of doubt when the institution thereafter extends his service beyond the period of probation and, correspondingly, to shift to the institution the obligation fairly to show why, if at all, that faculty member should nonetheless be fired. The presumption of the tenured faculty member's professional excellence thus remains rebuttable, exactly to the extent that when it can be shown that the individual possessing tenure has nonetheless fallen short or has otherwise misconducted himself as determined according to full academic due process, the presumption is lost and the individual is subject to dismissal.[18]

Academic due process requires a triallike hearing before a faculty body with the burden of proof resting upon the administration.[19] The faculty's power is only to make a recommendation to the institution's governing board, but the findings of the faculty are entitled considerable weight. The faculty is more familiar with professional standards and is in a better position to pass upon questions of mitigation and level of sanction than is a lay governing board.

The ground upon which a tenured appointment may be terminated is "adequate cause," usually meaning some significant dereliction or misconduct but including professional incompetence as well: physical or mental incapacity and financial exigency are additional bases for the termination of tenured appointments. The latter has been a major source of controversy in the past decade as higher education endured a significant depression. It suffices to say that the AAUP would allow an institution-wide financial crisis or the total elimination of a school or department as grounds to terminate tenured (and nontenured) appointments but would not view as permissible the asserted need merely to reallocate resources—to terminate tenured faculty in unpopular departments in order to free up resources for expansion elsewhere. To the faculty members and college presidents who drafted the 1940 *Statement*, against the immediate experience of the Great Depression, tenure was not to be sacrificed on an altar of evanescent shifts in student interest. Were tenure so to be limited it would be no tenure at all; faculty members would labor under the constant risk of summary termination at an administration's discretion to allocate funds. In my opinion, no decent administration should wish to claim such power, but, regrettably, several have made just that claim and taken just that action.

Now to what tenure is not. Tenure is neither a guarantee of lifetime employment nor a sinecure: it does *not* assure future rewards in rank or salary; it is *not* insurance against any and all forms of disapprobation, collegial or administrative; it does *not* insulate the tenured from any and all forms of subsequent evaluation. Tenure protects the professor's right, in the larger search for truth, to proclaim all manner of foolishness, but it does not insulate him from being thought a fool for having so proclaimed.

Probation

Most commonly, the new appointee will receive a written offer or a written confirmation of appointment. My impression is that an elaborate document entitled a "contract" of employment tends to be rare. The notice or letter of appointment customarily indicates rank, salary, department, and duration, that is, of one or more years. It may or may not expressly incorporate the institution's rules or regulations, most often found in a compilation labeled the "Faculty Handbook" or the like.

The 1940 *Statement* requires that all terms and conditions of employment should be stated in writing to the appointee prior to the commencement of the appointment, but my impression is that apart from the minimally essential terms just noted, new faculty members are rarely given a copy of the faculty handbook prior to appointment and may not actually see a copy until months later. Nevertheless, because the terse letter or notice obviously does not spell out all the terms, the courts have routinely held that the institution's rules bearing upon faculty status—and even its customary practices in that regard—supply part of its contractual obligations. The prospective appointee should ask to be provided with a copy of the institution's rules prior to acceptance in order to assure himself or herself of the nature of the institution's guarantees of academic freedom and due process. In addition, the new academic should peruse the AAUP's journal, *Academe*, to see if the institution is currently on the Association's list of Censured Administrations.

The 1940 *Statement* provides that the probationary period not exceed seven years, including a year's notice of termination in the event the tenure decision is negative. In contrast to tenure, the burden rests upon the assistant professor to establish his or her professional excellence and the promise of future performance as measured by the institution's standards.

The latter question, of ascertaining just what those standards are, has been the source of many a disappointed expectation and formal grievance. The AAUP's *Statement on Procedural Standards in the Renewal of Faculty Appointments* recommends:

1. *Criteria and Notice of Standards.* The faculty member should be advised, early in his appointment, of the substantive and procedural standards generally employed in decisions affecting renewal and tenure. Any special standards adopted by his department or school should also be brought to his attention.

2. *Periodic Review.* There should be provision for periodic review of the faculty member's situation during the probationary service.

3. *Opportunity to Submit Material.* The faculty member should be advised of the time when decisions affecting renewal and tenure are ordinarily made, and he should be given the opportunity to submit material that he believes will be helpful to an adequate consideration of his circumstances.

The major difficulty is that evaluation is necessarily subjective and, given the breadth of the standards adopted at most institutions—scholarship, teaching, and institutional service—each of those evaluating the candidate may assign different priorities to each category and weigh them differently vis-à-vis the candidate. One indication the candidate may have of what the operational standards are may be derived from observing, within the cohort of preceding assistant professors, who was recommended and who rejected for tenure, but the same caution noted above applies even to this weather vane (wholly apart from inevitable considerations of friendship, discipleship, personality, and departmental politics).

There are, in addition, three further imponderables: first, tenure standards vary over time—economists might say, in response to the labor market—so the fact that Jones, who would not secure a favorable recommendation today, was favorably recommended only a few years ago, does not lock the department into Jones's record as the standard of what is to be expected of all future tenure candidates. This means, in effect, that the fact that Jones received tenure with only four published articles does not assure you of tenure if you publish six.

Second, the decision may permissibly rest on educational grounds having nothing to do with the faculty member's professional excellence. A department of philosophy, for example, may vote to deny tenure to a very promising metaphysician because it wishes to allocate its scarce resources in areas of philosophic inquiry that it deems more promising.

Third, one of the more unhappy categories of cases I have dealt with is of the capable academic, who seems to meet all the institution's standards for tenure, but who is nevertheless rejected by the department on vague grounds of dissatisfaction. In some cases what may be involved is an issue of academic freedom; more on that in a moment. But in others, what I have found is a somnolent department, one composed of a senior faculty, rather set in their ways, who feel a deep anxiety about a young person who is "too" bright, "too" ambitious, and possibly, a little too abrasive. What is at work, in essence, is a lack of fit between the candidate and the institution, which should have become apparent before the appointment was made.

The disappointed tenure candidate is not without recourse. Most institutions observe AAUP standards for notification of nonrenewal of appointment: after two or more years of service in the institution, a year's notice is required if the appointment is not to be continued. This allows the faculty member time to seek a position elsewhere, as well as to pursue institutional review.

The review is subject to the rules of the particular institution, which, again, the prospective candidate should secure before accepting a position. The AAUP recommends that in the event the candidate claims that a violation of academic freedom played a role in the decision, he should have available a faculty body to which that complaint can be directed. If that body finds that the complaint is one that appears to have some foundation, it may require that a full hearing be held to decide the question. The procedure is the same as in a dismissal for cause except that the burden rests upon the faculty member rather than the administration. In the event the candidate claims simply that the decision was in error, the AAUP recommends that those allegations similarly be heard by a faculty grievance committee. It is generally recognized that such a grievance body is not to substitute its judgment for that of the department, but to decide whether the candidate was given adequate consideration. In the case of the candidate who appeared to be well qualified, but who proved too unsettling to senior colleagues, the appeal would test the willingness of the faculty at large and, more importantly, of the administration to alter the department's course. This is a prerogative that presidents, provosts, or deans are rarely eager to exercise.

An affirmative department or school tenure recommendation is not self-enforcing. It may be subject, depending upon the institution's regulatory system, to additional faculty oversight and is invariably subject to additional administrative review. This review tests how well the department has done its job—how powerful a case for tenure has been made. This review may also raise questions concerning the institution's direction—its willingness to commit the resources of a tenured position to one area or department rather than another. Again, the rejection of a favorable recommendation by higher authority is subject to the same avenues of redress by the aggrieved candidates that are available in the case of a negative departmental decision. A review of the tenure process from the candidate's perspective is supplied in Craufurd Goodwin's very helpful essay elsewhere in this volume.

The Future of Tenure

At the present time we are witnessing the growth of two none-too-subtle erosions of tenure. The first is the expanding use of "non-tenure-track" positions. These are either positions for a stated term that are not subject to renewal (the "folding chair"), or, more commonly, the term appointment that is potentially ever-renewable but not subject to a tenure decision (i.e., positions of perpetual probation). The administrative justification for these is "flexibility" in the face of an uncertain economic future, declining enrollment, and unpredictable shifts in student interest. In addition, some positions that are being designated as nontenure eligible are expressly identified as less "academic" and more practical or task-oriented, such as instruction in the basics of modern languages, clinical teaching in law schools, and "professors in the practice of" in a number of professions such as architecture, engineering, and business.

The arguments against the use of the latter position are fairly straightforward. First, those who hold such positions will never be secure and so will necessarily be inhibited in the exercise of academic freedom. Surely, even "applied" teachers have academic freedom. A clinical law teacher, for example, exercises academic freedom in case selection—that is part of his freedom of teaching—and, equally, the clinical teacher whose job may be at risk may be wary of taking on a pedagogically valuable case that pits the clinic against a powerful institution in the community (or a significant donor to the university). Even the professor who teaches only French I and II may shy away from speaking out against administrative—or departmental—programs to alter the curriculum. Second, the use of this device avoids the hard test that a tenure decision requires. It is difficult to conceive that an amiable, noncontroversial teacher of large undergraduate sections or applied professional training would be nonrenewed after nine or twelve years of service; the alluring alternative is neither tenure nor termination, but merely another term. Finally, the widespread use of "practice" professors creates a two-tiered faculty composed of academic Brahmans, who have tenure, and a permanent academic underclass, who can never secure tenure. The educational implications—to students as well as to faculty—of life in such an environment ought to give pause.

The irony is that by most accounts higher education is emerging from the depression it has experienced over the past fifteen years. In the next fifteen years, the grandchildren of the baby boom will start attending college and the demand for faculty will rise as those recruited in the 1960s start to retire. The legacy of the 1980s might well be an appointments structure that is antithetical to academic freedom and educationally unsound, and whose sole justification—a claimed need for "flexibility"—will have significantly diminished if not evaporated.

The second attack on tenure is a proposal, implemented so far at a very few institutions, for the periodic evaluation of tenured faculty, or "periodic posttenure review." As I mentioned earlier, tenure does not insulate the professor from any and all forms of later evaluation; indeed, professors are constantly evaluated—for promotions, salary increases, research leaves, honors and awards, summer teaching, sabbaticals, and the like. What is new in this scheme is that the evaluation is conducted at large, uncoupled to any particular kind of decision. The proposal proceeds necessarily upon the assumption that there is such slothfulness (or worse) in tenured ranks that a system of periodic evaluation is necessary to ferret it out.

One problem with the proposal lies precisely in the amorphousness of the end to which the evaluation will be put. In a termination for cause of a tenured professor, the burden of proof rests upon the administration to show that the faculty member is unfit for office. In such a case, the "evidence" accumulated in the periodic reevaluation process (student testimony, reviews by external referees of published work, and the like) would presumably be relevant to the incumbent's fitness or competence, to be decided in a hearing, but the fact of a negative evaluation could not itself be "cause" to discharge. Were a system of posttenure review devised to make a negative evaluation "cause" for dismissal, it would, in practical effect, substitute periodic evaluation for a dismissal hearing and would be indistinguishable from the abolition of tenure and the adoption in its stead of a system of periodic appointments.

A second problem with the proposal is administrative. Assuming that the interval of five years is chosen and that the evaluations are staggered accordingly, the consequence is that four-fifths of the tenured faculty of a school or department will be evaluating one another every year for the entirety of their professional lives. In addition to sheer burdensomeness, the implications to collegial relations are staggering.

Finally, the mere accumulation of evaluations and supporting files —squirreled away in some administrative office—must have a chilling effect on academic freedom and a dampening effect upon the individual's willingness to take on long-term research. As Kingman Brewster observed in his 1972 Presidential Report at Yale:

> I think that even with their privileges and immunities our academic communities are often too timid in their explorations. The fear of failure in the peerage inhibits some of our colleagues, even when they do have tenure. Too many seek the safe road of detailed elaboration of accepted truth rather than the riskier paths of true exploration, which might defy conventional assumptions. Boldness would suffer if the research and scholarship of a mature faculty were to be subject to periodic scorekeeping, on pain of dismissal if they did not score well. Then what should be a venture in creative discovery would for almost everyone degenerate into a safe-side devotion to riskless footnote gathering.

It remains to be seen whether these devices—the nontenure track and periodic posttenure review—will take hold and become permanent features of the academic world. The AAUP has condemned them and, in the latter case, so have leading administrators.[20] I suspect that posttenure review will not become widely accepted, but survey data reveal an alarming percentage of appointments are being made to the nontenure track. These figures betray a saddening complaisance on the part of senior faculty,[21] a lack of will (or ability) to resist on the part of those accepting such appointments, an even more disheartening shift of power to institutional management, or some combination of these.

The best corrective to the erosion of tenure, and so the freedom it protects, is through the work of the American Association of University

Professors, that is, through an agency that, since 1915, has brought the pressure of enlightened professorial judgment to bear upon institutional behavior. It is therefore appropriate to close by expressing my hope that you will join and become active in the association. In the academic no less than the civil setting is vigilance a condition of liberty.

Notes

1   See generally R. Hofstadter and W. Metzger, *The Development of Academic Freedom in the United States* (1955).

2   See e.g. *Sweezy v. New Hampshire*, 354 U.S. 234 (1957) and *Keyishian v. Board of Regents*, 385 U.S. 589 (1967).

3   *Pickering v. Board of Education*, 391 U.S. 563 (1968).

4   Ibid. at 568.

5   444 U.S. 672 (1980).

6   Ibid. at 689.

7   Ibid. at 687–88.

8   Van Alstyne, "The Specific Theory of Academic Freedom and the General Issue of Civil Liberty" in *The Concept of Academic Freedom* 59 (E. Pincoffs, ed., 1972).

9   Silber, "Poisoning the Wells of Academe," 43 *Encounter* 30, 37 (1974).

10   Ibid.

11   Ibid. at 39. A fuller account of the case is provided in R. Dugger, *Our Invaded Universities* 125–136 (1974).

12   The *Pickering* Court did allow in dictum that statements made with reckless disregard for the truth might place the teacher's fitness in question. 391 U.S. n. 5 at 573. But, "[T]he statements would merely be evidence of the teacher's general competence, or lack thereof, and not an independent basis for dismissal." Ibid. This coincides with AAUP's position on extramural utterance.

13   Van Alstyne, *The Constitutional Rights of Teachers and Professors*, 1970 Duke L.J. 841, 854 (emphasis in original):

  As a matter of common experience, however, the proposition is almost certainly unsound: while preserving the most rigorous personal standards within their professional specialty, teachers, like others, may occasionally be foolish almost beyond belief outside the area of their one particular discipline. Beyond this, moreover, if one must fear that even his extramural utterances on political matters wholly unrelated to his work can be seized upon as the pretext for questioning his entire professional competence and standing, his freedom of speech will surely be chilled and his teaching against the greater prerogatives of other private citizens gravely disadvantaged. In addition, elemental considerations of political realism suggest that even reckless inaccuracy in extramural expression is in fact unlikely to occasion any inquiry into the teacher's classroom competence *unless the point of the expression offends those with power to press the inquisition.* Precisely because the Court's suggested standard is too susceptible to abuse and misapplication for purposes of retaliatory dismissal, it should not be allowed at all.

14   So, for example, the Court saw nothing amiss in a state's allowing a union to take control of the faculty's system of participation in substantive academic policy formulation, even

though the profession would separate the professor's governance prerogatives from his status as a union member. Compare *Minnesota State Board for Community Colleges* v. *Knight*, U.S., 79 L. Ed. 2d 299 (1984), with the brief *amicus curiae* of the AAUP in that case. And, even more ominously, when a United States Court of Appeals struck down so much of a state law as precluded from public school teaching persons who "advocate" certain forms of homosexual activity, the United States Supreme Court affirmed the decision only by an equally divided Court. *Board of Education of the City of Oklahoma City* v. *National Gay Task Force*, U.S., 84 L. Ed. 2d 776 (1985); see the brief *amicus curiae* of the AAUP in that case for the nature of the legislation's intrusion in campus life.

15   Van Alstyne, "Tenure: A Summary, Explanation, and 'Defense'," 27 *AAUP Bull.* 328, 330 (1971).

16   Silber, *Poisoning the Wells of Academe, supra* n. 9 at 38–39.

17   Machlup, "Some Misconceptions Concerning Academic Freedom," reprinted in *Academic Freedom and Tenure* 177, 191 (L. Joughin, ed., 1969).

18   Van Alstyne, "Tenure: A Summary, Explanation, and 'Defense'," *supra* n. 15 at 329.

19   How radical a step this requirement was is explained by Walter Metzger:

To presidents opposed to predismissal hearings of any sort, predismissal hearings by the faculty were not a small step but two giant steps in the wrong direction. Moreover, many must surely have perceived that a faculty trial would not be just another bureaucratic bridging mechanism but the staging of a drama that would require a reversal of statuses and roles. A president who became a charge maker rather than a discharge maker would put himself on a level with the person he accuses; a president who must plead as a humble adversary for the favorable judgment of the staff in robes would suffer yet more severe displacements. A great deal was being asked of the executive ego: it was being asked to concede that high should be low, unequals equal, precisely at the most perilous junction—at the point where superior and subordinate have a falling-out. And this was being asked at a time when the executive ego was notably not of the shrinking sort.

Metzger, "Academic Tenure in America: A Historical Essay" in *Faculty Tenure: A Report and Recommendations by the Commission on Academic Tenure in Higher Education* 93, 145 (1973).

20   "On Periodic Evaluation of Tenured Faculty," 69 *Academe* 1a–14a (1983).

21   According to a survey conducted for the Carnegie Foundation, roughly half the professors surveyed, almost 70 percent of whom held tenured appointments, believed that academic freedom would be protected on their campuses whether faculty members could secure tenure or not. Fact File, *The Chronicle of Higher Education*, p. 26, 18 December 1985. Although there were significant variations according to the nature of the institution, indicating that those surveyed were sensitive to likely institutional behavior, the result may be of limited significance inasmuch as most of those surveyed were not living under a tenureless regime.

9 Some Tips on Getting Tenure

Craufurd D. Goodwin

You will spend some portion of your first few years as a young professor wondering if you have made the right choices about your career and about the institution where you find yourself. Over the same period, your colleagues in that institution will be puzzling over whether they made the right choice about you. Normally, at the end of six years they will decide whether they should invite you to spend a lifetime in their midst. Because it is typically conducted in secret, and because it involves so much human drama, there is more myth and misunderstanding about how the tenure decision is made than any other campus activity. Yet if you understand clearly and face squarely what is happening to you the likelihood is greatly increased that the result will be what you want.

Three separate groups on campus will take part in your tenure decision, each with its own methods, goals, and occasionally inconsistent criteria: your own department; the entire institutional faculty, represented usually by an advisory committee on tenure; and the college or university administration. A frequent reaction of a candidate for tenure combines anger with cynicism directed at all three groups. Both elements in the reaction are misplaced. There is no reason to be angry at your employer and associates for making this decision extremely carefully. They are making a judgment involving a commitment of possibly forty years or more and an investment running into the millions of dollars. If they guess right, you will bring luster to the institution, inspiration to your students, and joy to your colleagues. If they guess wrong, you may condemn a subdiscipline within your institution to shame or irrelevance and discourage and deter generations of students. You may increase, through your sloth, the work load of your colleagues, while injecting disharmony into the community of scholars. Nor, in most cases, are there grounds for cynicism. Those who are making the judgments on which your life depends are strikingly like you—with similar background, training, and values. There is no reason to think either that these people are out to get you or that the methods by which they proceed are inexplicable. In what follows I will try to illuminate how each of the three groups thinks through the problem of judging you and how they arrive at a conclusion.

Your Department

Your immediate colleagues will have several criteria by which to judge your suitability to become a permanent member of their department. They will be the first persons asked to make an evaluation of your "case" and their preparation of your tenure file will influence profoundly the probability of a positive outcome. The precise manner in which tenure is decided varies among institutions but typically the department has the responsibility of gathering relevant materials from you (curriculum vitae, copies of publications, student evaluations, statement of research agenda, course syllabi, and other appropriate items). A review committee of several department members, often in or near your own subfield, and perhaps an outsider or two, will read your materials and solicit letters of appraisal from a list of "peers" suggested by you and by themselves. The review committee will discuss the case and prepare a recommendation to the department. The review will, in all probability, bring to bear the most highly focused examination of your accomplishments and promise. Remember, however, that "promise" was the main criterion for your original appointment; now, after five years, you must have something to show. The committee will almost certainly contain the senior professors in or closest to your own field. They will be asked to show how you rank with your peers, how your interests complement theirs, and how together as a team you cover the subdiscipline. Other committee members from the department are likely to address the wider perception of your effectiveness as a teacher of nonmajors, majors, and graduate students. They will also testify to your qualities as a colleague and as an intellectual stimulus beyond the narrow coterie of specialization in your area. If those close to you and those distant from you in the department differ over your suitability for tenure, it may tell as much about relations among them as it does about you. But in any event such a division may be a serious obstacle to your successful progress through the tenure review. If the recommendation of the review committee is negative, the chances of departmental concurrence are high, although not certain, and ways will be discussed by which you can "move on," gracefully and with least damage to your career. If the probationary period is the customary seven years, you will learn of the negative decision in the sixth year and have one full year in which to find another appointment.

If the review committee submits a positive recommendation the full department will have to decide whether to join in the favorable judgment. Their decision will be based on several considerations similar to but somewhat more general than those of the review committee. The department will ask several questions. First, will you over a lifetime add to the reputation of the department? Is your research highly regarded by the field? Is it having a visible impact? Are you likely to remain productive? Is your success with students soundly based or is it rooted in flashy performance and the camaraderie of youth, which will not last? Are people a decade from now going to say "Oh, you're at State University, don't you have Professor X"? Or will they say "Professor who?"

A second issue for the department is whether you are a good colleague. Do you take your share of the burdens of teaching, advising, committee work, and other essential chores? Are you tolerant of others? Do you interact effectively in personal and professional terms?

A question often asked by candidates is whether teaching is really taken into account. This, of course, varies with the department. But don't be taken in by campus cynicism. Even departments and universities most on the make, and reaching desperately for improvement in reputation, will not ignore teaching effectiveness altogether. All teaching institutions are necessarily judged from time to time for their teaching success by their peers, legislators, students, or others; none wishes to be thought of as irresponsible or incompetent. Hence, even though teaching strength is not likely to overwhelm research weakness in a department that takes pride in a national reputation, it may go part of the way; in departments where teaching openly takes precedence over research, of course, your skills in that respect count a great deal.

With these considerations in mind you should plan carefully from the beginning a strategy of how best to use your six years to demonstrate your indisputable worth to your department. You must conduct research that will yield appreciable results within this time frame; you must teach effectively; and you must behave as a responsible member of the academic community. You must demonstrate that your career is on a proper upward trajectory and that you know how to get somewhere that is worth going. Remember that this responsible behavior does not include misusing your most scarce and precious resource—time, even if for the moment this might seem to answer a pressing need. For example, a young faculty member who volunteers for, or accepts readily, those extra sections of the freshman course or serves unstintingly on those innumerable committees is likely to encounter gratitude at the moment but a judgment of irresponsibility and unsuitability for a permanent appointment when the tenure decision is at hand.

So now you have passed over the department hurdle; the chairman writes an enthusiastic covering letter to the dean recommending your tenure and invites colleagues to include their endorsement. He then sends the entire file onward.

The Faculty

The dean or provost will probably submit your file immediately to a committee made up of faculty, or of faculty and administrators, for advice and recommendation. This committee's task is essentially to make certain that the department did a thorough and impartial appraisal of your candidacy —and especially to assure themselves that the reviewers were well chosen and balanced and that the proper weights were applied in reaching a conclusion. This faculty, or college or university-wide committee, will pay particular attention to the possibility that personal considerations have distorted the decision either way. They are fully aware that departments can be much like a family, where close bonds and deep enmities cloud professional judgments. Moreover, prejudices of all kinds may have full rein in the intense relationships within a department. The committee's task is to protect both the institution and the candidate; it should provide detachment and a level of objectivity comparable to that sought for in our larger society in the civil courts.

One function of the institution-wide review committee is to make certain that in considering your case the department is adhering to standards observed by, or aspired to by, the entire college or university. For you, this injects just one more element of complexity into the process of which you should be aware. The institution-wide review is complicated particularly if the institution is attempting at the moment to improve itself and to identify sources of strength and weakness. On the one hand you may have done all that has been traditionally required for tenure in your department only to find that the institution-wide standards have been moved up, perhaps without your having been clearly told. On the other hand, even though on the surface your case looks strong it may receive unusually close scrutiny at the institution-wide level if your department is perceived as weak. Especially during a time of institutional self-examination your tenure case will cause your department to be judged as much as you. This may cause several things to happen. The department will be reluctant to send on your candidacy to the higher level unless it is exceptionally strong; it will also cause the department to become an unusually vociferous advocate of your case because it perceives correctly that it too is to some extent before the bar of colleagues. Even though when considering your case among themselves your department colleagues were suitably judicious, weighing carefully the pros and cons of your candidacy, now before the larger court of the university and with their own reputations at stake, they will become your attorneys, exaggerating your virtues and suppressing your vices.

Many faculty committees will attempt to answer two questions about a candidate. First, how does he or she rank among the appropriate age cohort of peers in the relevant subdiscipline. Referees may be asked to give a specific ranking among a set of names. Naturally it is interesting to the committee to see if peers of roughly equivalent distinction at roughly equivalent institutions have yet gained tenure.

The second question asked is whether the candidate has established a successful scholarly career separate from graduate school mentors. Typically a new assistant professor will arrive at the first job with several articles or a book having come out of the doctoral dissertation. The hand of an advisor or an entire graduate school committee can usually be seen in these products. The next research "program" selected by the young scholar is crucial. Does it demonstrate independence and autonomy from the graduate school or is it further progress down the short road to diminishing returns? Was the candidate able to identify an interesting question and to provide the answer without external guidance? Clearly these are not easy questions to answer, and they may never be answered by the committee unambiguously. Neither the hope nor the expectation is that a young academic will abandon immediately old friends, former teachers, or valued associations. But a young faculty member is required during the probationary period to demonstrate independent intellectual qualities that will assure a rich and productive scholarly career long after the graduate school connections have necessarily grown old and cold. This demonstration may come through significant single-authored articles, selection of novel research projects, and in various other ways appropriate for particular disciplines.

Another one of the many myths that surround the tenure process is that tenure committees just sit around and count pages of publications. In some limited sense this is true; they do look for substantial and sustained scholarly effort. But they are also extremely sensitive to quality, both good and bad. If a candidate is found just to have been grinding out potboilers and textbook material during the probationary period, or has published only in inferior journals or nonrefereed media, these activities will sometimes count in the negative even more than inactivity would have done. Moreover, if referees comment repeatedly on sloppiness, misuse of tools and data, and hasty and careless preparation even in the presence of substantial quantity, that alone can sound the death knell. If, on the contrary, merely a single article of a candidate, though slight in size, is described as brilliant, exceptionally insightful, constructively provocative, or likely to make others in the discipline sit up and take notice, this alone may carry the day positively. Sometimes, to confirm such judgments, a tenure committee will examine citation counts published in the various "citation indexes" available in most college libraries. Tenure committees, especially at institutions with a clear research focus, want to know "does a candidate, or a candidate's work, really matter." The answer "yes" may come on the basis of as few as two or three important articles. A resounding "no" may come even in the presence of a dozen undistinguished articles or more and a book or two.

If you are told that your institution's tenure committee ignores teaching in its evaluations, can't tell quality if it is rubbed in their faces, and makes decisions either by log rolling or favoritism, remember that soon you may be in their place. If the committee has been well selected, it will contain senior colleagues who are respected for their fair-mindedness and for their scholarly distinction. The chances are that most of them will know you only slightly, if at all, before they see your file, and they will attempt to perform their task with justice to you and their institution.

The Administration

If you have passed successfully over the two hurdles of your department and the faculty advisory committee, you are probably home free. But not with absolute certainty. You must still pass the more-or-less serious scrutiny of the dean, the provost (or academic vice president), the president, and perhaps even the board of trustees. There are not many conditions under which any one of these parties is likely to reverse the earlier two judgments. But there are some of which you should be aware. First, if the decisions come on markedly split votes, the administrators will want to know why, and on the assumption that departments are likely to exaggerate the virtues of their candidates (for reasons discussed above), they may find themselves persuaded more by the arguments on the negative side than on the positive. Second, it is just possible that they may know something detrimental about you that the other two groups did not, and they will exercise their prerogative to block your tenure. Third, the administrators may come to the conclusion coincidentally with your tenure consideration that either your department, or the school of which it is a part, has become weak, lacking in vigor, and unable even to operate its own processes. In that event the administration may duplicate the inquiry into your suitability for tenure through additional phone calls, letters, and discussions. In these circumstances your tenure might be denied as a prelude to some larger remedial action toward the department or school. Finally, the administration has the authority to deny your tenure on grounds of financial exigency: they find suddenly that they cannot see ahead the means to guarantee your salary to retirement without imperiling earlier commitments to already tenured faculty. Obviously a responsible and farsighted administration should not allow a tenure consideration to begin if financial exigency looms but legislators do cut budgets without announcements, depressions strike, and other untoward financial events occur that just might catch you and others in the tenure process.

The word that your tenure has indeed been approved or denied will come to you in a letter from an administrator: provost, dean, or department chairperson. Some form of explanation will probably accompany the terse communication, more in the case of a negative than of a positive decision, but not much in either case because none of the parties to the decision wishes to enter into a protracted discussion with you about details. From beginning to end the process is likely to take six months to a year. This may turn out to be one of the most anxious and stressful periods of life, for you and for your family. If the final word is "yes," it will all seem worthwhile.

But what should you do if it's "No"?

If the dreaded conclusion of the process of evaluation for tenure is that your employer decides you should go elsewhere, you have several courses of action. Once more, just as when preparing to make your case for tenure, you should plan your strategy carefully. You have at least three alternative paths to follow.

First, you can appeal the negative tenure decision, initially to the administrative officer who made the final decision, and then up the line until ultimately you reach the governing board (trustees, regents, etc.) of the institution and even the civil courts. However, you should recognize two facts of life when you consider such an appeal. First, reversals of decisions do happen, but not often, and they seldom occur when they are carried beyond the major administrative officer who communicated the decision to you. Second, appeals are not costless, either in time, money, or the goodwill of persons upon whom you may have to depend in seeking a new position. Your best hope for a successful appeal is on grounds of due process. You may charge that the review committee wrote systematically to your enemies but not to your friends, that they neglected a recent manuscript that has just been accepted for publication in the discipline's most prestigious journal, or some other claim at this level. It is least likely that an appeal will be successful if it is simply an assertion of a different judgment from that of the institution. You may point out "My friends and former professors all say I'm the most promising person of my generation. How could they be wrong?" This is seldom persuasive. Above all, present any appeal in a careful, well-modulated fashion. An hysterical harangue (which may be your instinctive reaction) against the process and on your own behalf will almost certainly put the last nail in your coffin.

Your second possible course is to request more time and a second tenure hearing at some later date. Your argument in this instance must be that some new facts in the case are imminent: a significant work is soon to appear that will change the whole complexion of your case; you are about to receive a great honor or prize; the excellent reviews of your book are just now being published. If you were given your first unsuccessful tenure review before the customary six years of probation, a second review may not present any technical problems for the administration, so long as several reviews are permitted at all. If the review took place at the usual time you will be required to sign a waiver of your right to tenure under the seven-year rule. From your own perspective you should calculate as carefully as you can whether a second review is likely to go better than the first. If not you are simply wasting a year or two of precious time. Be encouraged, however, by the thought that the university is unlikely to grant you a second review unless it concludes that there is a strong likelihood of a positive outcome.

Your third possible path is to accept the fact that tenure is not likely to come to you at this institution under any circumstances and make plans to move elsewhere. If you accept the outcome with grace and good humor the likelihood is increased that your colleagues will assist you in the search and will support your candidacy at another institution. You will normally have a full year to conduct the search, and you will do so with the hard-earned wisdom of your recent experience to guide you.

The depressing reality is, of course, that if you decide to remain in academic life, and if you are not able to gain a tenured appointment at your new location, the whole agonizing cycle will begin again.

Conclusions

A tenure review is not something that anyone but a masochist would endure voluntarily, but it is a rite of passage that must be accepted for the benefits that tenure does confer. Like so many other of life's experiences, it looks less formidable in retrospect than when in progress. And like mumps, you will probably have to go through it only once. But unlike mumps, its discomfort can be minimized if it is well understood and it is approached in the right spirit. It is hoped that these observations will set you in the right direction.

10 Academic Salaries, Benefits, and Taxes

A. Leigh DeNeef

No one enters academia, pursues a Ph.D., or becomes a college professor to make money. We have all heard some such platitude many times en route to the degree. I recall even saying it myself to a father who many years ago voiced concern over the bleak financial future of my chosen profession. I'm sure there was some validity in my response then, but more likely than not the stock answer served as well to disguise the fact that I had absolutely no idea how well or how poorly college professors were paid and knew even less about such things as fringe benefits, retirement plans, or special tax issues I was about to confront.

This is not to say, of course, that my own professors never mentioned salaries: salaries, in general and in generally complaining terms, were a frequent topic of conversation; *their* salaries or *mine* rarely were. As a result, I finished graduate school relatively ignorant about what entry-level assistant professors in my field made across the country and about whether I would make substantially more or less than a peer in a different discipline, or than a colleague in another kind of school or in another area of the country. A few interviews and campus visits later, I had a rough idea about some direct and indirect fringe benefits, but no sense about whether these were ever negotiable or whether I had a right openly to ask about them. Now, many years later, I am still puzzled by the tax laws and still not always sure whether I am appropriately using the structures that have been established for my benefit or simply avoiding paying my own fair share.

As that last confession may suggest, I make no claims here to speaking the "final word" on academic salaries, benefits, or income taxes. What I can provide is a general survey of the financial side of an academic's life and a sense of a few of the issues that any new academic will want to consider.

Academic Salaries

I will begin again with another anecdote from my own past. In 1967, when I first entered the job market, the average salary offer I received was $11,000 per year. Individual offers ranged from $9,000 to $15,000. With that kind of range, salary alone became an important consideration when it came to the actual decision about which offer to accept. That I eventually took the *lowest* offer obviously meant it was not the most important consideration, but I now marvel that I did not know at the time where that offer stood in relation to the national mean. Had I had that information, or bothered to look it up, I might well have negotiated a bit further with my subsequent department and dean. Salaries, of course, are not always negotiable, especially for entry-level positions, but no school seeking the best candidates available can afford to deviate very much from the national or regional averages, and therefore some flexibility may exist for candidates who are alert enough to seize it.

Current starting salaries for assistant professors are considerably higher today than they were in 1968. In my own university and discipline, they are about $12,000 a year higher. Generalizations about historical fluctuations are not likely to be of much help to the budding academic, however, so it is better to focus on current variations. Among the factors most significantly affecting average salary levels are the kind of institution involved, its geographical region, and disciplinary competition from nonacademic employers. In fields that offer multiple career options, academic salaries are likely to be substantially higher than in disciplines with fewer employment options. A glance at table 10.1 will show that Ph.D.'s in law, business, computer science, and engineering command very different initial salaries than those in most humanities or social science departments. One conclusion that might be drawn here is that salary negotiations should be more possible in the competitive employment areas and the new Ph.D. might tactfully and tentatively explore them.

As others in this manual have noted, there is a wide variety of institutions in the national system of higher education today. Table 10.2 shows the average salary for all ranks in institutions distinguished along two axes. Vertically, the categories of schools represented are: I = major Ph.D. research institutions; II A = comprehensive institutions not engaging in significant doctoral-level study; II B = general undergraduate schools; II C = institutions specializing in one area, such as business or engineering; III = two-year colleges; and IV = two-year colleges that

Table 10.1   Average Salary Levels for Full Professors and New Assistant Professors 1985–86 and Percentage Change from 1984–85 to 1985–86, by Discipline[1] (Listed in Descending Order of Salary Levels)

	Full Professor			New Assistant Professor	
Discipline	Average Salary	Percentage Change	Discipline	Average Salary	Percentage Change
Law	62,177	7.3	Law	38,092	3.3
Computer Info.	51,840	8.2	Business	35,670	8.1
Business	50,792	7.7	Computer Info.	35,414	8.4
Engineering	50,390	6.8	Engineering	34,523	8.1
Physical Sci.	47,639	6.2	Agriculture	27,567	10.2
Mathematics	46,053	5.6	Mathematics	26,627	7.9
Social Sci.	45,519	5.4	Physical Sci.	26,512	7.4
Biology	45,050	5.6	Biology	25,999	9.0
Psychology	44,812	5.8	Tech. & Occup.	25,971	13.6
Library	43,821	4.0	Home Econ.	25,237	10.3
Public Aff.	43,757	5.8	Public Aff.	25,208	7.2
Tech. & Occup.	43,472	9.8	Communications	25,106	13.3
Foreign Langs.	43,317	4.8	Architecture	24,957	3.4
Letters	43,283	5.6	Social Sci.	24,277	8.9
Architecture	43,032	5.4	Education	23,916	8.6
Interdisc. Stud.	42,828	3.2	Psychology	23,527	5.9
Agriculture	42,147	5.4	Library	23,338	4.5
Home Econ.	41,836	4.8	Fine Arts	22,435	6.9
Area Studies	41,309	4.8	Foreign Langs.	22,358	9.0
Communications	41,151	5.4	Area Studies	21,250	−3.4
Education	40,577	5.8	Letters	22,197	4.9
Fine Arts	39,845	5.6	Interdisc. Stud.	20,500	−2.1
All Major Fields	46,338	5.8	All Major Fields	27,839	6.8

[1]Taken from the 1985–86 and 1984–85 Faculty Salary Surveys by Discipline of Institutions Belonging to the National Association of State Universities and Land-Grant Colleges, conducted by the Office of Institutional Research, Oklahoma State University.
Source: *Academe* (March–April 1986).

do not use standard academic ranks. Horizontally, the categories are public, private, and church related. Here the distinctions are more complex. Looking at Category I schools, one might assume that private institutions always pay more than public ones; but the same examination of Category II B muddies that conclusion; with Category III, it is absolutely reversed. What is clear, however, is that across all schools, the average salary for an assistant professor (here not a *new* assistant, by the way) is around $25,000.

Geographic distribution also affects salary levels. Table 10.3 presents another tabulation of average salary by academic rank, school category, and region. The ranges displayed vary considerably, from $10,000 in the professor rank of Category I schools to but $2,000 in the assistant professor rank at the same schools. Some of the discrepancies, of course, are necessitated by differing cost-of-living adjustments, but not all. It would be to a prospective employee's advantage to check the statistics for all schools in which he or she is seriously interested. (The most available source is the *Chronicle of Higher Education*, which publishes general salary data annually.) Has that school met, exceeded, or failed to meet its category or regional average? Are the higher ranks substantially better or worse in relation to national salary levels? This question would give some sense of your financial future were you to receive tenure, stay at the institution, and progress through the ranks. Where choice of geographical region is not a personal priority on some other grounds, salary distinctions could prove a useful factor in deciding what offer to accept.

I would be remiss were I to neglect the continuing lower salaries paid to women in academia. The discrepancies between salaries at all ranks and in all categories are not, I think, as great as they were a few years ago, but the following summary clearly suggests that higher education still has a way to go to equalize its pay scales for both genders. (See table 10.4.)

With these various salary factors and ranges in mind, two conclusions might be drawn. The first is that in comparison to business and industry, academic salaries are uniformly low in relation to the expense in both years of training and educational costs. Twenty years in the profession will not substantially improve one's economic lot. No one—not even those who rise to the very top of their disciplines—is going to get rich by teaching. The implications of this fact are far-reaching. Academic households are frequently driven by simple economic necessity to double vocations and double incomes. The high cost of living in certain areas of the country may well prove impossible at current and future salary levels. And given the relatively fixed ceilings on most academic salaries, professors at all ranks are more likely than not forced to find supplementary incomes.

The necessity of supplements, in fact, is my second conclusion. For the new academic trying to raise a family or buying a first home, salary supplements are not a luxury: without them, real sacrifices may be required. For this reason many new faculty will find themselves virtually forced into summer school teaching, hectic quests for internal and external grants to support research, and various kinds of consulting work. The case of a colleague

Table 10.2   Weighted Average Salary and Average Compensation, by Category, Affiliation, and Academic Rank, 1985–86[1]

Academic Rank	Salary			
	All Combined	Public	Private Independent	Church-Related
Category I				
Professor	47,280	45,560	53,190	48,350
Associate	34,040	33,430	36,360	35,380
Assistant	28,460	28,050	29,850	28,940
Instructor	20,990	20,430	23,370	23,510
Lecturer	24,440	24,430	24,860	22,400
All Ranks	37,330	36,230	41,730	36,980
Category IIA				
Professor	39,740	39,720	40,170	39,320
Associate	31,550	31,580	31,790	31,010
Assistant	25,930	25,950	26,070	25,550
Instructor	20,820	20,820	21,270	20,180
Lecturer	21,720	21,310	22,940	25,020
All Ranks	31,990	32,090	31,980	31,010
Category IIB				
Professor	34,280	35,610	38,200	30,660
Associate	27,600	29,750	28,990	25,380
Assistant	22,980	24,890	23,640	21,370
Instructor	18,730	20,140	18,690	17,890
Lecturer	21,910	22,240	24,280	17,620
All Ranks	26,920	28,430	29,040	24,580
Category IIC				
Professor	40,280	45,000	42,040	28,490
Associate	32,050	35,040	31,650	24,200
Assistant	26,520	29,630	26,100	20,230
Instructor	21,520	23,860	21,220	17,230
Lecturer	24,040	24,140	23,950	19,000
All Ranks	32,100	35,820	31,690	24,600
Category III				
Professor	34,560	34,870	25,970	24,820
Associate	29,490	29,760	22,140	21,210
Assistant	25,140	25,480	19,960	18,980
Instructor	20,520	21,420	13,090	16,030
Lecturer	18,210	18,550	—	13,740
All Ranks	27,990	28,510	18,220	19,770
Category IV				
No Rank	28,320	28,620	18,980	19,080

Compensation			
All Combined	Public	Private Independent	Church-Related
57,240	54,860	65,310	59,030
41,620	40,730	45,050	43,560
34,720	34,240	36,440	35,020
25,740	25,100	28,720	28,060
30,410	30,420	30,920	27,010
45,410	43,920	51,310	45,150
48,270	48,160	49,080	48,200
38,610	38,620	38,980	37,970
31,740	31,840	31,630	31,120
25,490	25,510	25,960	24,540
26,880	26,420	28,190	30,510
39,020	39,130	39,060	37,910
42,000	43,150	47,310	37,470
33,680	36,300	35,580	30,850
27,700	30,330	28,580	25,530
22,340	24,510	22,100	21,140
26,750	27,090	30,650	21,010
32,740	34,610	35,570	29,710
49,420	54,160	51,640	36,690
39,310	42,700	39,040	29,810
32,450	36,390	31,870	24,640
26,200	29,420	25,790	20,390
30,060	30,400	28,810	22,810
39,330	43,550	38,860	30,870
42,830	43,260	30,710	29,880
36,630	37,000	26,140	25,630
31,380	31,870	23,630	22,680
25,620	26,870	15,320	19,560
23,500	24,020	—	16,820
34,810	35,510	21,480	23,810
34,330	34,700	22,850	22,770

Table 10.2   (continued)

Academic Rank	All Combined	Public	Salary Private Independent	Church-Related
All Categories Combined Except IV				
Professor	42,500	42,260	46,950	35,280
Associate	31,800	32,150	32,900	28,310
Assistant	26,240	26,740	26,770	23,150
Instructor	20,350	20,860	19,770	18,540
Lecturer	23,310	23,210	24,330	21,530
All Ranks	33,090	33,390	35,350	27,730

[1]Sample includes 2,159 institutions.

at a neighboring institution may be representative. As an assistant professor of technical writing at a state university, his nine-month academic salary was about $22,000. To support his family and to purchase his first house, he has taught summer school for twelve consecutive years (an additional $4,000 for two months each summer) and developed a variety of external consulting programs for businesses to teach their own employees the fundamentals of technical writing. This work was usually consigned to the two months of the year during which he was not teaching, but its financial rewards were considerable. From a minimum of $2,000–3,000 in supplementary income, the consulting practice grew to close to $20,000 a year. Obviously at this point, my friend faced a genuine crisis, for business and industry were paying almost the same amount for two months of teaching that his university was paying for nine. It may not come as a surprise that he shortly left academia for greener pastures.

Not all academics, of course, will have or want this career option, but it is reasonable to assume that most will have to develop sources of alternative and secondary incomes. That is simply a fact of academic existence, or subsistence, and it is important that the new academic confront that future as soon and as openly as possible. The choices for secondary or supplementary income vary, of course, with your particular discipline, and they may divide between academic and nonacademic prospects. Developing a new textbook, contracting with a press for copyediting or indexing jobs, and developing various consulting practices are common strategies employing your academic skills. Nonacademic examples from among my own colleagues include part-time real estate, preparation of income tax returns, weekend carpentry and masonry, tree trimming and removal, and, in my own case,

Compensation			
All Combined	Public	Private Independent	Church-Related
51,630	51,120	57,680	51,630
38,940	39,310	40,560	38,940
32,060	32,800	32,540	32,060
24,890	25,770	23,830	24,890
28,960	28,890	30,150	28,960
40,360	40,680	43,340	40,360

Source: Academe (March–April 1986).

teaching technical courses in bird photography. I must emphasize, however, that there is one cardinal rule governing all such supplemental options: whether financially necessary or merely desirable, they cannot be pursued at the expense, either in time or energy, of your academic responsibilities. It would hardly make sense to jeopardize your primary income by overcommitting to a secondary one.

Fringe Benefits

Although both the specific dollar levels and the particular kinds of fringe benefits vary widely, the majority of academic institutions participate in at least eight standard ones (some, like workman's compensation, mandated by current law): (1) some form of retirement investment; (2) medical and (3) life insurance plans; (4) disability, (5) unemployment, and (6) workman's compensation plans; (7) social security and medicare contributions; and (8) tuition benefits for employee dependents.

Since few of these institutional dollars come directly to you as a faculty member, they are often overlooked when figuring the total compensation received or income tax owed. But the figures are significant, as a second look at the right-hand columns of table 10.2 will reveal. In every institutional category, the average assistant professor salary is supplemented by between $5,000 and $6,000 in additional benefits; full professor salaries are supplemented by almost double that amount. This means, of course, that the institutional investment in you is considerably higher than a mere accumulation of direct salary payments: on the average, an amount equal to 22 percent of your salary level is paid directly to these plans by the college or

Table 10.3 Weighted Average Salary, by Region, Category, and Academic Rank, 1985–86[1]

Academic Rank	West		North Central	
	Pacific	Mountain	West N. Central	East N. Central
Category I				
Professor	52,150	41,610	42,450	46,210
Associate	34,710	31,690	31,460	34,090
Assistant	29,930	26,920	27,030	28,680
Instructor	21,430	21,790	20,050	20,830
Lecturer	28,910	22,380	18,900	22,110
All Ranks	41,840	34,440	34,700	36,950
Category IIA				
Professor	43,860	36,560	35,990	37,300
Associate	33,640	29,810	29,820	30,840
Assistant	27,380	23,630	24,940	25,790
Instructor	23,330	21,660	20,540	20,850
Lecturer	29,540	21,740	17,080	20,950
All Ranks	38,030	29,280	28,760	30,710
Category IIB				
Professor	36,580	33,870	31,580	33,170
Associate	28,950	27,730	25,740	26,930
Assistant	24,020	23,420	21,930	22,390
Instructor	19,330	19,650	18,880	19,130
Lecturer	31,170	18,080	21,690	18,970
All Ranks	29,660	27,960	25,040	26,690
Category IIC				
Professor	43,770	40,790	31,910	39,130
Associate	32,330	30,380	27,660	31,160
Assistant	28,970	26,070	23,580	25,260
Instructor	19,380	21,540	18,960	18,940
Lecturer	30,670	27,500	16,390	21,950
All Ranks	34,310	32,280	27,250	31,260
Category III				
Professor	30,820	29,180	34,750	35,690
Associate	30,190	25,750	28,920	31,480
Assistant	26,020	23,400	24,040	26,960
Instructor	25,400	22,320	19,430	23,330
Lecturer	—	21,870	—	19,120
All Ranks	29,420	24,510	27,450	30,310
Category IV				
No Rank	33,100	28,450	24,080	28,430

[1]Sample includes 2,159 institutions.

Northeast		South		
Middle Atlantic	New England	West S. Central	East S. Central	South Atlantic
51,540	51,940	44,350	42,240	47,460
36,390	36,090	32,860	32,160	31,420
29,350	29,440	27,690	26,760	28,680
20,900	24,010	20,220	19,550	21,800
24,150	27,230	21,420	27,720	23,100
40,050	40,900	34,510	33,600	36,630
40,530	42,050	36,540	35,210	39,000
32,640	33,150	30,280	29,450	31,730
26,530	27,150	25,380	24,810	26,410
21,140	22,090	20,530	20,670	20,490
23,510	25,370	19,440	18,660	21,770
32,750	34,000	29,090	28,710	30,990
38,540	40,780	31,250	30,010	32,460
30,340	30,380	26,900	24,910	26,870
24,240	25,290	23,660	21,090	22,710
19,640	21,270	20,190	17,380	17,950
21,930	25,640	20,150	17,150	21,870
29,160	31,150	25,920	24,000	25,810
44,430	39,700	33,870	31,080	42,300
33,770	32,440	28,810	26,980	34,260
26,970	26,510	23,150	22,390	28,160
21,060	22,670	19,660	17,290	24,300
24,090	28,560	19,040	—	35,470
34,030	31,780	27,800	26,830	33,400
36,670	32,370	35,300	28,760	33,500
31,290	27,890	30,600	24,810	28,040
26,160	24,640	26,400	21,470	23,890
20,290	22,640	23,130	19,350	19,980
18,110	20,940	24,210	15,950	17,310
29,340	27,980	28,350	23,040	26,830
18,370	21,120	24,240	23,290	22,790

urce: *Academe* (March–April 1986).

Table 10.4   Weighted Average Salary for Men and Women Faculty, by Category, Affiliation, and Academic Rank, 1985–86[1]

Academic Rank	Men			
	All Combined	Public	Private Independent	Church-Related
Category I				
Professor	47,660	45,890	53,690	48,790
Associate	34,480	33,850	36,910	36,040
Assistant	29,330	28,910	30,700	29,800
Instructor	22,130	21,510	24,320	25,080
Lecturer	26,140	26,170	26,230	24,440
Category IIA				
Professor	39,960	39,890	40,550	39,790
Associate	31,930	31,900	32,320	31,650
Assistant	26,670	26,670	26,860	26,360
Instructor	21,590	21,590	21,810	21,250
Lecturer	23,130	22,570	24,570	27,430
Category IIB				
Professor	34,820	36,430	38,530	31,110
Associate	28,230	30,430	29,390	25,970
Assistant	23,620	25,540	24,090	21,990
Instructor	19,250	20,840	18,790	18,430
Lecturer	23,090	23,660	24,900	18,360
Category IIC				
Professor	40,830	45,550	42,690	28,660
Associate	32,690	35,490	32,450	24,330
Assistant	27,560	30,690	27,070	20,350
Instructor	21,930	25,500	21,480	17,380
Lecturer	25,800	25,430	29,570	19,000
Category III				
Professor	35,000	35,290	26,910	25,110
Associate	30,000	30,270	22,640	20,890
Assistant	25,780	26,090	20,890	19,370
Instructor	21,020	22,070	17,270	16,160
Lecturer	19,750	20,290	—	14,210
Category IV				
No Rank	29,840	30,080	19,780	20,110

[1]Sample includes 2,155 institutions providing data by gender.

| | Women | | |
All Combined	Public	Private Independent	Church-Related
42,470	41,350	46,410	43,860
32,320	31,750	34,380	33,190
26,650	26,310	27,840	27,330
20,050	19,600	22,250	22,500
22,650	22,550	23,410	20,990
38,400	38,660	37,760	36,130
30,350	30,550	30,130	28,990
24,790	24,850	24,880	24,180
20,170	20,170	20,820	19,240
20,220	20,010	20,790	22,290
32,300	34,860	36,190	28,180
26,470	29,570	27,880	23,860
22,230	24,440	22,970	20,570
18,290	19,520	18,580	17,470
21,340	21,490	23,870	16,830
33,900	37,560	34,940	26,680
29,180	32,530	28,570	23,720
24,260	27,000	24,010	20,040
20,630	22,530	20,020	17,030
21,730	22,350	19,190	—
33,320	33,670	24,150	23,560
28,560	28,820	21,490	22,130
24,310	24,670	18,970	18,460
20,040	20,800	15,910	15,830
17,060	17,300	—	13,200
24,560	24,900	18,010	17,910

Source: *Academe* (March–April 1986).

university. Of more immediate concern to the new academic, however, is how fringe benefits provide both immediate services and long-range investments that an entry-level faculty member probably could not afford himself.

The most obvious instances of immediate benefits are medical and life insurance plans. Although the cost of medical insurance is frequently affected by the presence or absence of a major medical center, for the average private citizen such plans can be extremely costly. Current subscriber fees for a typical Blue Cross–Blue Shield comprehensive family plan covering basic hospital and major medical expenses can run as much as $2,400 per year. In contrast, university group coverages for essentially the same plan could cost as little as $960 per year. The same difference generally applies with life insurance plans. Obviously these plans will differ widely among various colleges and universities, and their advantages to you will depend upon marital status and number of children (present or anticipated). The difference, for example, between Blue Cross–Blue Shield medical plans and university plans is not nearly as great for individuals as it is for family coverage. A husband and wife both employed by the university might therefore decide that two individual policies would be far more economical than the university family plan (so long, that is, as no children were anticipated).

In any event, you should be prepared for two things shortly after arriving on your new campus. One will be a mandatory physical examination prior to enrolling in any health or life plan, and the other will be a visit to your institution's benefits office to select the appropriate plan for you. Your options will be explained to you, but typically the choices will involve how much you need to contribute (if any) and how much the university contributes (if any) to each plan. Differences in the medical plans themselves usually involve deductible amounts (that is, the dollars you must pay on any bill before the insurance takes over) and coverages. Another is that some plans allow you free choice of hospitals and doctors whereas others will prescribe those. That distinction may not seem important initially, but it could become a major one. Another question you may find important to ask is to what extent dental insurance is available under any given plan. You should also remember that most institutional group life plans are decreasing term insurance. That means that for a typical family in later years such coverage will probably need to be supplemented by some other form of straight life insurance.

Disability, unemployment, work compensation, social security, and medicare contributions paid by your institution are federally mandated programs and do not involve any options for you. You may request, however, that the benefits office explain the current levels of such compensation and what benefits accrue to you as a result of them.

The two benefits that vary most among institutions are retirement plans and tuition benefit plans. Retirement plans may be strictly institutional, national, or state, and it is extremely important that you understand the benefits and the options of each. Some common questions to ask are: What is the institutional contribution over and above whatever amount you defer from your own annual salary to such a plan? What has been the record in recent years of investment return on the plan or the annual yield for retirees? Are optional investment opportunities available to you? Is the retirement plan transferable should you decide at some point to leave the institution for another one? What survivor benefits are incorporated into the plan in case you die? What are the minimum and maximum amounts you may contribute to the plan, and does the university offer multiple plans? At what point would such contributions be subject to federal tax?

Perhaps the most widespread plan in academia today is the Teacher's Insurance and Annuity Association (TIAA) and the College Retirement Equities Fund (CREF). Under this plan a typical arrangement might look something like this. You contribute directly out of your annual salary an amount equal to, but not limited to, 5–7 percent of that salary. The university will contribute 7 percent of that portion of your salary subject to social security tax and 14 percent of the basic monthly salary in excess of that amount. Although this last figure is not likely to affect an entry-level position, it will be important as you progress upward through the academic ranks and consequently receive salary increments.

You will have to decide what portion of these contributions you wish to go into the TIAA plan and what portion to CREF. The difference, on the simplest level, is that TIAA premiums accrue on a guaranteed rate of interest whereas CREF fluxuates according to the stock market, cost of living, and other variables. In effect, then, TIAA is a more dependable plan but you may receive a smaller yield when you retire; CREF's yield is not determined until you retire and at that far-distant point could be substantially higher than present market levels (although, by the same token, it could be considerably lower too). A typical choice is to put one-half of the retirement contribution into one plan, one-half into the other. It is probably very difficult for a new academic to consider these options thoughtfully since the eventual returns are so far in the future. If your benefits office shows you the projected monthly income you may receive upon retirement, it may come as a real shock to find it two or three times your present monthly salary. Remember, therefore, that you must examine your choices comparatively among themselves, not relative to present salary limits. And you must remember as well that under current social security policies, the federal retirement income is only about $730.00 a month, so obviously that amount will have to be supplemented by some other source.

Tuition benefits also vary greatly among schools, but at current and future levels this benefit may be among the most important you will have to consider. Does the institution, for example, offer tuition remission for any or all of your children? Does it limit that option to your own school or offer to pay an amount equivalent to its tuition to a school of your (or your child's) choice? If you are at a state university, are these amounts computed on in-state or out-of-state tuition levels? Is this benefit subject to periodic review by the institution? Is the benefit subject, when used, to either state or federal tax? Since tuition benefits are applied across the university, you will probably not have any room to negotiate them. You do, however, have the chance to weigh the benefits of one school against another when initially considering your job offers.

Given the difficulty of projecting future tuition levels, it is not easy to judge the real significance of such a benefit. But if one took even a conservative estimate—that an average annual tuition at a state university fifteen years from now would be $15,000—the cost to you for every child who attended college would be $60,000. With four children, your cost could be $240,000 over the years the children attend college. That, obviously, is an incredible amount to save over the initial years of your employment, especially when you will probably also be buying such things as new cars, a house, and so forth. Any institutional contribution toward that potential debt is certainly worth careful consideration.

Other institutional benefits, such as laboratory and equipment start-up costs, moving expenses, housing, and other cash options, may be up-front money negotiable with your college or university. Not all institutions offer such benefits, however, so you must be prepared to ask after a specific offer has been extended.

Tax Issues

Because the federal income tax laws are revised often, it is not possible in this section to be precise, but we can highlight a few of the general areas in which academics may confront special tax issues. One of these concerns the fringe benefits just discussed. Contributions to retirement plans, for example, may or may not be subject to income tax. Employer contributions up to a certain level, under current policy, are not taxable, regardless of which retirement plan is used. Employee contributions, however, are taxable unless they are paid directly by the employer under some form of a salary reduction agreement. That is, again under existing law, if you agree to, say, a 7 percent reduction in salary, the university will contribute that amount, in addition to its own contribution, directly into your retirement plan and you will pay taxes only when the annuity is actually withdrawn. You will also not be liable for taxes on any interest the contributions accrue until such time as payments are received. You should be aware, however, that while salary reduction agreements currently provide a shelter from federal taxes, they may not affect state or local tax liabilities. Again, your benefits office should be able to explain what portion of your contributions would be subject to those taxes.

Under the Tax Reform Act of 1986, there is a ceiling on individual contributions to retirement plans. Such a limit (whether a percentage or a fixed dollar amount) requires faculty to pay immediate taxes on any amount in excess of that minimum. In effect, this limit severely restricts tax sheltering options, especially the special supplementary shelter now provided by IRAs. Given these restrictions, the choice of institutional retirement plans may become that much more important.

Tuition remission plans, prior to July 1985, were exempt from federal and state taxes. Beginning with that date, however, such benefits are subject to tax unless the institution makes them available to all employees, not just to faculty. You must be certain to ask, therefore, not only whether the school offers such a benefit, but also whether it does so for all employees.

Most of the other special tax options for college and university teachers involve deductions and unique tax exemptions. A few of the more common are: deductions for the cost of books, periodicals, supplies, and equipment you use in either your teaching or research; deductions for unrecovered expenses incurred while attending professional meetings or traveling to necessary laboratory or research facilities; tax exemptions for certain research grants you may receive; and deductions for use of a home office or laboratory. All of these are explained in the comprehensive *Tax Guide for College Teachers*, which is published every year by Academic Information Services, Inc., and which is your best home assistance for keeping abreast of any changes in federal and state income tax regulations. Let me summarize, though, a few points on each of the deductions/exemptions mentioned above.

Your own personal library, including the professional journals to which you subscribe, are deductible under two different plans: under the expensing option you can deduct the cost of the item in the year you purchase it up to a limit of $5,000; under the depreciation option, a specified percentage of the cost is deducted each year of the depreciation period, which is also specified by federal guidelines. To the new academic, this deduction will be extremely useful, for the capacity to purchase books and to subscribe to professional periodicals during the graduate school years probably was severely limited. Now, with a "real," if modest, income, that capacity will be increased substantially. Knowing that at least some if not all such expenses can be recovered, generally over a five-year period, will increase it even more and allow you to keep up with current publications in your field.

The same principle applies to attending professional meetings and research travel to particular libraries or laboratories. Frequently your university will reimburse you for some of these expenses, either through direct departmental funds or through a university research council, but most schools have strict limits on the total amounts they will reimburse in any given year. Rather than restrict your own professional activity to that amount, you can retrieve at least a portion of the unrecovered expenses through this deduction. The benefit is especially important to those who need to travel overseas to conduct research, since the cost of such trips will almost inevitably exceed the institution's reimbursement limits. However, there are very different conditions for deducting travel outside the United States than travel within, and you will need to check the *Tax Guide* carefully *before* planning any research or "business-with-pleasure" trip. In both of these instances it should also be noted that the 1986 Tax Reform Act restricts employee business expenses to the amount *in excess* of 2 percent of your adjusted gross income. This means, of course, that a significant portion of such expenses are not recoverable at all, and this may be particularly true of your initial years in the university.

In an age when a home computer has become more of a professional necessity than a luxury, you also should examine carefully the restrictions and the log requirements forthcoming from the IRS. The federal concern over this particular deduction seems to be founded on the difficulty of distinguishing business or professional use of computers from personal and leisure use of them. This means that the restrictions may be stringent, and you will probably have to keep verifiable records of use in order to claim a deduction. Recent case law seems to further restrict this expense by allowing only employer-required computers.

While you are applying for either university or nonuniversity research grants, you should pay cautious attention to whether or not such grants are tax exempt. Recent rulings by the IRS suggest that in cases of National Endowment for the Humanities and National Science Foundation grants, for example, exemption was dependent upon whether the original proposal stressed the *study* aspect of the research over the *result* aspect and whether the research tended to benefit the recipient of the grant rather than the grantor. As a general rule, grants that are exempt from social security payments are also exempt from income tax. Institutional monies received for research while you are on a sabbatical or during the summer are usually subject to income tax, but again see the *Tax Guide* for exceptions.

A majority of academics perform a considerable amount of their professional work at home and deductions for an office or laboratory in the home can result in substantial tax savings. In recent years, however, the IRS has tightened the rules according to which such a deduction can be claimed. For the new professor just beginning a career and probably buying a house for the first time, an alert eye to those rules could prove highly beneficial so long as current policies remain in place.

As already mentioned, I would strongly advise that every new academic study thoroughly the *Tax Guide for College Teachers* each year, but even this will not answer all your tax questions. At the relatively modest level of your present salary and probably the relatively few complications your finances will involve, it may well be to your advantage to consult a tax accountant for assistance in preparing both federal and state returns. The fees for such a service are reasonable and themselves deductible (although, like other business deductions, they are limited by the 2 percent adjusted gross income floor), and if you can locate a specialist in academic taxes the savings to you could be considerable. After all, you will have worked hard for that initial salary and, given the limited resources of the first professional years, it would be nice to keep as much of it as possible.

THREE

Teaching and Advising

Like most new Ph.D.s, you are well prepared and eager to begin independent research; your entire graduate career has been designed precisely to that end. What happens, then, when you suddenly discover that you are scheduled to teach four courses in the first semester of the new appointment? Sometimes the four courses really are four: four different preparations, four different syllabi, two mass lectures, and two small seminars. The simple demand upon your time is unlike anything you have experienced in graduate school and unless you served a year or so as a teaching assistant the mere prospect of teaching may be fraught with terror. Of course, we all decided upon this profession because on some level we wanted to teach. But now the realities of that decision can seem overwhelming.

As the following essays suggest, successful teaching is never easy and does not, as it were, come naturally. It requires serious dedication, careful preparation, tremendous energy, flexibility, and understanding. Some of these requirements can be negotiated by advanced planning and a few tricks learned from experienced colleagues; some are dependent upon more individual characteristics, on your own senses of commitment and care. In either case, advice can help to smooth the transition from student to teacher, as well as that from teacher to advisor and counselor.

In the first two essays of this chapter, two exceptionally distinguished teachers attempt to explain the principles that have made them so successful in their very different styles. Professor Christensen offers advice on teaching large lecture courses; Professor Scott on the challenges of small group discussions. The remaining essays suggest additional factors that continuously impinge upon actual classroom experience and therefore complicate the demands upon those who dare to take up the challenge to "profess."

Dr. Sandler explores a variety of sexist responses that still pervade the classroom; Dean Nathans explains the complex and various functions of advising; Drs. Butters and Kennedy address the unique challenges of "special admits." Each of these essays is directed toward additional demands upon every teacher's time and effort. But each makes the more important point that all successful teaching depends upon your continued awareness of and sensitivity to the varied constituency you have chosen to serve.

Ideally, of course, teaching and research publishing go hand in hand, but many young faculty cannot help seeing them as competitive, even conflicting demands. It is very difficult, at times, to see any tangible institutional reward for good teaching, whereas the effects of successful research are easily noted. The researcher who actually learns from and therefore depends upon his teaching seems to be the exception rather than the rule. And yet most of us, when asked what we do for a living, say "teach" much more frequently than "publish." The challenge, therefore, is to bring these two aspects of our enterprise into mutually enriching relation. The essays that follow attempt to describe some of the strategies by which this can be done.

Norman L. Christensen, Jr., is Associate Professor of Botany and Forestry at Duke University. He is a specialist in plant ecology and forest ecosystems and has long been one of the most successful teachers in Duke's distinguished botany department. Professor Christensen has also been committed for several years to the advising and training of science teachers, particularly in the MAT program at Duke.

Anne Firor Scott, Professor of History at Duke, has long been one of the most challenging and distinguished teachers at the University. Author of many volumes on American women, Professor Scott has also been an active champion of women within the academy and has served on a number of state and national commissions on the status of women. Most recently she has been a fellow at the Center for Advanced Study in the Behavioral Sciences at Stanford.

Bernice Resnick Sandler is Executive Director of the Project on the Status and Education of Women for the Association of American Colleges. She has long been an advocate of women's rights, a consultant on a wide variety of legislation concerning women, and author of important position papers published by the Project.

Elizabeth Studley Nathans is Assistant Dean of Trinity College of Arts and Sciences at Duke University and Director of that college's award-winning Pre-Major Advising Center. She is a frequent consultant to universities and to state boards of education on advising and student retention programs.

Ronald Richard Butters is Associate Professor and Director of Undergraduate Studies in English at Duke University. Professor Butters is an acclaimed linguist, but he has also taught for several years in the University's Summer Transitional Program for selected precollege students.

Christopher B. Kennedy is Assistant to the Athletic Director at Duke and Director of Academic Support. He has, since 1977, been instrumental in ensuring the highly successful graduation rates of Duke athletes and during his tenure the University has been recognized three times by the College Football Association for graduating the highest national percentage of scholarship football players.

11 The "Nuts and Bolts" of Running a Lecture Course

Norman Christensen

It could be argued that the lecture became an anachronism with the invention of the printing press. Although most of what is covered in undergraduate courses, especially courses at the introductory level, can be found in textbooks, we persist in this archaic tradition. This persistence might be due to our unwillingness to part with the past or our need to bolster our egos by publicly parading our knowledge in front of admiring students. However, I believe that the survival of the lecture format can be attributed to at least three more laudable factors. (1) Pedagogical effectiveness—I suspect (though I might not be able to conjure up data to support my suspicion) that ideas and facts presented orally and visually and reinforced by writing (i.e., note taking) are more likely to find their way into our long-term memories than ideas and facts encountered in reading alone. Certainly, the lecture format offers opportunities for demonstration and illustration not available in a text. (2) Interaction—Lectures offer the opportunity for feedback and exchange between teacher and student. I suppose this most often takes the form of questions and clarification, but it can (and should) also facilitate challenge and debate. Compared to communication by textbook, it is much more difficult for either teacher or student to become isolated. (3) Synthesis—A lecture course is, regardless of topic and for better or worse, an individual creation or personal synthesis. The lecturer provides the service of distilling from a broad field those ideas he or she feels are most relevant or important. At its worst it may give a distorted or narrow view, but at its best it can bring together apparently disjointed ideas leading to insight at a higher level.

Much of what follows in this brief summary of "dos and don'ts" in preparing and running a large lecture course is simply common sense. Furthermore, aside from problems of scale (i.e., course administration, grading large numbers of exams, etc.), I am not convinced that lecture hall teaching differs (or should differ) from teaching a small group. In fact, the most successful large lecture classes are those in which instructors are able to break down the barriers between the podium and the multitude, destroy student anonymity, and create the sense of a small seminar room. I should also warn the reader that I have drawn heavily in this exegesis on personal experience. What advice I give should be judged in the context of your own personal traits and aspirations; successful teaching is necessarily a very personal process.

Course Organization

If there is an unforgivable sin in the eyes of students, it is lack of organization. This is true regardless of class format, but is particularly so in large lecture courses. Furthermore, attention must be given to organization at several levels, from the construction of the syllabus to the preparation of lectures.

If, indeed, one value of the large lecture is to abstract and synthesize information and ideas from a diverse field, then the first step in organizing a course is deciding exactly what will and will not be included. In some cases, such as introductory courses in a discipline, a certain portion of the curriculum will be almost mandatory. I cannot imagine an introductory biology course that did not cover cell division, DNA, or metabolism, or an introductory psychology course that did not touch on Freud, Jung, and Erickson. Nevertheless, successful lecture courses covering the same material may be remarkably different from one another. To use the example I know best, three courses taught at Duke by different instructors all go by the title of Biology 14. All three cover those elements deemed essential in such introductory courses (about 50 percent of the material), but they differ markedly in the content of the remainder of the course and in overall organization. My course places heavy emphasis on organism structure and function, and evolution. One of my colleagues emphasizes systematics and ecology, and much more time is spent in the third course on cell biology and physiology. The courses are equally well received, and there is no significant difference in performance in upper-level courses among alumni of the three courses. If you were to compare the syllabi from the three courses you might conclude that any organization of material is possible: one course begins with molecular and cellular biology and progresses eventually to global ecology; another begins with global ecology and ends with evolution and genetics. In each case, the content and organization of the course reflects the interests and priorities of the instructor, but each course has a clear sense of direction. Students know where they are headed and why.

No doubt every individual has a different technique for outlining a new course. You may find the following suggestions useful. Make a list of those topics you feel are essential, estimate the amount of time required to give them adequate coverage, and then increase that by fifty percent. Arrange the items on this list with respect to an overall plan or rationale. This rationale should be stated explicitly at the beginning of the course. I once took an introductory course in genetics that amounted to forty isolated lectures. Each lecture was reasonably organized, but the course had no global organization. I must admit that, by not providing such organization, the instructor caused me to develop one for myself, but I discovered later that the wheel I invented had a number of flat spots.

Leave room in the schedule to fit in items of special interest to you. Students are usually annoyed by digressions into the backwaters of a discipline except when they feel they are being guided through the swamp by an expert. Such digressions provide students with a glimpse of how research is actually done by someone who is actually doing it.

Organizing lectures is necessarily a discipline-specific process. For the sort of material I cover, a three-step process seems to work best. I begin with a list of points, ideas, and facts that I feel should be covered on a particular topic. This list includes all the vocabulary I feel is essential. On some topics in my introductory biology course, all I know and all the students need to know are identical sets. However, on topics near to my heart, I constantly have to fight the urge to say it all. I have to remind myself that the goals of each lecture at the introductory level should be to stimulate interest in the topic and to provide sufficient vocabulary to pursue that interest. In the second step, I construct a rough outline that provides the overall rationale of the lecture. Finally, I prepare a detailed outline from which I will lecture.

The actual structure of lecture notes varies from individual to individual. Some people can stop at step 2 above. Many of my colleagues actually write their lectures word for word. I have relatively detailed notes arranged in a loose outline form. I have managed over the past several years to transfer all my lectures to word processor disks and each year print a new set that has been appropriately updated. I include in these notes illustrations I plan to use, as well as notes to myself regarding emphasis of particular points, items to be left out if time runs short, and instructions for the organization of material on the board.

Lecturing

Be suspicious of anyone who tells you exactly how you ought to lecture. If you consider all the lecture courses you have had, I am sure you will agree that there was no particular style associated with success or failure. There are, however, three common denominators to successful lecturing.

(1) Know your stuff, but be willing to admit when you do not. This may be a minor problem when teaching a specialized course in your own subdiscipline, but it becomes a major challenge in an introductory course. During the semester of the introductory biology course I lecture on topics ranging from ecology and evolution (my own areas of expertise) to cardiac physiology and biochemistry. It is not difficult to find fifty minutes worth of verbiage on the kidney, for example, but my confidence in presenting that material (and therefore the quality of my presentation) is bolstered by the fact that I spend considerable time anticipating questions and reading on this topic. I make it clear to students at the outset that I am not an expert in most of the lecture topics. Students will forgive (indeed, they are often encouraged by) a certain amount of professorial ignorance, particularly if it is coupled with a willingness on the part of the professor to pursue an answer. However, routine lack of understanding of material and inability to anticipate rather obvious questions that will arise from particular lectures are considered by most students to represent professorial sloth.

(2) Know exactly how you are going to say what you are going to say. I have a colleague who maintains that if you have to use notes to lecture on a particular topic, you are not intellectually fit to speak on that topic. I do not mind adding that he is a notoriously poor lecturer. After twelve years of lecturing on the kidney, I can almost recite the notes in my sleep. Nevertheless, I would never appear before two hundred students without my notes in front of me. Although I confess that I use them only casually, they provide the structure for a coherent presentation. They are also a marvelous security blanket. Indeed, the lectures in which I rely on notes most are those in my own subject areas. Without the discipline of notes, I am quite likely to launch off into some ethereal digression on these subjects.

In smaller lecture courses a certain level of disorientation is sometimes forgiven for the sake of a "less structured atmosphere." Success in a large lecture hall setting demands polish. I found it necessary during my first years of lecturing to large classes actually to give the lecture a couple of times to an empty room. I still do this with new lectures covering unfamiliar territory. This not only improves the quality of your presentation, but gives you an accurate idea of how much time a lecture will take.

(3) Be yourself. The most successful lecture courses are those that, while organized and polished, engage the students personally or create a small class atmosphere. A polished and organized lecture can be delivered in a relaxed and conversational manner not all that different from the way you might explain the same material to a small group over lunch. You should make every effort to let your enthusiasm for the topic come through (if you have none, do what you can to conjure some up). If you approach a lecture as something that is preventing you from getting something else done (and it frequently is), students will approach the material you present in the same manner.

Humor, if it is natural and appropriate, is an excellent way to engage students. In my first outing in introductory biology, I felt led to write jokes into my notes and attempted to "be funny" in every lecture. I was demolished by one honest student's evaluation that read "if I had wanted a comedian I would have hired one." As I have relaxed, I have found ample opportunity for ad lib humor (frequently centered on my own foibles) that reinforces a particular point or, more often, simply breaks down the isolation of standing alone at a podium before two hundred quiet faces.

I would like also to pass along a few technical ideas that I have found helpful in large lecture courses. It is often useful to supplement lectures with illustrations or charts using slides or an overhead projection. When I first tried this, students found it aided understanding on the one hand, but often made note taking difficult on the other. I began to provide copies of these graphs and illustrations on handouts and included a fairly detailed outline of the lecture as well. Over the years this practice has evolved into a bound course guide that includes a detailed syllabus, a statement of philosophy and policy, copies of the previous year's exams, and handouts for each lecture. In fact, for one particularly difficult lecture on meiosis and genetics, I include a verbatim copy of my notes. Not only has this guide proved helpful to students, but I find it allows me to cover more material in each lecture.

Another technical matter that is often given little thought is the use of the blackboard. Another student evaluation following my first lecture course suggested that I should learn to use that board.

It is very annoying when a lecturer writes everything (or worse, random snitches of everything) on the board. Even more frustrating is the individual who seems to scribble messages on the board that only he or she can decipher. I have found it useful to plan exactly what I will write on the board, and how I will arrange it. I also had to learn to leave things up sufficiently long to allow them to be copied.

Taking questions during lectures can contribute a great deal to student involvement, but, if not controlled, it can be distracting and lead to unnecessary digressions. I encourage questions during lectures and indeed solicit them when I am going over what I know to be difficult material. However, I encourage students with questions that go well beyond the scope of the material to see me individually. I also know that there are certain topics that will not be understood by even the majority of students without some thought outside of class. Students usually feel a bit relieved when told that it is all right to not understand at this moment and encouraged to consider the problem on their own.

Evaluation and Grading

I now and then consider that teaching would be the ideal profession were it not for the need to construct, administer, and grade exams. I am skeptical of the notion that any instrument I develop can, in fifty minutes, completely and fairly evaluate a student's understanding of what I have covered in a span ten times that long. I dislike the processes of exam writing and grading. Most of all, I resent the attitude that our evaluation-oriented educational system encourages among students that the grade is *the* final product of a course.

One could lay blame upon our A–F grading system, but I have seen little evidence that alternative systems are much better. During the 1960s and 1970s a number of colleges experimented with gradeless transcripts. Students were evaluated by letters compiled throughout their tenures. Not only were such letters difficult and time consuming to prepare, they were equally difficult and time consuming to read and interpret. The experiment deteriorated when professors began ending their letters with the phrase, "if we were using a conventional grading scale, this student would receive a . . . ."

Having said all that, I firmly believe that evaluations (flawed as they may be) are a necessary part of the educational process. They not only give us a comparative measure of student performance, but they also provide the best measure I know of the effectiveness of our teaching. Their success is entirely dependent upon the thought and care that go into their preparation and execution.

Students should be informed at the outset exactly how they are to be evaluated. Will the course be graded by strict percentage guidelines or by some sort of curve? What proportion of the final grade will be determined by midterm and final exams, papers, and labs? Do you plan to drop a low quiz or exam? I suggest that this information have a prominent place in the course syllabus. Once stated, you should view this as a contractual agreement to be violated only by mutual consent. Have a clearly stated policy regarding late assignments and missed exams. For example, missed classes and assignments should be excused only by clearance from an academic dean. This arrangement puts the burden on the student to show just cause for missing a course event and leaves the decision in the hands of individuals most able to judge whether a particular excuse is legitimate.

In large courses, it is necessary to schedule the dates of the exams at the outset. Students will adjust their schedules to such dates if they have them well in advance. Trying to get a large class to agree at midterm on an exam date is a simple recipe for chaos.

In most large courses grades are heavily determined by exams. Regardless of its format, an exam measures two things: how well the student knows the material and how well the examiner and examinee communicate with one another. Ideally, the variance in exam scores due to communication problems should be small.

Constructing exams presents a real dilemma. Objective-style tests (multiple-choice, true-false, completion, etc.) are the simplest and fastest to grade. Answers are either correct or not and grading can often be done by machine. While I do not use such exams, I believe they can be very effective instruments in many disciplines when properly constructed. It is possible, for example, to write multiple-choice questions that require thought and synthesis. Nevertheless, such exams are incredibly difficult to write and are subject to abuse. Every now and then I get it in my head to write an objective exam for the general biology course. It takes me a minimum of an hour to write each multiple choice question and, therefore, several days of hard work to construct the exam. Even with careful editing, I seem always to find serious glitches in one to several questions after the exam has been given. Furthermore, I have more difficulties with academic dishonesty on this style of exam than any other. Essay exams are generally easier to construct, but much more difficult to grade. I do feel it is easier with such questions to test a student's understanding of concepts and ability to synthesize material. As with objective exams, it is important that essay questions be carefully edited so that what is being asked for is absolutely clear. When I first started using such exams, I had a tendency to write wordy, "interesting" questions. I soon discovered that, in the turmoil of an exam, such questions were often confusing and misinterpreted.

In large courses, unless exams are machine graded, multiple graders are almost a necessity. This can lead to a certain amount of unevenness in grading across the class. The problem can be minimized if each question is graded for the entire class by a single person. Graders should read a significant number of exams prior to grading to calibrate themselves and to be sure that the expectations of the key are reasonable. They should be as explicit as possible regarding lost points. A copy of the exam key, with indications of how credit was assigned on each question, should be posted. I feel (though not all my colleagues agree) that students should have some recourse if they feel they lost points unfairly. My students are allowed to submit their exams for regrade within a specified time period following receipt of the exam. A written justification for regrade is also required. Each grader then responds by making appropriate changes or providing a detailed explanation for points lost. I should add that on a couple of occasions I have caught students altering their exams before submitting them for regrade. This problem was solved by xeroxing the exams prior to returning them to the students (the cost of such xeroxing is included in the fee for their course guides).

Large courses present many opportunities for academic dishonesty. While I am not convinced that the problem is as large as the popular press would lead one to believe, I do feel it is the responsibility of an instructor to be cognizant of the problem and to make certain that opportunities for cheating are minimal. The first time I was confronted with a cheating problem, I was informed by an angry (signed) note from a student. Her anger was directed not only at the cheaters, but also at my naiveté. I have found it best to meet this problem head on. I devote a section of my course guide to defining what I believe to be academic dishonesty and to describing the "wages of sin." I have discovered from experience that it is essential to be explicit about what is and is not cheating. Clearly, copying an exam and plagiarism are cheating. But is it cheating when students turn in nearly identical laboratory exercises after being encouraged to cooperate? In all cases of academic dishonesty the student is entitled to "due process." At most universities this means referral to a judicial board. Such hearings can be very time consuming and intimidating for both student and instructor, and it is very tempting to try to handle the matter "internally." This not only leads to unfair or uneven treatment, but also leaves the instructor open to potential future litigation.

Class Rapport and Instructor Accessibility

I am convinced that successful lecture hall teaching depends upon breaking down barriers between the lecturer and the students. I have also discovered that some barriers will always remain and, indeed, probably should. I arrived at Duke with a disdain for titles and hierarchy characteristic of a student of the sixties. Furthermore, I had the phenotype of an eighteen-year-old, and therefore I had great difficulty convincing various offices on campus that I was a professor; indeed, I was not all that convinced myself. I was very concerned with student interaction and tried hard to "be one of the kids." Student reaction was quite mixed. Some students liked that sort of familiarity, but many felt it bordered on patronizing. Several students commented in evaluations that they were not paying tuition to be taught by "one of the kids." Because of the simple fact that the lecturer is also sitting in judgment with regard to grades, there are necessarily going to be barriers. I also quickly discovered that I did not have time to be constantly available. Indeed, with a large class I found it necessary to set rather strict limits on accessibility. Students understand, in general, that young faculty have many competing demands, and they are quite willing to take advantage of office hours or appointments. If you have additional course staff, such as teaching assistants, do not hesitate to delegate some of this work. Occasional review sessions will allow you to deal with the most frequently asked questions and will greatly diminish demands for individual conferences.

Duke University Press   Durham and London

The

Academic's

Handbook

12   Why I Teach by Discussion

Anne Firor Scott

Teaching and learning are among the most complex activities in which human beings engage, and neither is fully understood. Why can a boy who cannot remember the dates of the War of 1812 tell you who was up to bat in the ninth inning of the 1929 Red Sox–Yankees game? Why is a teacher who seems to whisper in the classroom, who never looks up and whose tone of voice seldom changes, remembered by her students for years after as the high point of the college experience? These are the kinds of mysteries that make us humble.

What I am about to write, therefore, represents one person's experience of nearly thirty years teaching undergraduates, and a good many forays into teaching adults. My pedagogical theory developed as I tried to understand what I could see (or thought I could see) happening in the classroom. It is offered here in the hope of stimulating new teachers to think hard about what they are doing.

Real learning changes the way people think. It occurs when the learner is actively engaged in discovery—discovery of "facts," of what other people have thought, of the way in which knowledge in a particular field is created, or of the existence of unanswered questions.

It follows that an important part of a teacher's responsibility is to plan classroom experiences that promote that sense of discovery. One is not engaged in pouring knowledge into an empty vessel; one is trying to activate an intelligence to begin learning on its own. My purpose in any course is less to communicate a body of knowledge than to help students learn how that knowledge came to be and how it can be used to think through problems and organize concepts. There are many ways to do this, and they differ from one subject to another. My examples and anecdotes grow out of the experience of teaching history, but I think some variation of these methods could be developed for virtually every field of knowledge.

What follows can only be a bare outline, to be filled in with experience. Its purpose is to encourage the beginning teacher to experiment.

Let us suppose that the new teacher is assigned a course about which she knows at least something and knows, further, how to learn more. In preparing to teach the course the first question must be: what do I want to accomplish? What do I hope my students will know how to do at the end that they do not know now? At this stage be as idealistic as you like; you will fall short no matter what, but it is better to fall short of a lofty goal than to achieve a puny one.

Having established your goal, try to put it in straightforward words so that you can offer it to the class at the beginning. "This is what I hope we shall achieve this semester—I would also like to find out what *your* goals are." Since some will have no goal whatever, beyond filling a requirement or taking a course that meets at a convenient hour, this challenge gets you off to the right start. From the beginning eschew passivity; *assume* they are anxious to learn.

How do you design a syllabus for a course based on active learning? Choose reading assignments and research projects that introduce students to the basic knowledge that you consider essential. This means reading must be carefully chosen and small writing and research projects (which keep the students fully involved) must be planned so that they are not overwhelming and so that they promote an incremental growth in competence. They should gradually become more demanding as the semester goes along.

The syllabus should be clear and complete. Each day's responsibility should be spelled out, along with a few questions to guide the student's reading. "Upon what evidence does the author build his argument? Is that evidence convincing to you? Come to class prepared to discuss two or three concrete examples." If the students know these questions will be discussed in class, they will usually read carefully.

A class of this kind requires attendance. I point out on the first day that this class will produce very little that can be gotten by reading someone else's notes, that attendance is therefore expected, and that anyone who is unavoidably absent will be expected to turn in an essay on the day's assignment. Under this rule cutting is infrequent.

To prepare for the actual class meeting the instructor needs a list of logically articulated questions that will elicit the principal ideas covered in the day's reading. In practice, however, it is well to allow room for the unexpected. Sometimes the discussion takes off after the first question, and then the class develops its own direction and may develop ideas quite new to the instructor. On bad days (say the Monday after Homecoming) a fair bit of extempore lecturing may be the only way to move ahead. But, by and large, when there has been adequate preparation on the part of both student and teacher, most of the day's work can be carried along with discussion.

The nature of the instructor's questions is crucial. They should only occasionally be answerable with information. Mostly they should ask students to think and to bring to bear what they have read, and their own knowledge of the world, on the issue at hand. "Have you had even a brief experience in your life that helps you understand what it was like to be a slave? A master?" "What was Lincoln trying to accomplish in his First Inaugural? Why is the Second Inaugural so different?" "What would you need to know if you wanted to understand the real motivation for the founding of Hull House?" "What do the Mexican War, the Spanish-American War and the First World War have in common?" And so on.

If we come down to the nuts and bolts: how does one begin? With a provocative, if possible an unexpected, question that wakes up the drowsy and challenges the alert. How does one bring everybody in? By assigning specific questions ahead of time it is possible to bring along the shy students whose inclination is to sit still and listen. For example: "John, would you find out before next time what happened to the cost of living during the depression of 1893?" How does one handle the loquacious who never know when to stop? First, by not always calling on the first person who raises a hand; second, by being prepared to say "Ah—let's stop there and ask what other people think."

People ask me over and over: how do you keep the discussion on track? This is where your own outline is critical. In the midst of a lively discussion of a minor issue it is often necessary to say: "this is all very interesting but before we leave today we simply must address. . . ." And thus bring everybody back to the main issues.

It is helpful to summarize frequently. After you feel enough has been said on a particular question, "Now, let me see, I gather that most of you think . . . and a few of you also think . . . and assuming for the moment that you are all right, the next question would be. . . ."

I like to begin sometimes with a summary of where we have come so far in the course, with some reference to the way our ideas are changing and developing as we go along.

Skeptics often ask me, "What do you do when there is dead silence?" There are many ways to deal with an absence of response—some spontaneous. "Is this rush week or what is wrong with you folks?" Or rephrase the question. Make sure it has no simple answer. Sometimes it is possible just to wait, looking expectant. One of the most successful discussion leaders I ever knew used to walk into class and sit down and simply look around in a friendly way. It wouldn't be long before someone would pipe up—and the class would be off to a lively session.

The point on which I differ with many colleagues, and about which we argue a good deal, is that of what is called "coverage." Discussion, they argue, is fine for making people think, but it takes so much time that one is in danger of not "covering" the subject at hand. My view is that what is called coverage is usually a matter of memorizing a body of material that the instructor, or the consensus of people in the field, has determined to be important. All the psychological evidence I have seen suggests that this kind of learning is lost in a few weeks or months and is almost all gone within a year. So, of what use is it to the developing mind?

My own view is that the kind of learning that I call active, if it succeeds, changes the student from a spectator into a participant, one who is capable of learning whatever, out of the vast body of what we call knowledge, she needs to know for a particular purpose. There is no space here to go into the history of educational thought since Plato, but I am convinced, from all I can read, that the truly great teachers have always tried to teach students how to teach themselves.

There are various practical cautions:

(1) Try to find out what students already know, since part of your task will be relating what they don't yet know to what they do.

(2) Learn names fast. There are a number of techniques for doing this, but the sooner you can do so, the better the discussion will go.

(3) Be willing to admit error. "After listening to you I can see that I missed the point." Then it is easier for *them* to admit error.

(4) Be willing to experiment, and if one question doesn't work leave it quickly and try another. Over the years you will develop a kind of sixth sense about what will work even though students change and each class is different.

(5) Keep on learning yourself all the time. This is the *only* way to communicate what we call the joy of learning. Remember that the adage: "what you do speaks so loud I can't hear what you say" is a vital principle in teaching.

(6) Try to help your students feel more and more competent as time goes on. Never, no matter what the provocation, make fun of a student or belittle his or her effort. The most confused statement can be rephrased in a way that makes a little sense—and if the student thinks "aha, that is what I meant," maybe the next effort won't be quite so confused.

(7) <u>Be accessible out of class</u>, which means not just that you are present and accounted for at your stated office hours but that your *mind* is accessible to what they have to say.

(8) <u>Keep thinking about the educational process</u>, what it ought to accomplish, <u>how one can make it work better.</u> The kind of teaching I have here described does not grow tiresome since it is always changing and developing. And since the teacher is not bored, students are not either.

A course taught in this mode requires different kinds of examinations and different standards of evaluation from a traditional lecture course. Examinations must be designed with the goals of the course in mind: they must set problems that students can tackle, using the information and tools they have learned daily in the classroom. Such examinations are more difficult to construct, but the reward is that they are also much more interesting to read, since each one is different.

One could write endlessly on this subject but—in keeping with its philosophy—I would much rather lead a discussion than write a didactic essay. However, perhaps enough has been said to stir the reader to experiment, and experience suggests that once you try it you'll never go back to straight lecturing!

13 The Classroom Climate: Chilly for Women?

Bernice R. Sandler

Although many overt barriers have fallen over the last decade so that the door to higher education is now open for women, once inside there are many subtle barriers that remain—barriers that may be almost invisible to both students and faculty. Yet faculty, men and women alike, often inadvertently treat men and women students differently and thereby subtly undermine women's confidence in their academic ability, lower their academic and occupational aspirations, inhibit their learning, and generally lower their self-esteem.

Let me tell you how my thinking on this topic got started. A few years ago I was attending a seminar for executives in Colorado. There were nineteen people there and four participants were female. After a few days, I began to realize that the women were getting interrupted quite a bit. I checked with the other women to see if they had noticed the interruptions, and they agreed with my observation. But because I am a committed researcher, and because I wanted to be absolutely sure, I made a little chart showing the number of male interrupters, male interruptees, female interrupters, and female interruptees. The next morning I didn't participate but merely observed the seminar and filled in my chart. It turned out that the women had about double the number of interruptions the men had. There was also a difference in the kind of interruption for men and women. For men the interruption was really a continuation or development of their comments, such as "What you are saying is that Confucius and Marx were not very far apart." For women, the interruptions were of a very different nature, more trivial and less focused on their comments. For example, one woman's husband was attending the conference; one of her interruptions consisted of "Well, what do you think your husband would say about that?"—an interruption that not so subtly communicated to her that what she had said was not quite as worthwhile as what other people (the men) had said. After the class, I showed my chart to the two coleaders, who denied the accuracy of my chart, but the next morning there were no interruptions of any kind for the women. In other words, the behavior—interruptions—was changeable.

If we can identify other subtle behaviors and make people aware of them, we might be able to change a good deal of behavior. As I thought about this, I came to realize that many of the so-called social "problems" of women could be related in part to how they are treated in the classroom. For example, women are seen as passive and may often act that way, do not participate in class as much as men, and often lower their academic aspirations during their college years. They still major in the traditionally female fields, fields that perpetuate sex segregation in the workplace and the system, whereby women earn less money. To test out these ideas, I looked both at ways in which women in the classroom are singled out and treated differently and ways in which women are ignored.

Let me state at the outset that these types of behaviors are not limited to men. Often women faculty are equally at fault. Faculty who are very concerned about discrimination may inadvertently and unknowingly treat men and women differently. Although these behaviors do not happen in every class or all the time, they do happen often enough that they constitute a pattern—a pattern of behavior that dampens women's ambition, lessens their classroom participation, and attacks their self confidence.

First, let me talk about some behaviors that are not subtle at all—obvious overt behaviors that are often disparaging. Overt discriminatory comments on the part of faculty are not only still surprisingly prevalent but these comments are also often intentional—although those teachers who engage in them may be unaware of their potential for real harm. They may occur not only in individual student-teacher exchanges, but also in classrooms, office consultations, academic advising situations, and other learning contexts. There are some indications that overtly sexist verbal behavior on the part of faculty may be more prevalent in those fields and institutions where women are relative newcomers and that it often increases in both intensity and effect at the graduate level.

The quotes and examples I'm going to give are real and recent. They are excerpted from interviews and conversations with women students and from campus reports. ". . . [I]n other classes they hear women described as 'fat housewives,' 'dumb blondes,' as physically 'dirty,' as 'broads,' 'chicks,' or 'dames,' depending on the age of the speaker." "Class time is taken up by some professors with dirty jokes which . . . often happen to be derogatory to women (i.e., referring to a woman by a part of her anatomy, portraying women in jokes as simple-minded or teases, showing women as part of the 'decoration' on a slide)."

The following suggest even more deep-seated negative attitudes toward women:

–comments that disparage women in general, such as habitual references to "busy-body middle-aged women"; statements to the effect that "women are no good at anything"; or the description of a class comprised solely of women as a "goddam chicken pen."

–comments that disparage women's intellectual ability, such as belittling women's competencies in spatial concepts, math, etc., or making statements in class discussion such as, "Well, you girls probably found this boring," or "You women wouldn't understand this feeling."

–comments that disparage women's seriousness and/or academic commitment, such as, "I know you're competent, and your thesis advisor knows you're competent. The question in our minds is, are you really serious about what you're doing?" or "You're so cute. I can't see you as a professor of anything."

–comments that divert discussion of a woman student's work toward a discussion of her physical attributes or appearance, such as cutting a student off in mid-sentence to praise her attractiveness or suggesting that a student's sweater "looks big enough for both of us." While such comments may seem harmless to some professors, and may even be made with the aim of complimenting the student, they often make women uncomfortable because essentially private matters related primarily to the sex of the student are made to take precedence over the exchange of ideas and information. One student noted: "I have yet to hear a professor comment on the daily appearance of a male colleague. I have yet to go through a week without some comment pertaining to my appearance."

–Many professors, while admitting awareness of sex stereotyping language, often justify their continued use of these labels. Frequently they joke about their continued male chauvinism, as though their admission serves as an exoneration for a continuation of sexism.

–Often professors rely on sexist humor as a classroom device, either "innocently" to "spice up a dull subject" or with the conscious or unconscious motive of making women feel uncomfortable. Sexist humor can range from the blatantly sexual, such as a physics lecture in which the effects of a vacuum are shown by changes in the size of a crudely drawn woman's "boobs," or the depiction of women in anatomy teaching slides in Playboy centerfold poses, to "jokes about dating, about women students waiting to be called by men, etc."—that is, the usual fooling around that relies on a certain bad taste in order to create a lively atmosphere in class.

Sexual harassment can also have a devastating effect on some women's participation in the classroom and elsewhere. Women have been known to drop or avoid courses, change majors, and even change schools or drop out of college altogether. Even when the effect of sexual harassment is less drastic, sexual harassment, like other overt remarks, tells a woman that she is viewed in sexual terms, rather than as an individual capable of scholastic and professional achievement—that she is not viewed as an individual learner, but as a woman who, like "all women," is of limited intellectual ability, operating out of her appropriate "sphere," and likely to fail.

The subtle behaviors about which I want to talk next are of different order. Often neither the professor nor the student may notice that anything special has occurred. Singly, these behaviors probably have little effect. But when they occur again and again, they give a powerful message to women: they are not as worthwhile as men nor are they expected to participate fully in class, in college, or in life at large. For example, faculty make more eye contact with men than with women, so that individual men students are more likely to feel recognized and encouraged to participate in class. Even a female teacher I know discovered that when she asked a question she looked only at her male students, as if only men students were expected to respond.

Professors are more likely to nod and gesture in response to men's comments and questions than to women. Faculty often assume a position of attentiveness, such as leaning forward, when men are talking. When women talk, faculty may be inattentive, such as looking at the clock or shuffling papers.

Professors may group students according to sex, especially in a way that implies that women students are not as competent as men or do not have equal status with men. Some laboratory teachers insist that there be no all-women laboratory teams because "women can't handle the equipment on their own." Others may group the women together "so that they can help each other," or so that they "don't delay the men."

Professors may give men detailed instructions in how to complete a particular problem or lab assignment in the expectation they will eventually succeed on their own, but actually do the assignment for women—or allow them to fail with less instruction.

Further, despite the "popular notion" that in everyday situations women talk more than men, studies show that in formal groups containing men and women not only do men talk more, but they control the topic and direction of the conversation. What men say often carries more weight. A suggestion made by a man is more likely to be listened to, credited to him, developed in further discussion, and adopted by a group than the same suggestion made by a woman.

Teachers themselves may inadvertently reinforce women students' "invisibility," and/or communicate different expectations for women than for men students. Faculty behaviors that can have this effect include ignoring women students while recognizing men students, even when women clearly volunteer to participate in class, or calling directly on men students but not on women students. Male faculty, especially, may tend to call directly on men students significantly more often than on women students. Sometimes the faculty wish to "protect" women students from the "embarrassment" they assume women may feel about speaking in class and thus simply discount them as participants.

Also, faculty call men students by name more often than women students. Sometimes faculty are surprised to discover that they *know* the names of proportionately more men students than women students in their classes. Calling a student by name reinforces the student's sense of being recognized as an individual. Calling men by *last* name but women by *first* name implies that women are not on a par with men as adults or as future professionals. Additionally, faculty may address the class as if no women were present. Asking a question with "Suppose your wife . . ." or "When you were a boy . . ." discounts women students as potential contributors. Or faculty may "coach" men but not women students in working toward a fuller answer by probing for additional elaboration or explanation or wait longer for men than for women to answer a question before going on to another student. Some teachers are more likely to ask women students questions that require factual answers while asking men questions that demand personal evaluation and critical thinking.

Faculty often respond more extensively to men's comments than to women's comments. This pattern may be exacerbated because men *students* may also be more likely to pay more attention to and pick up on each other's comments but to overlook those made by women. Thus, men students may receive far more reinforcement than women for intellectual participation. Also, many teachers credit men's comments to their "author" ("as Bill pointed out") but don't do the same for women. They may use classroom examples that reflect stereotyped ideas about men's and women's social and professional roles, as when the scientist, doctor, or accountant is always "he," while the lab assistant, patient, or secretary is always "she." Last, some faculty use the generic "he" or "man" meant to represent both men and women. Often when a professor is criticized for using the generic "he" or "man," the professor will label the issue as "trivial." It makes one wonder: if the issue is indeed trivial, why is it so difficult for professors and others to change it?

Why should these behaviors occur? Many, of course, have their origins long before students reach the college classroom, some perhaps as early as the cradle. This differential treatment may spring from two basic concepts. One is different expectations and perceptions. If we expect girls and women to be passive and dependent and not interested in math or science, we may well set up self-fulfilling prophecies. The second—and perhaps this underlies the expectations and perceptions—is the *devaluation* of what is female. Throughout our society, what women do is seen as less valuable than what men do.

There have been numerous experiments when two groups of people "rate" things such as articles, works of art, resumes. The creators' names are changed for each group. Those items ascribed to women for the first group are ascribed to men for the second group, and those items ascribed to men for the first group are ascribed to women in the second group. The results of these experiments are singularly consistent: if people believe a woman was the creator, they rank it lower than when they believe it was created by a male. Both men and women do this: they devalue those items ascribed to females. Studies of how women's success is viewed show a similar pattern: men's success is attributed to talent; women's success is attributed to luck. Even when men and women act the same, their behavior is viewed differently. He is "assertive"; she is "aggressive" or "hostile." He "lost his cool," implying it was an aberration; she's "emotional" or "menopausal." Thus, her behavior is devalued, even when it is the same as his.

So, if you believe—without perhaps even knowing that that's what you believe—women are not as intellectual, not as capable, not as serious as men, you may simply ignore them or simply treat them differently or simply view them as peripheral to the classroom, to the college, and to life itself. As overt discrimination disappears, we become increasingly aware of the subtle forms and less obvious barriers to women's development. We also become increasingly aware of the different ways in which men and women view discrimination. For example, men are more likely to acknowledge and understand overt, intentional discrimination. But when overt barriers are dismantled (such as when a department chair no longer excludes women from his department), many men assume that the problem of discrimination is thereby solved. On the other hand, many women view discrimination as being more than just the formal overt barriers. They see a host of subtle behaviors. For example, women may view social behavior, such as male faculty always having lunch together, as having a discriminatory effect because women thereby are excluded from informal sources of information and the subsequent opportunity to learn more about their profession.

Thus, many men tend to *overestimate* the progress that has been made, and many women tend to *understate* the progress. Men think in terms of how far we have come, and women think in terms of how far we have to go.

Making the classroom a welcome place for women is not easy. Delineating the myriad of attitudes and behaviors by faculty that undermine confidence and/or blatantly discriminate against women is only useful if people understand the harm their actions may cause and are willing to undertake a concerted effort to reverse the behavior. Women teachers and women students also need to know the underlying causes of their discomfort as well as how to react to these attitudes and actions.

I say to you—the new Ph.D. about to enter the classroom as the person in charge—"read the foregoing and be aware of how subtle behaviors can contradict your efforts to be a fair teacher. I hope you will not only reflect on the type of intellectual role model you will be, but also the social role model you must be for all students, so that each will enjoy and feel comfortable learning from you. Your power is really quite tremendous, even as you begin your teaching career, to shape and influence the course of others' lives, just as you similarly were molded. Let your example be open and honest to men and women alike."

14   New Faculty Members and Advising

Elizabeth Studley Nathans

Time-consuming, demanding, anxiety-provoking, expected, and exceptionally rewarding if often unrewarded: such is advising. As a newly minted Ph.D., or in some institutions even as an ABD instructor, you will advise. You will advise whether or not your department assigns you formal counseling responsibilities, whether or not you are commandeered for a "general" or underclass advising program, whether or not you want to advise. If you teach, you will advise. Your advisees will undoubtedly survive their encounters with you, whether you advise well or badly. How can you survive yours with them—and both contribute to your students' development and enjoy the advising experience?

Departmental (Major) Advising

Some advising, the easiest when you are new to the faculty, will be that done within your own department. Your department (through the chair, the director of undergraduate studies, or perhaps even a department secretary) will present you a list of majors, probably several more-or-less complete folders containing transcripts, scribbled notes from your predecessors, and other miscellaneous items. In large departments, individual faculty members may advise as many as thirty or more students; more often, you will carry ten to fifteen advisees. Declared majors all, some of your advisees will be sophomores; probably most will be juniors or seniors. In your first year on the faculty, most may know far more about the institution, your colleagues, and your department than do you.

What do major advisees expect of you, and how do you deliver? The basic desiderata are easy to enumerate. You must know your college's requirements for graduation, and you must know your department's own major requirements. If you do not know them, you cannot advise effectively—and in extreme cases, you may even share legal liability for your deficiencies. As an undergraduate and as a graduate student, you doubtless avoided slogging through the murky prose of the institutional bulletin. You can avoid it no longer.

Nor can you avoid the handouts that your department will surely bestow upon you: advertisements for this course and that seminar, special notes about what will "count" for which requirement and what will not, endless errata sheets that correct the errors in the supposedly infallible bulletin. Your temptation to "trash" all such scraps of information will be strong. Resist temptation—and devise a filing system. Your advisees won't automatically understand or remember the requirements, and your colleagues will expect you to tout their courses and seminars. A minimal investment of time to file bits of paper as they accumulate can save you precious minutes when your appointment schedule becomes crowded and information needs to be at your fingertips.

Let's assume that your department does advising well: that it has given you a list of students (perhaps even with pictures and local addresses), relatively complete transcripts, and all the information you need to be a "good advisor." You are told that advisees know your name and that each advisee will see you "at least once" each semester, to talk over progress and academic plans. Fresh, enthusiastic, and eager to impress, you look forward to meeting "your" students. You post your office hours on your door, perhaps even list them with the department secretary. You are careful to add extended hours during the registrar's designated course selection period each term. And you wait. No "real" work gets done during office hours: it would scarcely pay to write when you might be interrupted at any moment, and even serious reading of more than book reviews is problematic. So you wait some more—and few or no students come.

This, indeed, is the frustration particularly of upper-class advising. Students profess to want good advising, and in several schools, student governments have literally begged the undergraduate administration to leave in force requirements that students meet with advisors at least once each semester. But relatively few of your advisees will seek you out until (or unless) compelled to acquire your signature on their registration forms. And then many will appear (some without appointments), completed course cards in hand: "would you please sign this." For such encounters, all your careful preparation, the hours of making sense out of requirements, of planning how to justify your recommendations, seem wasted. The students seem not to want advice—and they certainly resist investing the time to receive at your hands the best you can offer them.

And yet, if you recall your own undergraduate days, you probably sense that they need advice. Not, perhaps, about what courses to take next semester; of those choices, they may be quite certain. But more important advice, of the sort they cannot get from their peers or from institutional publications. What should they do during the summer? Should they go to graduate school? What will it be like? How can they cope with the inevitable "down" times? Should they take a semester (or a year, or more) off? What courses outside the major should they consider taking—and why? What, in short, should they know about both the present and the future that they cannot readily learn through the student grapevine?

These are precisely the things that you—even (and perhaps especially) as a young faculty member—are well equipped to help them decide. The trick is to involve them, to get them to want what you have to give.

You will find the devices that work best for you. Some advisors invite their advisees to lunch (one-on-one) each semester. Departments often have funds to cover such entertainment, and if they don't, students are generally happy to pay for their own food. Others invite groups of advisees to their homes for informal suppers. Again, departments will often pay, and some colleges even provide meals or snacks catered by the campus food service. Other advisors send a note to their advisees each term (sometimes, different notes for juniors and seniors). Here, the department secretary and the word processor can combine to produce something better than a photocopied form letter, and the advisor can add a handwritten "p.s." mentioning some item he or she has noticed in the record that might initiate a discussion.

Whatever devices you choose, the temptation to be a friend to your advisees will be strong. The age differences may be minimal, and you will be fresh from the teaching assistant mode of easy first-name informality. Informality is fine; collegiality based on common interests is encouraged. Genuine friendship between equals, however, is probably out of the question. Advisors occasionally must do things students find difficult to accept in friends: they must reject choices; they must interject a note of reality into what may be a student's overoptimistic plans; ultimately, they must produce realistic and balanced letters of evaluation and recommendation. One can be informal and still maintain a certain distance and the ability to make judgments when the occasion demands; one can be friendly and open and welcoming without again becoming a student. It will take time to find your own right approach and niche. Being aware of the ramifications of the advisor's role, however—and being aware that undergraduates often welcome an adult who will tell them honestly where they stand—may help.

Whatever the requirements of your institution, whatever its advising procedures, and whatever the records and future plans of your advisees, the students majoring in your discipline will want and expect of you certain types of information. As you prepare for one of the first administrative tasks you will undertake as a faculty member, be certain that from reading your department's own materials, from conversations with experienced colleagues, from (if necessary) research in the library and contacts with colleagues in other campus offices, you can discuss the topics listed below authoritatively and can provide guidance to the student who wants more detailed information. Be sure, too, that you know what services and support your department's director of undergraduate studies or similar officer will provide your advisees and you. Attend any meetings convened by your department for its majors —partly because senior faculty will expect attendance of you and students will welcome it as a sign of interest and commitment, but mostly because you can glean valuable information. Read your institution's "teacher-course evaluation" booklet, if only so that you will know the student grapevine wisdom on the courses and colleagues you will be discussing with advisees. Do not ally yourself with the legions of advisors who are always underprepared. Even if you use only a fraction of your information in working with students, you will benefit from learning more about your institution and its resources. Consider the following:

–Departmental and institutional degree requirements
–Special requirements (e.g., languages? statistics? etc.)
–Graduate and professional school requirements/procedures
–Nonacademic job markets for graduates
–Summer internship/job possibilities
–Special programs (study abroad, research programs, etc.)

If you can handle these topics comfortably, you will be prepared, as a new departmental advisor, to go beyond your role of providing competent technical advice and ready to do that which your students in the end will prize more than any specific assistance you offer. You will be prepared—however busy you are, however rarely you may see many of your advisees—to make majoring in your department a personal experience for each of your students. For you will, in the course of acquiring the technical expertise, also begin to acquire the judgment to apply it to individual circumstances.

Advising of Nondeclared Students

Occasionally, you may be asked to advise nondeclared (usually freshman and/or sophomore) students. Many selective colleges and universities avoid requiring this task of new faculty members, preferring to wait a year or so until new professors are acclimated to the institution and know its curriculum, practices, and personnel. If as a first-year faculty member you are asked to perform this service, discreet enquiries are appropriate among other junior colleagues or (if you are lucky enough to have one) of a trusted senior mentor in the department. Is such service customary for first-year faculty at your institution? If it is, you are certainly willing to serve; you want only to ensure that you acquire quickly the information you will need to do a commendable job for the department and for your students.

If you are assigned nondeclared or general education students in your first faculty year, your advising tasks will be vastly more difficult and more demanding than those you will assume in the department. You will have to know the whole curriculum; you may even need a nodding acquaintance with other schools and colleges in your university, if your institution is a comprehensive one that permits students to transfer among undergraduate programs during their first two years of enrollment. You will need to know at least the rudiments of your institution's policies on such matters as housing, Greek rush, financial aid, and the like, for nondeclared students will expect you to be the source of all such knowledge, not merely that which pertains to your academic discipline. And you will need a comprehensive storehouse of referral information: to whom should you send the former would-be English major who awoke this morning certain that her future lies in electrical engineering? What do you do with a tearful freshman, cut from his single-shot rush choice, who can't take his chemistry test because he's "too upset"?

Most comprehensive state-supported institutions and many of the selective private colleges and universities recognize the enormity of the nonmajor advising task, and they genuinely try to support those who work with undeclared or nonmajor students. Support for advisors will generally take one of several forms. Advisors may work within a central facility where they have access to deans, to more experienced senior colleagues, and to some all-knowing individual called variously an advising coordinator, advising director, or some such, who schedules appointments, keeps track of students' records, and is available on a moment's notice to answer questions and provide referral guidance. Often, in such a system, advisors leave their offices and go to a central location for their appointments with students. This can seem an inconvenience, to be sure, but it is a boon to inexperienced advisors who are not left on their own, isolated in their departmental offices, to deal with matters beyond the depth of their experience or knowledge in the institution. Centralized systems generally provide other forms of support, as well: comprehensive advising handbooks, often organized around the "questions most asked" by freshmen and sophomores; training workshops and meetings to update advisors on specific topics before and during the academic year. Handbooks can be cumbersome to read from cover to cover, but the best are indexed, and most advisors ultimately find them useful. Workshops are undeniably tedious in the heat of late summer or the slush of winter, but again they can alert inexperienced advisors not only to facts they need to know, but also to approaches, to tricks of the trade that can save time for both faculty and students.

In decentralized systems, advisors to freshmen and sophomores generally work out of their departmental offices, often with some sort of handbook as a guide, but otherwise on their own to deal with any and all questions as they arise. To the uncaring and cavalier, such an arrangement may be welcome: it demands little of the advisor and imposes few restrictions. To the conscientious, it can be terrifying: what to do about the question the advisor can't answer? Whom to call? To whom to refer? The new advisor would do well in such circumstances to call on a more experienced colleague, either within the department or in the office of the dean. However decentralized their advising systems, all colleges and universities employ vast numbers of deans, assistant deans, and assistants to the dean. Such persons are paid to know the rules—and the best also know how and when to circumvent them. Most would rather field a question—any question—from an advisor, than pick up the pieces of disaster later. Often, the campus telephone or staff directory will make clear to which office questions should be directed, and new faculty members can profitably spend some time familiarizing themselves with their institution's roster of counseling services and personnel. Lacking a handbook or other guide that suggests where to go or whom to call, the advisor can direct questions to the person who appears to rank lowest in the hierarchy—in arts and sciences, for instance, an assistant dean or an assistant to the dean. If the individual taking the call is not the appropriate person to field the particular query, no harm is done: the call will be referred by a secretary to a more appropriate member of the staff.

Whatever the system in which the advisor labors, he or she will find that nonmajor advising demands special skills. It demands, first, tolerance. Nondeclared students are, sometimes on successive days, absolutely certain that they will become Nobel laureates in medicine and that they will win next year's Pulitzer prize for literature. They are, in turn, arrogant and overconfident and paralyzed with self-doubts. Eager, compliant, and seemingly grateful for your suggestions at one conference, they may return a week later to berate you for your supposed incompetence, your lack of interest, your inability to help them. Or, worse yet, they may report your alleged shortcomings to their parents—who won't bother with you, having long since learned that going straight to the president gets prompt attention. (There are ways to survive even this eventuality; see the hints below.)

In any event, your nonmajor advisees will need from you, first and foremost, interest. They will forgive your lack of expertise; they can learn to accept "I don't know," if it's accompanied by "Let's find out." They may break appointments with you, but they will not forgive your breaking appointments with them. Most likely, you are the first faculty member with whom they have spoken face-to-face. Whatever you think of yourself, you are to them an awesome and exalted figure—idealized, in some ways, beyond any reasonable standards. Often, they generalize their impressions of the faculty as a whole from their specific impressions of you. You will develop the expertise to answer your advisees' technical questions over the course of your career. The interest, and the willingness to communicate that interest, must be there from the start.

The Classroom Teacher as Advisor

Much of your advising will be done not as formally designated advisor to either major or nonmajor students specifically assigned to you, but in the context of classroom teaching and the conferences and casual conversations you have with students in your courses. Your own preferences will dictate how open to such informal contacts you should be: for most junior faculty members, it takes time to strike a balance between appearing overly accessible and protecting the time that is essential to complete research and writing that will be necessary to your survival in the institution.

The size of your classes will dictate to some extent how well you know your students. If you are lecturing to a group of two hundred, you will likely know only the few individuals bold enough to seek you out—unless you are unusually good at associating names with faces or determined to resort to such relatively outmoded and unpopular devices as a seating chart. Even if you occasionally teach "sections" normally presided over by your own teaching assistants, you will not have the frequent contact with small groups of students that invites individual conferences or close relationships.

If you teach smaller sections, however, and if you are comfortable enough in the classroom to convey a sense of informality (not, note, incompatible with being perceived as tough or demanding) and interest, you will likely be approached by individual students, either before or after class or during office hours.

Generally, the initial approach will be limited to the course material: the student will profess not to have understood a certain point in the reading or to be encountering difficulty with a particular experiment or with a paper topic. First, of course, you deal with the concern the student presents, and your interest in the subject matter and the student's concern to master it give you common ground for a productive conversation. Whether to go beyond — whether to inquire, for instance, if the student who has yet to submit a paper when it was due in your class is having similar difficulties in other courses — is more problematic. Young instructors often shy away from posing such questions, fearful, perhaps, of learning more than they want to know or cope with. Some, almost brazen in their disinterest, announce flatly that they don't care whether the student is having difficulty, that conversations must be restricted to the work at hand, and that any problems the student has should be taken up with someone else, somewhere else. For the latter group of instructors, the problem of advising students outside the classroom is generally short-lived: one edition of the institution's teacher-course evaluation booklet suffices to spread the word, and the faculty members in question will likely be troubled little by students in future years.

When confronted with student concerns that go beyond the scope of a single course, what can the classroom instructor appropriately do? First, and probably most important, recognize the limitations of his or her perspective. The professor sees the student in only one course: if a student hints at a concern or problem that goes beyond the scope of a class, that problem probably also transcends anything with which an individual instructor should be expected to deal. The instructor can play a crucial role by explaining to the student that, while he or she can help within the context of the particular class, the problem is one that deserves the attention of someone with broader expertise than the instructor possesses. This is the time for a call to a dean, and for encouragement to the student to seek the help that even the most cumbersome and insensitive bureaucracies can offer in such situations. And it is the time for follow-up, both to assure the student of continuing interest, and to ensure that appropriate attention is being paid to the student's problem.

The instructor who spots a problem not reported to him or her by a student faces a more difficult dilemma. The playground ethic remains strong even among Ph.D.s, and the temptation not to tell on the student will be overwhelming. Often, young instructors will confront the student, hoping to deal with problems themselves. Most commonly: "Bill, you haven't turned in the last four papers in the course. You know that the syllabus announces a penalty for late papers, but if you have a really good reason for not turning them in, we can talk about it." This approach invites the student to devise an appropriately heartrending story — and virtually forces the instructor to waive the penalty. Naively, the instructor accepts the student's assurances that it will never happen again — only to go around the same circle once more, when the next paper falls due. Or an instructor may notice that a student misses class regularly or, attending, dozes brazenly, often in the front row. Again, the temptation to do nothing is strong: students are, after all, responsible for their own attendance at most colleges and universities, and if confronted by their negligence, most will simply excuse themselves as having been ill or having had a lot of tests this month. Not wanting to doubt the student's word by demanding the written, official excuse for which most colleges make provision, the faculty member is trapped: either accept the story and forgive the transgression or brand the student a liar.

Again, more experienced colleagues and particularly the college deans can and should be asked for help. The deans keep comprehensive records on students in all but the largest universities: if anyone knows whether a student is genuinely encountering difficulty, they will. They will also know, in many cases, whether a particular student seems to become ill before every scheduled test, whether there has been a consistent problem with late submission of work, whether there have been in the student's past a remarkable number of inept instructors who have failed to recognize the student's talents and have (in the student's eyes and those of his or her parents) evaluated work unfairly. The dean's office is both resource and protection for the instructor in such circumstances, and it can even reassure the inexperienced of their own expertise and sanity. The dean's records may suggest, simply, that the problem student is lazy or distracted. Or they may reveal genuine difficulties: learning disabilities, underdeveloped skills in reading or quantitative reasoning, lack of adequate secondary school preparation in certain fields. Occasionally the record points to marginal intellectual abilities and to Herculean efforts by the student in question to meet parental or societal expectations which may be beyond the student's reach. In any event, the dean's staff will have a breadth of perspective and experience which you, as a relatively new instructor, will lack. They can be of inestimable help to you in your efforts to aid the student in your class. And your care and concern in reporting apparent problems will in turn assist the deans in their task of identifying students in difficulty and directing those students to appropriate sources of aid.

Those Awkward Situations

Inevitably, there will arise those awkward situations when the best preparation, all your efforts to anticipate your responses, and everything you've read and learned won't be much help. A few of the more common:

Cheating. No one ever prepares for his or her first cheating case, and most of us have probably been "burned" several times, because we neither suspect cheating as often as we might nor feel comfortable confronting it when it occurs. If you encounter cheating, it will generally take one of two forms: the plagiarized (or, perhaps, the borrowed or stolen) paper or lab report, or the cribbed or copied exam. Most often, instructors suspect cheating when they receive a paper markedly better—and more intellectually sophisticated—than its predecessors; occasionally, another student will drop a broad hint that the instructor should "check on" student behavior on a recent exam or the integrity of submitted papers. Some prudent instructors in grading objective or short-answer submissions photocopy papers before returning them; a relatively modern but all-too-common form of cheating is the submission of a paper for regrading, with original answers altered on the basis of in-class discussion of the test or perhaps a posted exam key. In any event, if you confront the cheater, he or she will either profess innocence and outrage (and you will feel off-guard and threatened) or dissolve in tears of remorse and protestations that the incident will never again be repeated.

In neither case are you in a position to judge the events objectively or to assess the appropriate penalty. Every institution has judicial and counseling procedures for students accused of academic offenses. The faculty member who fails to use the proper procedures in cases of suspected cheating subverts the system that upholds the integrity of the whole community. And he or she may be subject to charges of violating the student's due process rights by assessing a penalty within the course that the student finds unreasonable or damaging and subsequently elects to challenge. In all cases of suspected cheating photocopy everything, tell the student that you are holding the grade on the work in question, and report the matter to your institution's designated administrator. The faculty handbook provided at most institutions will guide you through the procedure; if in doubt, consult your departmental chairman or the office of your institution's academic dean.

The Poison Pen Letter. Almost every faculty member, sooner or later, is the object of a spiteful letter to the president, the chancellor, or the dean from a disgruntled student or parent. Often, the information in the letter is secondhand; often, the student will excuse his or her own poor performance by complaining to the parents that the advisor recommended the "wrong" courses or the professor "didn't tell us" what would be on the test or was "unfair" in assessing the student's work. The parents then write to the administrator, presenting the student's side of the tale as Gospel, and demanding anything and everything from tuition refunds to the faculty member's decapitation. Such letters can be devastating to inexperienced instructors; most often, the charges are unfair and the complaints unfounded, but administrators, who are far removed from the daily round of classroom teaching and advising, take them seriously and forward them to deans or to departmental chairmen for response. Your temptation when confronted by your first such complaint—whether from a student or a parent—will be to panic. The student pays tuition; you are a hired hand. Who will believe your story? Relax! Your best defense is a good offense: routine, accurate recordkeeping that indicates what advice was given, and why, or in your classes, when papers were due, when they were submitted, and how they were evaluated; a comprehensive syllabus that indicates what is required in your course and when; and notes, written immediately after the fact, about any classroom or advising encounter with a student that your instincts tell you may be problematic (a controversy over a grade, a student's protest that you failed to accept a class excuse, an undergraduate's insistence that you lost a paper you are convinced the student failed to submit, an accusation that you "didn't tell" a student about a particular requirement). Contemporary notes will be vastly more convincing than those written weeks or months after the fact; they require little of your time, but they will prove immensely useful in the one situation in a hundred that proves problematic for you. And they will endear you to the department chair or dean who must draft a diplomatic but firm response to the parents, the provost, or the president.

Crushes. Most times, you will not see as much of your students as you wish. At some point, however, you will see too much of the student who develops a "crush" on you and who seems to need and demand a major share of your attention. Quite likely, you won't initially recognize the situation for what it is. Flattered by the student's seeming interest in your course or discipline and by the way he or she hangs on every word in advising sessions or in the classroom, grateful, perhaps, for the visits that relieve the tedium of office hours, you will notice too late that the student turns up wherever you do; that the visits become longer and the occasion for them less clear; that, perhaps, social invitations even become explicit. Phone calls at home are commonplace; late evening visits aren't unheard of (nor are irate spouses). Sometimes, the student who acquires the crush is physically unattractive and socially inept; idealized from afar, you become the friend he or she has never had. Perhaps more often, however, the student is highly intelligent, serious about intellectual endeavors, deeply involved with you as a potential role model—and socially too immature to fit readily into the college social scene. Either way, even the slightest attention from you will become a precious commodity, and your every glance and word endowed with a significance (described, often, to roommates and corridor-mates) you never intended. In one instance of this sort, a faculty member found himself pursued to Europe during his sabbatical by an especially ardent young woman who delayed arranging her own study abroad until she knew where he would be working and living. Fortunately, his wife is both balanced and understanding.

What to do? First, the obvious things. Minimize opportunities for the student to speak with you alone, and avoid absolutely situations where you meet behind closed doors! Confide in a trusted senior colleague and in your mate: the former can offer protection within the department if rumors ultimately start to fly, and the latter can fend off phone calls and late-evening visits and at the same time establish to the student the fact of his or her presence. Encourage the student to take courses with others next term when the student wants to do advanced work—or, heaven forbid, independent study!—with you. And, if all else fails, confront the student, gently but firmly: "I'm flattered that you enjoy my course and that you find conversations with me interesting and helpful. But I must spend time this spring finishing an article for publication, so I'm going to have to cut back the time I have available to any one student. And I'm sure you'll understand that my time at home is so limited that I won't be able to take calls there from students any longer." Such comments get the message across, without demeaning or embarrassing a student who is likely to be quite vulnerable— and without damaging a classroom or advising relationship that must, after all, last at least until the end of the current semester.

Your department, your dean, your institution, will reward you for the research you do and the articles, papers, and books you contribute to the store of your profession's knowledge. Inevitably, however, your greatest satisfactions as an academic will often come from your interactions with students.

The days will be long, the tangible rewards few, and the frustrations of student interactions many.

But for virtually everyone who embarks upon an academic career, there was, somewhere at some time, one individual who—with a word of advice, a chance comment, a bit of encouragement—made a difference. Degree in hand, faculty status (however temporary or precarious) conferred, you will be the one now who, probably at the time and under circumstances you least expect, will make that difference for one of your students. That, in the end, is what advising comes down to—that and caring enough about your students to do the job well.

15 The Problems of Special-Admission Undergraduates

Ronald R. Butters and

Christopher B. Kennedy

Every young scholar enters college or university teaching with certain dreams. One of them is almost certainly the vision of exciting Socratic exchanges with bright, committed, knowledgeable students. Such exchanges sometimes actually take place. Sometimes the instructor leaves the classroom with the sense that something important has just happened and that he or she is actually a Teacher. But such moments, which all of us yearn for and remember fondly, are the exception; much of teaching is routine rather than incandescent. Even at the best of colleges, the range in quality of students often prevents any one class from maintaining a consistently high level of discourse. Even at the best of colleges, even at those institutions that select their students most carefully, there are groups of students that have been admitted under different standards than the rest of the student body have. It may be your dream to teach only the best, but it will certainly be your task to confront the problems of those students euphemistically referred to as "special admits."

Every college makes allowances, to one degree or another, for applicants who, although inadmissible under regular standards, are desirable for other reasons. Children of faculty or alumni, applicants in whom the development office has an interest, some minorities, athletes, and other potential students whose talents or abilities distinguish them—all may be admitted and some will eventually find their way into your classroom. There they may well act as an anchor upon the class's voyage of intellectual discovery as, numbed with incomprehension of class discussion, they vainly inscribe disjointed, mysterious notes that will be no more meaningful to them upon review than the contents of the Rosetta Stone.

It is natural, perhaps inevitable, that you view these students with a certain lack of enthusiasm. They may be unprepared for college work; their lack of comprehension of, and interest in, the class material can make attempts to teach them every bit as satisfying and pleasurable as driving a nail into cement; you may fear that their mute, baffled presence in the classroom will affect the other students, particularly in small classes. And in many cases, your apprehensions about special admissions students will be justified. However beneficial their presence may be to the rest of the university, it may be a decided trial for you. Yet there they sit, usually in the back row. You are their instructor. How do you approach them? How do you help them?

There are two sides to your response to special students. The first is the teaching side. You must confront them, and their problems, in the classroom. You may not like or agree with your institution's admissions policies, but you, and not the admissions officers, are responsible for educating your students, however they gained admission. You are, as it were, on the front line, and you must be prepared to accept the responsibilities of your position. Fortunately, you are not alone. While you must teach these students, almost all institutions maintain a variety of counseling services to assist the students, and you, if the need arises.

Alas, there is no magic formula that will solve the difficult part of the equation: the day-to-day classroom contact. The fact is that, while the problems of special admission students manifest themselves in similar ways, they may arise from circumstances so varied that no single approach or response will work consistently. In the same class, you may encounter a rural, black football player and the daughter of wealthy parents whose interest in the school's endowment was instrumental in her admission. The only thing these two students have in common is their presence in your class and the difficulties it causes them.

The academic problems of the football player may arise as much from nonacademic factors as from any lack of high school preparation. It is not uncommon for so-called big-time athletic programs to recruit players who otherwise would have no interest in their institutions. Often, these students find themselves feeling out-of-place when they arrive at their chosen school. A southern, rural black may find that the life of the majority of students at a private institution is almost entirely unfamiliar. Among white, affluent, northern prep-school graduates, such students may see themselves as outsiders, feel that they do not belong, decide that they have made a mistake in their college choice, and so be desperately unhappy. The student who is feeling unsure of his place in the school as a whole is almost certain to be acutely uncomfortable in the classroom as well. Even the complications of athletic participation have a disproportionate effect on academic performance. Many high-school stars find themselves relegated to bench warming in college. Some of these, for whom success in athletic competition has always been the foundation upon which their sense of self-worth is constructed, are shattered by the experience. Their self-image changes; they suddenly see themselves as failures. Such a radical shift in self-perception cannot fail to affect the student's classroom performance.

The daughter of wealthy parents may not be doing any better in your class than the football player, but for different reasons. In fact, students who have gained admission through the support of the development office are sometimes the least qualified to do college-level work of all special admits. At the same time, their parents, many of whom are highly successful, impose unrealistic demands upon them. Caught between their academic deficiencies and severe pressure from home, they sometimes suffer a kind of paralysis. Fearful of earning only C's, they stop trying and earn D's and F's instead.

What can you, as a faculty member, do about such cases? There may not be much; in fact, in large courses you may not even be aware of special admission students. Because they often do not want to be noticed as special, many develop the chameleon's talent for blending into the background. It sometimes seems that teacher and student are working at cross-purposes: your task is to identify the potential problem student; theirs is to evade notice. The best advice that we can offer is simply to be alert, to be sensitive to the performance, both written and oral, of your students. Perhaps the most consistent early sign of impending academic disaster is sporadic class attendance. Rather than attend a class in which they feel lost, marginal students may simply stay away. When signs of academic trouble appear, consult at once the student's dean; if the student is a "special admit" the dean will know it. No one will expect you to hound your students, but good teaching does require attention to *all* students. If you ask if you can help them and at the same time remind them of the importance of regular attendance, your show of interest and concern may be an important first step toward gaining their confidence.

In the classroom, perhaps the most important thing is one's attitude. More than any concrete measures one can take, an open and receptive attitude frequently works wonders with struggling students. Special admission students are usually aware of their status and often very sensitive about it. They tend to be easily intimidated by faculty members and even by their fellow students. Sensitive about their "special" position, they may interpret reserve or preoccupation on your part as disapproval. If they understand, however, that you are sympathetic to their plight and willing to help, a considerable portion of their trepidation about your class may disappear. You may not think that you are a particularly threatening individual, but the insecure freshman or sophomore may see you entirely differently. It is sometimes hard for us to understand (or remember) how fraught with dread the very act of walking into a classroom can be for the student who regards each class as another forum in which he will publicly demonstrate his ignorance. Although your demeanor may not seem especially significant to you, it can go a long way toward dispelling such a student's dread and open the way for more concrete forms of assistance.

Accessibility of the instructor can be a crucial factor. Students who are afraid to appear foolish in front of others may benefit significantly from one-to-one contact with the instructor during office hours. In private, the student may be more willing to open up and express concerns about his or her abilities or about difficulties in your class. If you provide convenient, open office hours and encourage students to take advantage of them, you may well be providing the student with an avenue into the course that he cannot find in the confines of the classroom. Sometimes a personal invitation to take advantage of office hours may be necessary; sometimes such invitations will go unheeded. More often, however, your demonstrated willingness to go beyond the confines of the classroom means a great deal to the student; any measure that helps him to see that you are an approachable ally rather than some implacable inquisitor is likely to be productive.

One of the most significant dangers that we have found in dealing with minority or special admissions students is falling under the influence of our prejudices. We don't believe that we ever completely escape some of our preconceived notions about groups. For example, the popular image of the college football player—hulking, semiliterate, somewhere between the gibbon and the mountain gorilla on the scale of evolution—is a powerful one. We may recognize it for the stereotype it is, but it nonetheless contributes, however slightly, to our expectations about the large person in the back row. And unless we guard against them, our expectations may well distort our perceptions of a student's work. In this respect, knowledge is a powerful antidote: the more one knows about, for example, American dialects, the less likely one is to stigmatize speakers of ethnic and regional varieties of English as lacking in native intelligence.

We have suggested that you be an active, almost an interventionist, instructor, seeking out problem students, offering them what assistance you can. But you have only so much time, and you are not, after all, a trained counselor. If you feel that your potential responses to special admits in your classes need to be supplemented, it is important to be aware of the counseling resources your institution offers. Most institutions, for example, maintain some kind of minority counseling or assistance center to which students can be referred. Frequently, these centers offer academic tutoring as well as personal counseling. They can serve a particularly valuable function in giving the student a place where he or she feels comfortable. In the case of athletes, virtually every big-time athletic program offers some kind of tutoring and advising service that provides much the same kind of support that the minority office does for its students. It is a good idea when you first arrive at your institution to find out what services are available for students so that, if the need arises, you will be prepared to refer them to the proper form of assistance.

Such services are set up to help you as well as the student. A call to the minority or athletic office about a student who has not been attending will more often than not produce the student and an explanation in short order. Moreover, if you have the opportunity to discuss your concerns about a student with someone else who is working with that student, the likelihood of your being able to help him or her increases dramatically.

Familiarity with specialty academic services can be helpful for other, more immediately practical reasons. It is, for example, unfortunately possible that at some institutions coaches or other university officials may attempt to pressure faculty members into changing poor grades in order to preserve the athletic eligibility of marginal student-athletes, or to protect the grades of a politically important student. Even more likely is parental pressure. It is not uncommon for parents to call instructors, departmental chairmen, and deans, insisting that failing grades be changed. ("How could she have failed when she had a 'C' at mid-term?")

The pressure problem can be distressing, but one way to deal with it is by anticipation. We all hope and believe that we are impervious to strong-arm tactics, but you may avoid the problem entirely by notifying the student's academic dean or the athletic advisor of any difficulties the student is having in your class as soon as you are aware of them. By doing so, you may ensure that the student has a chance to get the help he or she needs or discover how you yourself can help the student in time to avert a low grade. At the very least, this kind of early notification makes it harder for the parents or the athletic department to apply pressure at the end of the semester in the event the student does not do well in your course.

There are no magic spells that will allow us to understand all of our students all of the time. There are no formulae that instantly improve one's ability to bridge cultural or racial gaps. Be sensitive to your own attitudes, distrust your immediate impressions, be willing to listen to your students and communicate with them. Some problems will not be solved, some students will refuse to be helped, but the persistent effort to be of help, the readiness to assist students as individuals, will ensure at least a chance at success.

FOUR

Funding Academic Research

For a new assistant professor whose credentials are yet to be proved and whose research skills are yet to be tested, research funding can be difficult to obtain. In the humanities, small grants from a college or university research council may suffice, at least for a while; in the basic and social sciences or in technical and professional areas, such grants will not go very far. Indeed, in these disciplines the amount of external funding obtained is one form of professional validation and may be every bit as important in the eventual tenure decision as your publications. Applying for government or foundation grants may consume large portions of your academic time and give rise to untold worries and fears. But where external funding is a necessity, not merely an academic luxury, it is essential that you enter the competition boldly and optimistically. Yet this is not easily done. In the essays that follow, two specialists on funding sources and procedures try to clarify the grant-making process and offer suggestions that may help to ensure your success. As both stress, a research proposal that is truly worthy will probably be funded, but not, perhaps, without considerable effort, preparation, persistence, and patience.

Louise Knight draws upon her considerable experience with government agencies to summarize the range of sources available and the general strategies for approaching them. Fred Crossland also draws upon personal experience, especially upon his service in the Ford Foundation, to explain the essential contours of the quest for private funding. Since your own course of seeking adequate funding to underwrite your basic research will likely involve both public and private sectors, it will be important to know from the beginning some of the fundamental differences and similarities between them.

Louise Knight is Director of Foundation and Corporate Relations at Wheaton College. She has also edited a national newsletter on federal funding for school districts and served on the staff of a federal grants program in the (then) Office of Education. She has taught proposal and grant-writing to many academic and nonacademic groups.

Fred E. Crossland, who is now retired, served for many years as Program Officer for Higher Education and Research for the Ford Foundation. He also served as Vice President of the W. Alton Jones Foundation, as well as both faculty member (History) and administrator at New York University. He has been an advisor and consultant on higher education policy issues for many colleges, universities, and federal agencies.

16 Seeking Federal Funding for Research

Louise W. Knight

The process of seeking funding for research is never as simple as one would like. Who would not prefer to make one telephone call and receive a check in the mail soon after? Unfortunately for the busy researcher, there are a number of intermediate steps involved, all of them time-consuming. This is the terrible knowledge possessed by the experienced faculty member: finding research funding takes time, persistence, and patience.

In this essay I will outline the particular steps involved in the process of applying to the federal government, but first a few preliminary observations are in order. Consider your expectations: they probably include the hope that somewhere there is a funding program interested in exactly the type of research you do. For the humanist, this hope may be fulfilled because the scarce federal funding that is available for humanities research is rarely restricted to specific research topics. Federal humanities programs, primarily those of the National Endowment for the Humanities, tend to support "the best humanities research" that fits their general guidelines. Your priorities by definition become their priorities.

Nonhumanists are not so lucky. Although there is some "open-ended" federal funding available for the natural sciences and engineering (e.g., through the National Science Foundation), most of the federal research dollars are spent on research that responds directly or indirectly to the responsibilities and activities of the agencies themselves. For the researcher, the most important implication of that fact is that some research may simply not be fundable by the federal government.

At the same time, you will be amazed to discover the range of research interests the government pursues. Social scientists in particular can, with luck and some extra effort, discover a number of unique sources of research support within the policymaking branches of various federal agencies. For the social scientist and the natural scientist and engineer, although a successful search for funding sources is no guarantee of eventual support, you should always assume that somewhere an agency or bureau exists to fund your project. Your initial task is simply to take the time to look.

When you find a source that seems "to fit," you may be faced with a common dilemma. To make the "fit" better, should you modify your research in some way? This is a continual question that has no general answer. Each researcher must evaluate honestly the limits of his or her flexibility. A key issue is how far the agency's program interests will take you from your research goal. Moderation is probably advisable if the variance is not too great. It is also possible to avoid the problem by dividing your project into smaller units: one agency might then be appropriate for part of the funding and a different source or sources can be found for the rest. However you confront the problem of "fit," do not without careful thought allow the availability of funding to divert you from the project at hand. You are seeking funding in order to do research, not seeking a research topic in order to get a federal grant.

In the end, all the choices are yours. The goal, in looking for research support, is to be flexible and to have as many options as your project permits.

The Federal Agencies

Although the federal government's executive branch is a single organization with one person, the president, at its head, this does not mean that the various agencies operate in the same way or relate to university research in a single pattern or fashion. Diversity, in many dimensions, is the norm. The challenge the researcher faces is to discern the habits and methods of the agency being approached. Thus, you should begin with the assumption that each agency is unique.

Federal agencies can be grouped in three categories according to their views toward research. The first and smallest group sees the support of research, whether conducted by an agency staff or external researchers, as a central part of the agency's mission. Indeed, for a few agencies, the funding of basic research *is* their mission. Agencies in this category include the National Science Foundation, the National Endowment for the Humanities, and the National Institutes of Health (which is part of the Department of Health and Human Services). Each of these organizations is well equipped to assist the faculty researcher in finding support. Inquiries are expected and welcomed; printed guidelines are furnished upon request. Some programs have deadlines for submitting applications. In general, these are the agencies that are the most approachable, and, not coincidentally, those with which you are already likely to be familiar.

The second category includes subunits of larger agencies. These subunits are also organized to support basic research and operate much like the basic research agencies already mentioned above. The two agencies with these types of basic research subunits are:

(1) the Department of Defense (subunits: the Army Research Office, the Office of Naval Research, and the Air Force Office of Scientific Research) and

(2) the Department of Energy (subunit: the Office of Energy Research).

Although these units usually have no deadlines and few detailed guidelines, they view university researchers as a primary constituency and receive inquiries from faculty on a regular basis.

Finally, there are a number of agencies and subunits of the already mentioned agencies that fund research at universities through a myriad of programs, none of which is expressly designed to fund research but all of which perceive university research as a part of their mission. Such programs fund both basic and applied research, but, in either case, their research agendas are thoroughly and immediately shaped by the agency's mission. These agencies include:

(1) the Department of Defense: outside of the basic research offices listed above, DOD supports extensive research, most of it applied, through a number of other offices and programs;

(2) the Department of Energy: outside of the Office of Energy Research listed above, DOE, like DOD, has a number of applied research programs, all of which provide limited research funds to university researchers;

(3) the Environmental Protection Agency: this agency has an extensive, mainly applied, set of research programs organized under its Office of Research and Development. University researchers most frequently apply to ORD's Office of Exploratory Development, which funds primarily basic research;

(4) the National Aeronautics and Space Administration: this mission-oriented agency funds university research in a manner similar to EPA. There is no single office, however, that specializes in funding basic research, because much of the basic (and applied) research NASA supports is managed by installations (Field Centers) located around the country. As a consequence,

most university research is funded directly by the installations themselves, even though some funding is available from the agency's headquarters in Washington.

One further pattern—that of supporting some university research via government laboratories—can be traced across several agencies. Indeed, all of the agencies listed in the last group have major laboratory facilities and fund university research directly through them. Typically, these labs conduct both basic and applied research, but the emphasis is on the latter. The agency with the biggest budget for laboratories is DOE, but DOD probably has the most complex system of laboratories. To date, none of these agencies has done a particularly effective job of facilitating relations between their labs and university researchers. Indeed, a recent White House report was critical of this very failure and one can only hope that a change in the pattern will soon occur. Both the laboratories and the universities could benefit from closer contact.

This list of the more prominent and important sources of research funding for university faculty is intended primarily to convey the basic patterns the agencies follow in their relations with universities. There is not space here to describe programs for all disciplines in any detail.

Equally varied is the range in grant awards one might receive (from $500 to $1 million or more) and the kinds of research federal agencies support. Topics range from research on the splitting of genes to research on the splitting of mountains, to research on the splitting of opinions over U.S. relations with a foreign country. As in other matters relating to the federal government, diversity is the rule.

It is important to know where the agency you end up dealing with fits into this typology. Such knowledge will help you understand the kind of response you receive. For example, if you are dealing with a research agency (like NSF or NEH), you will find that relations are easy. They have materials to send you, a deadline (often) established, and you also have quite a bit of latitude regarding what their research interests are (this varies from program to program, of course). You will find much the same ease in relations when you deal with the research subunits, like the Army Research Office. Although their agenda is shaped by nonresearch issues, the office itself is devoted solely to basic research (or mostly) and the people you deal with, as in the research agencies, are researchers.

The challenge comes in dealing with the mission agencies and the programs that are not primarily research programs. Here you will encounter some puzzlement and skepticism. There will be initial hesitation that your research and their interests really intersect (even though they might). You will find yourself needing to spend more time explaining the significance of your research to their interests (which means you need to spend some time understanding their interests first), and you will need to be more persistent. In general, it will take far longer to determine whether research support is really going to come out of this contact. And you may find that, at least initially, there is no funding at all, but only some consulting with a laboratory that is affiliated with the office you called, or an invitation to visit, the next time you are in Washington. The contacts are important and could well lead to major funding later, but the process is very long term. The type of agency you are dealing with should therefore shape your expectations.

First Steps

Having reviewed the range of federal research programs, we can consider next how the new researcher might best approach an agency. Where to begin?

The most accessible sources for printed material on the federal programs are your university's office of research administration and the reference and document sections of the library. One of the most useful publications, if you can locate it, is *The Federal Executive Telephone Directory*. The *Directory*, published not by the government, but by a private company (Carroll Publishing, Washington, D.C.), is updated every two months, and lists the titles, names, and telephone numbers of selected federal administrators. It is a good place to familiarize yourself with an agency and its organization. The *Directory* will provide you with telephone numbers of offices whose names strike you as interesting. This makes it a good place to start.

If you cannot find a copy of the *Directory*, and your institution has little information available on research funding from the federal government, then try the Washington, D.C., telephone book. Although it contains less detail about each federal agency's offices and telephone numbers, it is a place to start (look under "United States, Government of").

Once you have a telephone number either for the office you are interested in, or even the entire agency, you can call that number and request publications. (Again, if your office of research collects these, it is far easier to consult their collection.) The kinds of publications to ask for include an agency telephone directory, a compilation of grants awarded by that agency to universities over a certain period, a brochure describing a group of programs and program guidelines.

In trying to track down such information by telephone be patient. As a general rule, no one ever reaches the right office in the federal government with just one telephone call. Expect to be referred endlessly. But hang in there. Each referral is bringing you closer to your goal (even if you are not sure at the time!). The key at this stage is to persevere. Getting frustrated and quitting will guarantee you find no research funding. Persevering can almost guarantee you will. If, during this frustrating process, you can also find it within your heart to be cheerful, so much the better for you. There is no doubt that the strangers on the other end of the line will be more helpful to you if you are pleasant.

Now, we will assume you have received the program guidelines (and remember, many programs publish no such guidelines). Read them carefully to see how your research interests fit into theirs. If you are not sure, you should call the program officer.

Indeed, with government agencies, and in contrast to the procedures in dealing with private foundations, you should always call the program officer before sending in an application. This is obviously necessary if you are dealing with a program that has little printed material about its research funding interests, but it is also a good idea even for the more formally organized programs, including those of the National Science Foundation. During the conversation, you can confirm that your research fits their interests and also get answers to any questions you may have about the program (e.g., whether it will fund the purchase of equipment, whether you fit the eligibility restrictions, and so forth). Be sure, though, before you ask any questions, that the answers are not tucked into some corner of the printed material. Asking questions that have been answered in the program guidelines will not win you friends among program officers.

In cases where there are no guidelines, your goal during the telephone call will be to describe your own research very briefly and to learn whether the program officer finds it relevant to his/her program. If there is a good match, the officer may make a few comments about the particular aspect of your research that is of interest and suggest that you prepare a brief preliminary draft proposal (probably no more than three pages long). This is an encouraging sign. If the suggestion is not made by the program officer, feel free to make it yourself. It is a sign to the program officer of your interest.

If you do prepare a preliminary proposal, mail it to the agency within a week or two of your telephone conversation, while the program officer's memory of the conversation is still fresh. A prompt response will demonstrate that you have a "professional" attitude and will alleviate fears that you are just "fishing." In your cover letter to the proposal, you can describe your research in a few sentences and remind the program officer of the ways, as you discussed earlier, that your research might be relevant to the program's interests.

Most important of all, promise in the letter that you will call in about ten days to discuss the response to your preliminary proposal. This is much better than merely saying that you look forward to hearing from the program officer, because that leaves the ball in his court, where it may well sit gathering dust while you wait nervously back at the university with fading hopes. His silence may signify little, but to you it may be very discouraging. By promising to call him, you retain the initiative. You also alert him to the fact that he should read your proposal and share it with colleagues by the time you call. Done in the right spirit, your follow-up telephone call need imply no discourteous pressure. Indeed, if you call and he has not read your draft, be careful to sound casual and chat with him about whether you should call back in a week or two, or perhaps a month? Be responsive to the demands on his time, but keep the ball in your court.

What about paying a visit? This can be a very good idea, depending on the circumstances. If your initial telephone call goes especially well, for example, and you sense that the program officer is quite interested in your work, you might ask if you could stop by the next time you are in Washington. In this case, be sure to send your three-page draft several weeks before your visit. And be sure to set up an appointment. Face-to-face meetings can help both you and the officer learn more about each other's research interests and can be the beginning of a longer relationship. For the program officer, your visit can be a stimulating break in the day and an opportunity to learn about some interesting research. For you the point of the visit is not to persuade the officer to fund your research but to share information and to learn more about the agency's program. A visit can sometimes provide an opportunity for you to meet other staff who may also have a significant voice in whether or not your proposal is funded. There may be a time, of course, when a visit is not a good idea. Trust your instincts on this question and never force the issue.

Writing the Proposal

If the response to your preliminary draft is positive, you are now ready to write the proposal. Before starting, however, reread the program guidelines carefully, if there are any. That sounds like the usual advice, but it is extremely important. One of the most common errors inexperienced applicants make is to fail to follow the specific instructions of the program guidelines. A large number of applications to the federal government are rejected each year for this single reason. Be sure to include everything the guidelines require, address each point thoroughly that is listed in the criteria to be used for review, and include *all* the information and materials requested.

Finally, before you start writing, take a little time to think about the task you are undertaking. You are about to create a document that, on its own, must answer all the reviewers' most important questions. The typical reviewer will probably be trained in your discipline, but will not be as knowledgeable about your specialized field of research as you are. Your task, then, is to write about your project in something less than totally technical terms. Also, because the reviewers cannot read your mind, you must not omit discussions of "obvious" points. Any idea you forget to put down on the page will, from the reviewers' point of view, not exist.

All of this will be true whether your proposal is reviewed by a panel of academic advisors, convened by the agency, or by the internal staff of the agency, or both.

How do you organize your proposal? Some programs instruct you on this in their guidelines. If not, there are some standard formats. For researchers in the natural and social sciences and engineering, the format is:

Cover Page

Summary/Abstract

Project Description
   (1) Background
   (2) Problem (including literature review)
   (3) Objectives
   (4) Methods/Methodology/Design (flow chart, time line)
   (5) Results/Implications
   (6) Illustrations
   (7) References

Personnel and Facilities
   (1) Brief biographical sketch(es)
   (2) Other relevant resources

Budget

Current and Pending Support

Appendices (full vita goes here)

Faculty doing research in the humanities face a wider variety of formats to choose from. Indeed, in humanities proposals, there is no standard format at all. A few programs may list topics to cover in their guidelines. It is always a good idea to use these "topics" as subheadings around which to organize your proposal. That way, you are sure to cover the material they want, and they are sure to be able to follow your organization.

In cases where no real guidance is given, researchers may wish to use the following format:

Summary (usually one paragraph)

Description of Project

  –how you came to choose this topic (i.e., a description of the evolution of your research interests, and the development of your knowledge of this field);

  –a brief statement of what you want to study and how you propose to study it (where and when are important to mention) and what methods you will use (and why);

  –some more detailed discussion of the research questions you wish to investigate and what you think your research results will contribute to the field;

  –a clear statement about what the final product will be (article, book?) and why this project is essential to completion of that product. (If the product is a book whose research you have already begun, be sure to explain in detail how far you have come and what you will be able to accomplish further with additional funds).

Having provided this format, let me add that, as long as these elements are present in the final proposal, the order may be varied. The single most important thing to remember in writing a humanities proposal is that you discuss all these points and that your discussion has its own coherency and natural flow to it. Use the first person and allow your interest and excitement about the project to be conveyed. More than in a scientist's proposal, the humanist's proposal is a personal statement. The reviewers will respond best to a clearly conceived, obviously intelligent proposal whose author is present on the page.

The Review

Now your proposal is ready to be reviewed. At this step, diversity among federal agencies continues to be the norm. While it is true that the basic science agencies (NSF, NEH, and NIH) make the greatest use of external peer review, each agency follows different procedures (often within an agency there may be different policies: NIH and NEH have agency-wide practices, but NSF has a wide variety). Among the practices that vary are whether reviewers read the proposals at home and send their comments in or travel to Washington to meet as a panel to review and rate the proposals. A second variation is the role the program officer plays in providing reviewers with background information on proposals. If there are panel sessions, the program officer is likely to play a larger role. The review process itself is traditionally seen as one of the "black boxes" of life. Yet the process, though beyond your view, is not so mysterious. In fact, except for the cases where the reviewing is shaped by politicized issues within the discipline (about which see below), it is very human and very predictable. Basically, all the reviewers try to be fair and to understand the research proposed. Their difficulty is that you are absent and they can only rely on your words on the page to guide them.

Understanding this, it becomes clear that the proposal writer's first job (beyond conceiving of an excellent and doable piece of research, as you were trained to do in graduate school) is to be clear. This is not so easy when the subject is your most absorbing interest and your readers have not thought at all about your research until the moment they sit down to read the proposal. Though they may be expert in your field (and many of them will not be), they still know very little or nothing about your research. Your challenge is to present its shape and substance and rationale to them via the written word, with no second chance to answer their questions later. This means you must anticipate their questions, even if you think the answers are obvious. They may be obvious to you, but the chances are very good they will not be obvious to them.

To state all of this most baldly, one of the things that reviewers most like in a proposal is that all of their important questions are answered in it. They also like the use of subheads (because these signposts help them find their way through the material) and a literature review that sticks to the point, that is, what is known about the research question you want to address, and what are the limitations or holes in that knowledge? They like a proposal that gives the researcher's reasons for designing his protocol in one way and not another ("I considered this method but decided against it because . . ."). And they like research designs that are neat and clean and produce useful results.

Conversely, they do not like proposals where the literature review is a laundry list of articles and books on many subjects (this effort to impress usually backfires), or where the research proposed seeks to answer a narrow and/or uninteresting question, or uses a method whose validity is not well established or uses a research design that doesn't suit the research question. They tend not to fund research whose research questions are vaguely formulated, because that is likely to produce weak research results.

From all of this, it is clear that the researcher has her job cut out for her. This is one reason it is a good idea to have three or four people read your draft proposal. Each new reader will point out something that is unclear or unpersuasive to him. You can then evaluate whether they are right (they usually are) and what to do about it. Each time you improve your draft proposal and your research rationale and design, you are improving your chances of being funded.

Rejection

The average applicant to NSF has the proposal funded on the third try. The statistics are similar for the other agencies. Although programs vary in their level of competitiveness (one NSF program has a funding rate of 55 percent; another, a rate of 17 percent), all receive more good proposals than they can fund. If your proposal is rejected the first time, the best advice is to swallow hard, sleep on it, and persist. Request the reviewers' comments if the agency has not already sent these to you. The government has the responsibility to provide you with this information if you request it and if there were external reviewers. If, after reading the comments, you have a real (as opposed to a defensive) question, call the program officer. But be careful. You are calling him not to point out why the reviewers were wrong, but to make sure you understand their comments. If the reviewers did misunderstand something you wrote, then your job is to make sure that doesn't happen again by being clearer in your next try. You can never change the review, only your next proposal. It is also dangerous to get into the game of trying to guess who the reviewers were. First, you might be wrong. Second, you can't know who they will be next time. It is better not to waste time on it.

Should you resubmit your proposal? Definitely. Unless the reviewers' comments indicate that your research topic was never appropriate to the program in the first place (in which case the program officer did not do his job well), you should rework your proposal in response to the comments and send it in again. This is a relatively small amount of work in order to have another chance to receive a grant. It is far less work than starting from scratch and you have the additional benefit of having specific comments about why your original proposal was not funded. You are now in a position of advantage in comparison to the first-time applicant. In short, whether your virgin proposal is accepted or rejected you are now an experienced grant-seeker; that alone increases your chances next time.

Conclusions

When you get your first job as an assistant professor and begin to establish your research plans, you are likely to meet a faculty member whose experience in seeking research funds contradicts most of what I have said. Over lunch some day, he will sit you down and give you the "real scoop." "It is a matter of connections," he'll advise, "and the rest is luck." You may get depressed, feeling that success in this crucial area is outside your control. But take a look at that faculty member's funding record. Not very successful? Interesting! Seek out the most funded researcher in your department and ask for more advice. You will probably hear about hard work, persistence, and patience. You will hear about submitting a good proposal and making sure it is complete and clear. You will hear about learning from your mistakes, as well as about being a good researcher. Luck and connections help, of course, this colleague will tell you, but a large part of funding success is in your own hands. That is your challenge and your opportunity.

17 New Academics and the Quest for Private Funds

Fred E. Crossland

One of the more difficult problems facing first-time faculty members is finding financial support for research. Academic promotion, tenure, and enhanced professional reputation ordinarily are based on the quality and quantity of published scholarship, so support for research is critical. Since it is virtually impossible for a young assistant professor to finance his own projects, he will have to turn elsewhere for funds. The three most common sources are:

(1) *The institution where you are employed.* A relatively modest sum may be available for faculty research projects, but there is likely to be keen competition for these funds, and staff newcomers may be at a disadvantage.

(2) *Public sources.* Scores of federal agencies underwrite research requiring the expertise of virtually all academic disciplines in one way or another. State governments—and to a much lesser degree, local governments—also occasionally subsidize specialized research by higher education faculty.

(3) *Private sources.* Possibilities include the following:

(a) Individuals. This is rather unusual, but not unheard of.

(b) Corporations. Ordinarily they are interested in research directly related to their products or services.

(c) Special-purpose, nonprofit agencies (often bearing the title of "foundation"), such as medical research entities, religious organizations, charitable societies, trade associations, and lobbying groups. Almost all have sharply focused program interests.

(d) Broad-based philanthropies or foundations conducting regular, ongoing grant programs. For the most part, the discussion in this paper will be limited to funders of this type.

Coping with Diversity

It is important to note the tremendous diversity that characterizes both higher education and private philanthropy in the United States. For each generalization about them there are uncounted exceptions, so in your quest for funds you must be sensitive to the differences and be flexible.

There are 3,200 degree-granting colleges and universities employing about 750,000 faculty members. These institutions are public and private, large and small, serve distinctive purposes, attract markedly different student bodies and staff, and hence do not present the same research opportunities and do not have the same expectations regarding faculty research. More than one thousand of these institutions are public two-year community colleges; typically, they are service- and career-oriented with strong local identification. Another eight hundred are private, four-year, liberal arts colleges; emphasis here tends to be on teaching and individualized service to students. Perhaps one hundred or so higher education institutions may properly be designated as major research universities; these include both public and private schools offering graduate and professional programs, with faculty expected to conduct sophisticated and original research in appropriate disciplines.

Faculty members from all these types of colleges and universities very likely will be seeking some sort of external support for some sort of project or activity from some sort of private funder. So you can be sure of three things: first, that the field of applicants will be both large and diverse; second, that requests will far exceed available resources; and third, that grant rejections will far exceed approvals.

American philanthropy is at least as diverse—in its forms, purposes, and procedures—as American higher education. One form is the private foundation. There are some 22,000 of them operating in the United States, and their total grant awards come to $4 billion annually. Although the combined value of their assets exceeds $50 billion, the holdings of individual organizations run from less than $100,000 to more than $4 billion at the Ford Foundation.

Only about 3,700—one-sixth of the 22,000 grant-makers—actually have assets exceeding $1 million and award more than $100,000 annually. The overwhelming majority are quite small, essentially family-run philanthropies with sharply limited program interests, and which operate rather informally without professional staff. Others are, in effect, the philanthropic arms of corporations; they vary considerably in size, purpose, and independence from their corporate parents. In fact, relatively few foundations—regardless of their size, stated purpose, or financial origins—are truly free and independent of control by the individual, family, or corporation that established them.

Parenthetically, you also should be aware that the designation "foundation," used to describe organizations with charitable purposes, is also used by groups that are actually grant-seekers rather than grant-makers. Such fundraising organizations are not included in the 22,000 figure noted above.

All grant-makers find it necessary to restrict their program interests. Many have self-imposed geographical limitations. Others may support only certain religious groups, research relating to a particular disease, projects dealing with specific social or economic problems, or members of certain groups in society. Only a handful of the largest grant-makers could appropriately be called "general purpose foundations," but even they can't cover all possible fields of interest.

Almost certainly there are no more than fifty private foundations that have assets of more than $100 million, annually award $5 million or more in grants, have reasonably broad objectives, operate on the national scene, have full-time professional staffs, and evince interest in higher education activities. Even among these few large private foundations, most grant dollars are awarded to colleges and universities for general institutional support, endowment, facilities and equipment, or student assistance rather than to individual faculty research projects.

You should be aware, moreover, that even among the very few large philanthropies willing to consider seriously requests of the latter type, several limitations are often applied. For example, foundations usually emphasize "practical" research likely to lead to early, demonstrable results. It is important to remember that most of the large, professionally staffed philanthropies do not perceive themselves to be "charities" doling out dollars to the worthy or needy, but organizations "investing" in ideas, projects, and people that hold promise of finding solutions to specific problems.

Among the larger and better-known foundations meeting many of the criteria set forth in the preceding paragraphs are the following: Carnegie, Danforth, Exxon, Ford, Hewlett, Robert Wood Johnson, Kresge, Lilly, MacArthur, Mellon, and Sloan. Some are relative newcomers to the philanthropic scene; some have demonstrated interest only in specialized areas or problems of higher education; some were active in the national arena twenty or thirty years ago and subsequently became more local in orientation; some are relatively passive bankrollers while others clearly are activists; some could appropriately be labeled liberal and others clearly are conservative.

As a group, these few large organizations continue to exert considerable influence on both the philanthropic community and higher education, and it would be wise for you, as a new faculty member, to learn more about them. It is not likely, however, that you personally will have direct contact with these foundations during your early years in academe; initially, you probably will be seeking support from smaller, local, less well-known potential funders.

To find out about these, large and small, there are certain resources to which you can turn. The most important and useful is the Foundation Center, located at 79 Fifth Avenue, New York, New York, 10003. Established and supported by foundations and corporate grant-makers, it is the primary source of public information about private foundations. The center also operates reference libraries in Cleveland, New York, San Francisco, and Washington, D.C., and is affiliated with a network of cooperating libraries. The center provides a range of specialized services and produces a number of publications, including a booklet issued every couple of years entitled, *Foundations Today: Current Facts and Figures on Private Foundations*. The latest edition is available from the center at modest cost.

There is also a Council on Foundations, but it resembles a "trade association" for grant-makers and does not purport to be a public information agency. Rather, it seeks to advance professionalism within its ranks, to encourage better management of foundations and their resources, and to keep an eye on federal and state legislation likely to have bearing on philanthropic activities.

Given the diversity and complexity of the funders' landscape, no wonder most new academics are intimidated and despair of ever mastering the so-called art of grantsmanship. In fact, many resources will be available to you, but you will be trying to find a productive match between your interests, talents, and concerns and those of a potential funder. This is not easy to achieve, but several simple and practical steps can be taken to increase the likelihood of finding that ideal match. The suggestions offered below should be helpful as you make your first moves into the foundation community.

Taking Those Important Preliminary Steps

The essential starting point is this: be confident that you really do have something to offer—a *new* idea, a *different* approach, a *distinctive* solution to a *significant* problem, the *time, talent, and energy* to get the job done, and the *qualifications* (if a fellowship competition). This is no time for either false modesty or an overly inflated ego. Be realistic, and always remember that you must have something to offer that is truly worthy of support.

To be sure you meet this essential first criterion, check with others in your discipline, in your professional associations, in neighboring institutions. Know what they are doing. Know what else has been tried, has succeeded, has failed. Read your journals and keep up-to-date. Don't reinvent the wheel. Don't automatically dismiss the possibility of collaborating with others in developing and carrying out your project. Since it is still early in your career, consider playing the role of junior investigator in a joint proposal. It may provide exactly the sort of experience and visibility you need.

It is extremely important for you to check with colleagues in your own academic department and with administrators in your institution before you start seeking outside funds. There will probably be established procedures that you are expected to follow, and certain clearances may be required. Check them out, for they vary considerably from one campus to another. Also remember that it is unwise to spring surprises on your department chairman or senior faculty colleagues. At some crucial time, you may need them for references, advice, or assistance.

Even at this early stage, it is useful to put your ideas on paper. Preparation of a draft proposal (with a fair amount of detail, a projected time frame, and an estimated budget) will help clarify in your own mind what you hope to achieve and how you would go about it. This draft will probably be for your eyes only, but it would not be amiss to test it out with colleagues who have your full respect and confidence. Weigh their advice judiciously and remember that as successful grant-seekers themselves they may be an invaluable source of promising leads.

Deciding Where to Apply

Now it is time to take an initial survey of possible private funding sources. First, sit down with the key people in your institution's development office. Their advice and help may be crucial. After all, the overwhelming majority of grants are made to *institutions*, not individual faculty members. Universities receive the funds, must account for them, and accept responsibility for funded activities. In deciding where to apply, and in all subsequent steps in the funding quest, it is very important for you to go through institutional channels. The foundation field initially will appear discouragingly large, but almost certainly there are only a very few realistic possibilities for your specific project or proposal. Your institution's library undoubtedly has reference books and directories with pertinent information, and they should be consulted. In several locations in the United States there are centers where data about foundations are kept on file. A visit is best, but you can get some help by mail or telephone. Your local research development office probably has copies of recent annual reports, lists of program priorities and interests, and grant application guidelines issued by several of the larger foundations. With advice from the local fund-raising staff and others, try to reduce the field of potential funders to no more than a half dozen of the most promising.

In this winnowing process, by no means limit your consideration to the well-known, big-name, national, or wealthiest philanthropies. The important thing to remember is that you are trying to find a match. If by some chance your research project happens to have a local or regional focus, you will probably be much better off seeking support from a local or regional foundation, even if it happens to have only modest resources. Generally speaking, if you are a young faculty member with limited foundation contacts and if your proposal clearly falls within its range of program interests, it may be easier for you to get the attention of a smaller funder. In any event and regardless of where you apply, you certainly will be better off if your proposal does not attempt to be global, but focuses on something carefully defined and limited, and hence more likely to be accomplished. With that limited definition and focus in mind, look for foundations—large or small, near or far, specialized or general purpose, corporate or otherwise—with a similar program focus.

Once you have reduced the field, it is time to review your draft proposal in light of the programs and procedures of the funders you have identified. Consult the professionals in your development office. Consider modifying your draft, taking into account specific funder interests. Perhaps one foundation would be interested in only a part of your proposal; perhaps another with somewhat different concerns would be responsive to a different aspect of your project. Don't hesitate to adapt to donor priorities so long as you keep clearly in mind, and do not distort, your own basic objectives. Getting the grant is not an end of itself; it is merely the means for achieving your project.

Look further into the foundations you have identified and feel comfortable and confident in dealing with. If you know someone on the staff of a potential funder on your list, place a telephone call asking for advice on next steps. This would not be out of order, but don't ask for or expect a definitive judgment about funding prospects for your draft proposal; that question would be premature and possibly counterproductive.

If you know someone who recently received a grant from one of the foundations you have identified, you might call that person for advice on how to proceed. Do not be disappointed if the help you receive is minimal. Remember that competition for grants is keen and many who have been successful may be reluctant to share their secrets. But don't be afraid to ask.

If the printed materials you have reviewed about a particular foundation do not appear to be adequate or are out-of-date, write a brief letter on institutional stationery requesting more current information—new guidelines for grant applications, a list of program interests, the latest annual report. At this juncture there is no point in providing any details about the project or proposal you may have in mind or are developing. The nature of the response you receive may give you some clues about your prospects. The likelihood is, however, that you will receive very general information, much of it couched in the vaguest of terms and seemingly designed to discourage potential applicants. Be realistic, but don't be put off too easily.

Now you should begin to prepare a "final" draft (or drafts) of your proposal, basing it on the information and advice you have received from several sources. Depending on circumstances and the advice of your local funding experts, it may be decided that your proposal should be submitted to more than one foundation. You may do that simultaneously, or perhaps serially if at first you don't succeed. In any event, do not send photocopies of a single proposal to all potential funders. Certain elements of it should be included in every version of your proposal, but it is wise to prepare an individually tailored document for each foundation you plan to approach.

Making Application for a Grant

Now you should be ready to approach a foundation directly with a specific grant request. Check first with your local research development office. Do you visit, write, or telephone? It depends. Foundations are often quite explicit on such matters, and it is best to follow their advice. Much depends, of course, on the specific nature and policy of the funders you hope to contact. Most of the smaller ones (for example, family foundations, modest community foundations, and the like) are little more than "mail drops," have no full-time professional staff, and meet only infrequently (usually with outside consultants and advisors) to review requests and make decisions. Many of the corporate foundations operate along similar lines. Often there simply is no one to visit and no one to talk to on the telephone. You have no option but to resort to the mails.

The large, well-known, professionally staffed philanthropies usually present different possibilities for a new faculty member hoping to make initial personal contacts. By no means, however, should a grant hopeful appear at a foundation office unannounced without a scheduled appointment. Sometimes foundation staff members will agree to a meeting set for a predetermined day and time, but in almost all instances a personal visit by a petitioner to make a grant request will prove to be of little value.

· A telephone inquiry—assuming it deals with substance and is not merely a request for an appointment—also is not likely to provide any satisfaction for the applicant. Almost certainly, the young faculty member's first contact with private funders will be through the mails.

Unlike most public funding programs that have prescribed (and often long, complicated, and detailed) application forms, virtually all private foundations suggest that you initiate your request by sending them a one-page letter setting forth briefly and informally what you hope to do and why. In this fashion the potential funder can quickly screen out the bulk of unsolicited inquiries.

If the one-pager does happen to generate foundation curiosity, the petitioner will be asked to provide more information, perhaps to submit a formal proposal along certain specified lines, or may even be asked to visit or be visited. Positive initial responses, however, are rare, and disappointed grant-seekers almost always—and too often with good reason—are certain their one-pagers were never carefully read or seriously considered.

What goes into that first piece of mail to a foundation? If a one-pager is asked for, that is what should be sent. But in most cases it would be quite acceptable to enclose with it a copy of your proposal (it would be wise at this stage to mark it "draft"), tailored to that foundation's programs and priorities.

The one-page covering letter obviously must be brief and should present a summary of the proposal, highlighting (a) the problem you hope to address, (b) what you propose to do, (c) why you are qualified to do it, (d) how long it will take you, (e) how your effort could be evaluated after the fact, (f) how much the total effort will cost, and (g) how much support you are seeking. It is difficult to compose such a letter within this space constraint. You would be well-advised to check very carefully for grammatical and factual accuracy, write very lean prose, avoid hyperbole, keep adverbs and adjectives to a minimum, and resist all temptations to butter up the addressee or the foundation. An effective letter, in this instance, is one that commands the respect of the reader and arouses sufficient interest to persuade the recipient actually to read the "draft" proposal you enclosed with it.

Institutional policy at your college or university, as well as the specific nature and scope of your project, will have a significant bearing on the content and style of your one-page letter and on the form and substance of your proposal. For example, the letter may have to be signed by the institution's president, some other senior academic administrator, or perhaps a representative of your local research development office. In any event, you will have to provide the basic information to be included in the letter, and probably you will be asked to draft it.

If your proposed project requires the use of institutional facilities or personnel, there may be certain direct charges or overhead considerations that will have to be included in your budget. Again this point must be emphasized: as a faculty member—and especially as a new and junior member of the staff—you must touch base with the appropriate people at your institution *before* knocking on foundation doors. Almost always, if a grant indeed is awarded in support of your project, it will be to your college or university, not to you personally.

Furthermore, your requests to specific potential funders quite properly must be set in institutional perspective. It is almost always counterproductive when several unrelated proposals from a single college or university descend simultaneously on a foundation, especially a smaller one, thus forcing the latter to ascertain what may or may not be considered important by that school. Coordination of fund-raising efforts is essential. By all means, your campus should have established its own priorities, and you will be expected to accommodate yourself to them.

Process, Patience, and Prospects

No two foundations operate exactly the same way. Some will acknowledge receipt of your proposal immediately, but say nothing of substance. Others will send you a rejection form letter by return mail. From still others you may hear nothing at all. If your proposal does strike a responsive chord, however faint, you may be asked to provide more information, clarify a point or two, defend your research design, or consider certain modifications. Such responses are encouraging, of course, but they are no guarantee of a positive final decision.

Since each foundation conducts its own business in its own way, you should anticipate great differences in decisionmaking procedures. As a general rule, your proposal will go through several screening steps (assuming it is not simply turned down out of hand); the number will depend upon the size and bureaucratic style of the particular foundation. If the proposal survives the winnowing process — which unfortunately may take several months and many reworkings of your draft — ultimately it will require approval by the foundation's governing board. This process cannot be hurried. Board meetings are infrequent and scheduled far in advance. If you push for an early and probably premature decision, it almost always will be "no." Even junior foundation staff members usually can reject a proposal; only the board (or in some cases the president) can say "yes."

If your proposal receives serious consideration, you can expect to engage in some negotiations with the potential funder. Rarely are projects funded exactly as originally submitted. Discussions may involve almost any aspect of your proposal. If you are dealing with experienced professionals at the funding agency, their advice and counsel may be very helpful. In any event, you would be well advised to be attentive, flexible, reasonable, and articulate in stating your positions, without compromising the essential elements of your proposal.

Unfortunately, the odds are that your requests for foundation support will be rejected. This should not be taken personally. The supply of philanthropic dollars always is exceeded by the demands of petitioners. Most likely, your turndown will come very early in the screening process, and most likely no significant substantive reason for the rejection will be given. You will find this frustrating, but you should resist the temptation to engage the foundation in debate. It is an argument you cannot win. It would be wiser to send a polite acknowledgement thanking the foundation and its staff for its consideration of your proposal. If you believe that no satisfactory reason has been given for the rejection, you might ask for additional information to enable you to do better next time. But don't be too optimistic about receiving a response; most foundation staff members are busy and don't encourage pen pals.

If you are among the fortunate few who do receive foundation support, there are several considerations to keep in mind. This is important: read carefully all the terms and conditions of the grant letter. Perhaps interim and final narrative and financial reports are required. Check with the appropriate officials at your institution about the financial administration of the grant and reporting responsibilities and procedures. In many respects, a grant resembles a contract; you have certain obligations and failure to carry them out will jeopardize any future proposals you may hope to submit.

Finally, here are three points to ponder. First, notwithstanding several observations made above, seeking a grant from private sources is neither a game nor a contest. It is a serious endeavor, to be sure, but grantor and grantee should not adopt adversarial postures. Ideally, they both must recognize that they are (or should be) partners seeking to achieve a common goal. If the process degenerates into a battle of wits, there likely will be no winners.

Second, there may well be a widespread sentiment in academic circles that foundations are insensitive, unresponsive, and given to making unwise and capricious decisions. These sentiments, although based largely on personal disappointments, may not be entirely incorrect. But the fact remains that private philanthropy has been and probably will continue to be a powerful and salutary force in American society generally, and in higher education particularly. You should not be blinded to the larger goals and accomplishments of foundations simply because you were not successful in gaining their support last time around. Of course, foundation personnel are not infallible, but they are not necessarily rascals either.

And third, do not be easily discouraged. As you embark on an academic career, there will be much to learn, important personal and professional contacts to be made, and ever-expanding opportunities to contribute to your discipline and to increased public understanding of it and its potentials. In your early years as a faculty member, patience will be both a virtue and a necessity. And in your quest for foundation dollars, the first grant very likely will be the most difficult to secure. It never will be easy, but then few things of lasting value merit that designation. May you have good fortune in your quest. And more importantly, may you deserve good fortune.

FIVE

Publishing Research

So you've gotten the coveted academic position, secured a foundation grant, and completed your research; another hurdle now appears, the mysterious and foreboding prospect of publishing your results. As many of the contributors to this volume emphasize, the publication of research is at the very core of academic existence. The aged exhortation to publish or perish is cited on more than one occasion. To this extent, of course, our authors may be reflecting, albeit subconsciously, their own careers in primarily research-oriented institutions. Certainly the pressures to publish vary widely across the academic landscape, but just as certainly the fundamental stages and procedures of publishing are reasonably standard across disciplines. The three essays that follow attempt to chart those stages and define the procedures.

Although each of the essays addresses a particular aspect of publishing, from articles to books, from matters of style to questions of content, all agree that the quality of scholarship, not its quantity, is the most important desideratum. And while each author has spoken to the obvious relations between publishing and making it through an impending tenure decision, all again agree that worthy scholarship that is well received by the profession at large and contributes significantly to the knowledge or thinking of a particular field is an end in itself. One might say, in fact, that it is *the* end of academic life, for the effective communication of the results of research brings scholar, student, professional peers, and lay community into intelligent and fruitful dialogue. In so doing, publication of any sort could be seen as the fulfillment of the academic mission.

Of course, not *any* sort of publishing is what you wish to do. Whether consciously or unconsciously, your reading in professional journals and books has already influenced your own scholarly aspirations. But how, other than being the best scholar-author you can be, do you set about fulfilling those aspirations? The suggestions that follow—how to select an appropriate journal or press, how to prepare and send off a manuscript, how to endure the sometimes lengthy review process—are designed to help alleviate some of the normal anxieties and to present a clearer picture of how publication really works.

Our three authors provide unique perspectives on the field of publication as a whole. Professor Budd speaks here largely from his experience as editor of a distinguished humanities journal. Professor Strain writes mainly from the perspective of an author, in particular a distinguished scientist. Mr. Rowson, who has considerable experience in both academic and nonacademic presses, offers an overview of the process by which a manuscript becomes an actual book.

Boyd R. Strain is Professor of Botany and Director of the Duke University Phytotron. He is a plant ecologist specializing in physiological studies of environmental stress. Professor Strain has published over 100 scientific papers, edited or coedited four books, and served on the editorial boards of four scientific journals.

Louis J. Budd is James B. Duke Professor of English at Duke University. Author of many articles and books, he is an acknowledged expert on the life and writings of Mark Twain. For several years Professor Budd was Managing Editor of the journal *American Literature* and is presently the Chairman of its Board of Editors.

Richard C. Rowson is currently the Director of the Duke University Press, but he has had a wide range of experience at several different publishing firms, including Pergamon Press, R. R. Bowker Co., and Praeger Publishers.

18   On Writing Scholarly Articles

Louis J. Budd

I will cheerfully admit to a squinting view because I am mostly going to discuss pitfalls, but the writing up of original research or new insights into a text or fundamental theory does bring deep satisfactions, and I intend finally to sound not only helpful but upbeat. I certainly intend to encourage beginners, if only for the sake of their professional self-development, which should include humility. Too many instructors who grade undergraduate term papers tyrannically have never run the gauntlet of their peers, have in fact not subjected their own work to criticism since they finished graduate studies.

I also admit to a hope that nobody will follow my advice blindly. In dealing with editors and, through them, with usually anonymous but very human referees, authors should trust their own reasoned sense of how they would behave from the other side of the transaction. Too many beginners listen gullibly to somebody who, elated by an acceptance (maybe a scratch single or even a bunt), is hot to explain the tricks of hitting a home run every time at bat. The accomplished scholars who have offered advice on how to get an article published don't bother with the tactics of outwitting editors. They know that a veteran editor, like a weathered traffic cop or a ticket-taker at the Super Bowl, has already seen most dodges many times.

Preparing a Manuscript

Although my details and examples draw on the field of literature, I believe that my advice applies more generally, for the humanities anyway. Experienced critics and scholars from many fields will agree on basic principles about content and style. First, and perhaps surprisingly, they will say: submit one article at a time. A common mistake is to add a loosely related but revealingly detachable section to an already substantial manuscript (which perhaps compresses a Ph.D. dissertation). Likewise, too many manuscripts include tangential mini-essays disguised as footnotes or endnotes. As a mechanical but generally sound rule: if a comment longer than two or three (brief!) sentences does not rate promotion to the main text, it is probably dispensable. In any case, most readers will pay little attention to long notes unless to decide that the article looks too heavy for mental transport. A corollary rule is to avoid inflating notes with information that is just marginally relevant but is "new," that is, supplies a lost fact or obscure linkage that happened to resurface along the research way. A scholarly article is not a personal essay (which is still harder to do successfully) or a "bet-you-didn't-know" kind of chat.

Another overdone feature of the notes is the phrase—literal or implied —that announces "on the other hand," and even "on the other, other hand," suggesting a scholarly octopus. I don't mean to grow supercilious. Sometimes the notes poll a mob of quarreling predecessors because the author wants to acknowledge all debts or, more anxiously, to avoid any hint of plagiarism. But I'm simpleminded enough to believe that anyone at the undergraduate level or above who is trying to operate honestly will refer here and there to the main sources being used and so has nothing to fear. I also believe that plagiarists know exactly what they are up to, no matter how skillfully they play the part of shocked innocence later. And I am content to believe that plagiarism, once published, is always spotted, that the diligent, bleary-eyed scholars who cover out-of-the-way journals will remember where they had already seen some passage. As for deliberately twisting or just bending the documentary sources to make a believable case, the *Chronicle of Higher Education* for 6 February 1985 features the attack of senior historians on an assistant professor for, allegedly, this cardinal offense.

The converse of the principles of relevance and unity is to have enough genuinely fresh material for an article, or else, still fresh and up-to-date. The starting Ph.D. is usually assigned a substantial load of students (and, these days, feels lucky to get it). By the time an article gets into the mail, four or six years (surprisingly) may have elapsed since the last careful search of the bibliographies for a dissertation. Referees comment regularly on a lost block of years in the citations. My point here is not to spread nervousness about getting "scooped." That very seldom happens, in fact. But other scholars and critics are, happily for them, working away and, happily for us, do keep adding insights and facts useful for our own immediate project.

As for enough fresh material, some of the submissions to every journal are dangerously inflated, ready to explode. No doubt, as rumor has it, a harried committee on tenure may be tempted to measure by quantity rather than brilliance. In the humanities, a new idea takes much explaining and defending, and I don't know of any major scholar-critic whose reputation grew out of a one-line equation. But that fact doesn't translate logically or practically into the law that the longer, the better. Most journals give a section over to notes, and that's respectable housing too, more impressive than a note that tries to last as long as a sonata by sounding all imaginable variations or by claiming cosmic reverberations for a down-home fact. But, to follow my own precept here, I now drop this point.

Two narrower matters also concern content rather than form. First, although wit and eloquence ordinarily give pleasure, titles of articles should be not only as short as functionally possible but so descriptive as to make sure that the reader starts out right. Incidentally, punning, ironic, allusive, or otherwise elusive titles can get an essay lost in bibliographies that are coming to depend on keywords for sorting more items than any employee or committee of volunteers can scan closely. Second, and increasingly important as long-range editing projects reach their multi-volume goal, a would-be scholar must use the most dependable text for primary sources. Citing *The Scarlet Letter* from an anthology or a cheap paperback rather than the centenary edition shakes the faith of better informed readers in a scholar's alertness. Or, to argue positively, finding and using the most authoritative text "expresses a simple preference for quality."[1]

Forty or fifty years ago, perhaps as a way of striving toward the prestige of the sciences, it was still common to counsel scholars in the humanities to aim for a no frills, objective style. The classic statement, itself enlivened by irony, came from a distinguished researcher and editor:

> We ought, I think, at the start to realize that no reader whom we are likely to have will be nearly as much interested in our views or discoveries as we ourselves are. Most of them will be people who are a little tired, a little bored, and who read us rather out of a sense of duty and a wish to keep up with what is being done than because they have any real interest in the subject; in return for our reader's complaisance it is our duty as well as our interest to put what we have to say before him with as little trouble to him as possible. It is our duty because we ought to be kind to our fellow creature; it is to our interest because if the view that we wish to put before him is clearly and competently expressed, so that he understands without trouble what we are trying to say, he will be

gratified at the smooth working of his own intelligence and will inevitably think better of our theory and of its author than if he had had to
puzzle himself over what we mean and then in the end doubt whether
he had really understood us, so raising in himself an uneasy doubt
whether his brains are quite what they used to be![2]

This statement proceeds to a set of commandments (No. 7: "Do not try to
be humorous") that are still useful to consider although, in practice, editorial
boards will grumble about a conspicuous lack of color or verve. The basic
wisdom here may be double: authors have to depend on their own judgment,
taste, and goals while expecting the usual human variability of response from
readers as well as an editor, the immediate lion in the path.

Beyond generalities and tips on niceties of detail, nobody can explain how
to compose a publishable article, although a senior scholar-critic has come
closest lately, after warning that "there is no formula."[3] Most cogent of all are
his rule that beginners "assume too little and tell too much" and his advice
that rather than worry that somebody may have scooped them, they should
think in terms of joining a "dialogue" about their subject. My own gloss on
that latter point warns against quickness to scold someone known only as a
signature to published work. The young scholar may eventually meet that
victim with embarrassment and, in some instances, with a blocked chance
for interplay. The wisdom of diplomacy aside, none of us should cry up our
own originality by running down predecessors. Indeed, we should blow the
annunciatory trumpet lightly, if at all. The experts, our key audience, know
what's already in print, and the other readers will infer that the fact of
publication certifies some degree of firstness. As a related misstep, beginners are too quick to conduct a census of the relevant bibliography in the
opening paragraph or first note. The expert audience knows all that, and the
cogency and balance of any article should quietly testify throughout to mastery of the recorded scholarship.

Two other tangential issues on content. First, the "most consistent reaction" of editorial boards is to call for "substantial cuts."[4] This call is not made
automatically and should not be anticipated by the tactic of submitting forty
pages while expecting to come down to twenty-five. Editing a journal uses a
more direct approach than selling used cars, and we all need to stay aware
that wordiness and overkill are standard mistakes. Second, my decades (I'm
sorry to be able to say) of scanning journals in my field lead to advice against
invoking the latest innovators of theory; the pollster would discount their
eminence for the recency effect. An idea is sound not because a sage said so

but because our minds accept it. Though we want to give credit where due, our readers will sense the difference between integrity and the urge to flaunt some name; especially glaring are those notes that conduct a mini-course in trendy wisdom. The guru-worshipping article will sound outdated sooner even than young scholars will hear a new instructor addressing them as "sir" or "ma'am."

The job-seeking ABD may wonder if a term paper is publishable right off. While real-life cases answer "Yes," one accomplished veteran, putting himself on the schedule of the seminar he was directing, found that he could not create a mailable article from scratch. Besides the pressure of time, it is most unlikely that a paper shaped for a seminar of one's peers or just its ayatollah will suit the editors as well as the format of some journal or—far more fundamental—will have squarely matched the gestalt of standards, tone, and niceties currently favored by the subprofession involved. Another veteran warns both young and old: "Resist the desire" to mail out an article "right away. After a week or two much which looked like very oak may well turn out to be slash pine instead."[5] To be sure, the job market pushes even ABDs into print, but if they recognize the underlying dilemma, they may decide more shrewdly: the home department often prefers speed and quantity, while out in the profession and for the long run, quality counts much more. In any case, no pressure for speed can excuse a submission that carries half-erased, term-paper stigmata such as the professor's red pencilings.

The fresh-minted Ph.D. may have to decide whether to aim for a book from the dissertation or to mine a few chapters. Again, the answer will differ from campus to campus. Where quick results are needed, it's not likely that a single article can condense a dissertation yet hold to an acceptable length, which very definitely includes the notes. It's plain improbable that any single chapter as once written will make a successful article; it will have to be reworked to look and sound freestanding. Then, like a revamped term paper or, indeed, any manuscript, it needs a critique from a tough-minded, candid friend. The editorial board can get still tougher, though not because the author is a beginner. In spite of rumors of cronyism, referees and editors can come down hardest on their peers who "ought to know better by now."

Submitting the Article

After the pressures and anxieties of getting an article ready, the author should stay keyed up for the decision of where to submit it. In the field of literature the *MLA Directory of Periodicals* can help you choose among scores of possibilities; for example, some journals refuse to consider a note-length item whereas others especially welcome it. Here and elsewhere, as I apologized at the beginning, common sense should make detailed advice superfluous. Choosing a journal that the author reads regularly should prevent an obvious misplacement.[6] Just leafing through several issues of a journal will reveal, for instance, that the *Sewanee Review* will "seldom publish analyses of single works (and never of short stories and poems)." *American Studies* warns that many manuscripts are rejected "not because of their quality but because they are too narrow for use: their authors seem unfamiliar with our editorial policies and the nature of our readers' interests." On the immediate level, someone who's been too busy getting through graduate school to feel surefooted among a forest of journals should consult an older colleague about the best matchup. In the longer run of course, the would-be author has to keep up with the relevant journals and books to nurture a realistic sense of what is publishable and where.

To come back to the rumors of cronyism, I state flatly: it's worthwhile for anybody to try the most prestigious journals. As calm analysis shows, they publish many first-time authors. Money, furthermore, is not a problem; no journal in the humanities exacts a fee for submission or "page charges" for printing. (On the other hand, very few journals pay at all and none pay handsomely for either articles or book reviews; anybody needing immediate income will earn more by selling encyclopedias door to door.) In choosing the level to try, however, the author has to judge realistically whether the manuscript itself is major or minor, whether—to adapt Herman Melville—it deals with a whale or a flea. But what if the subject is so major that some desirable journal has lately carried two or three articles related to it? *American Studies* takes the trouble to assert: "Articles are accepted or rejected because of our perception of their worth, and not because we have run too few or too many on given subjects." To put the matter positively, some editors believe that their subscribers like a cluster of articles, particularly on a major subject.

About ten years ago the younger cohort began pressing for anonymous submission. A few journals do now carefully hide the names of authors from the referees, but nobody has yet proved that such a policy raises the rate of acceptances for any group who consider themselves outsiders. Although *PMLA* had its first "all-female" issue in October 1984, its male editor doubted that anonymous submission made even part of the reason for that. Blind refereeing (no slyness intended) has the possible virtue of letting the young or otherwise supposedly excluded feel less suspicious. Still, in considering where to submit an article, I would not use this policy as a criterion.

To put another increasingly live matter as negatively as possible, nobody should even contemplate making a double (or multiple!) submission. After growling that "we strongly resent" it, *American Studies* threatens that "our policy when we identify" it is to "notify the [would-be] contributor's academic dean or chairman," who will, I predict, side grimly with the editor. Of the double-dealers who pretend surprise that anybody could object, I merely ask that they inform all editors concerned. A problem more cheerful and even amusing to those who look up from the bottom rung is whether it's wise to appear in the same journal a second or third time. As a yuppie might ask, should we diversify our portfolios? If that journal has at least average standing, I would seize the day. In the long run the quality of the article counts much more than its former companions.

Although I am focusing on articles, the tenure-track scholar will wonder about their payoff relative to a book. Coffee-break wisdom used to make six (or whatever) "solid" articles equal to a solo in hardcovers, but I seldom hear any such formula lately. Now the grimmest sages warn, "Go only for a book!" That's dismaying to those who don't believe they have as yet developed a line of thought that deserves and will find such a berth. But only the very attractive departments can insist on so high a price for tenure.

A specialized anxiety asks, "How much does an edited book count?" Even a showily decisive umpire would have to answer, "That depends." Depends on the variety of editing and on the person counting. Mere compilation rates close to zero while sophisticated handling of texts that pose intricate problems will impress anybody except the loftiest metatheorists (who could respond that a few textual enthusiasts deride analysis and speculation as ersatz whipped cream). In big-league calculation the ordinary textbook counts low and even may arouse scorn hiding envy of royalties. Getting back to articles, papers read at conferences may count much less with more dignity. However, if published later their tenure points will vary directly with the quality of the symposium and its publisher or the journal that prints it. As for the relative prestige of journals, there is probably measurable agreement among the members of any specialty.[7] But I grow uneasy as questions keep arising: "How's the Dow Jones on coauthors? on coeditors?" In such dogged calculating the figures can add up to a humanly wrong answer. I am idealistic enough to predict that young Ph.D.'s will find the most satisfaction—and material success, quite possibly—by allowing much to their own personal grain as well as that of the project itself.

For nitty-gritty details, the ideal is professionalism without bells and whistles. Because any would-be contributor to an established journal is bucking the odds, having all zippers secure can help in borderline decisions. For example, since editors do retire eventually or just choose another incarnation, an author should check the latest masthead before addressing a cover letter. The target journal will state or show what system of documentation it follows although most editors waive such criteria until acceptance is likely.[8] While neatness is desirable, editors understand that retypings to achieve supercleanliness will slip errors past the tiring author who has almost memorized the text. Sending the ribbon-copy (so long as that term still has meaning) tends to reassure all concerned and pleases the copy editor when the transaction gets that far. Word processor texts have graduated to full respectability and soon will rate as the natural format among those who have played with computers since kindergarten. Whatever the technology of the printout (or tape or disc), I can't imagine the day when editors won't want everything double-spaced. Everything, even the block quotations? Yes, everything! While as dazzled as anybody by electronic agility, editors also want the manuscript printed on one side of the sheet only. The savings will come in their bill for over-the-counter drugs.

Shifting to *don'ts* for emphasis, I repeat that an author merely wastes time by playing games with an experienced editor who long ago saw, for example, the trick of hiding length with margins so narrow that the copy editor will have to sit sideways to use them. Authors should not devise a table or diagram without realizing that it means added expense — higher than they're likely to estimate — for any journal. They are probably wiser to draw the diagram verbally or to tell readers where to find a painting already reproduced elsewhere. But I don't mean to make authors approach the editor on their knees. Publish or perish applies to a journal too, and it depends on volunteered articles. Furthermore, editors are just as upward-striving as the most ambitious author and will tolerate many annoyances in order to produce a better issue. Nevertheless, editing a journal entails borderline choices, just like shopping for tomatoes or selecting a patient for an artificial heart. In a few cases the editor has to decide irritably, at midnight, whether some article is worth all the niggling labor needed to tidy it up.

Editors, I must confess, tend to grin wryly over many a letter of inquiry. Too often it betrays that the writer has not bothered to read the journal or even the inside cover. Sometimes it tries for an advance commitment, which no editor of a refereed journal would dare to make; the only immediately definite answer can be "No." An offer of a rough draft is only slightly more welcome than a letter bomb. Offers of a sprawling manuscript that the editor would be free to trim are welcome only if signed by either Thomas or Tom Wolfe. An admirably scrupulous author may wonder if a seminar paper must confess that it was lately waxed and buffed into an article. I see no obligation or hope of benefit for doing that.

Editors, I confess further, laugh out loud at a few covering letters for the manuscript. Since one veteran flatly warns that the letter can do more harm than good, the safest tactic is to keep it short and of course mildly sweet. Editors do understand why an author might expect them to want a brief autobiography, a list of medals, or even a c.v., but their minds fasten on the self-contained manuscript. Its author can raise distracting hackles by quoting Professor Goodheart's praises, by pressing for a quick answer (through being jumped to the head of the queue), by threatening double-submission (if the wait for response grows "excessive"), or by puffing the article as the chapter of a soon to materialize book. Ironically, journals with a high rate of rejection judge that they serve the profession best by not squandering their pages on an article scheduled soon for hard covers.

Three _do's_ for a covering letter, the first to the author's benefit alone. It should explicitly ask for any criticism the editor can find time to transmit. Having felt the sting of rejection themselves, editors tend to filter out the harsher commentary from the referees, and to transmit all of it only when urged. I'm not preaching masochism, but in order to revise effectively the author needs the frankest critiques. A second positive feature for a covering letter is to show, where necessary, alertness to problems of quoting restricted materials. Although the author will have to accept the legal responsibility in writing, journals balk at any chance of getting drawn into litigation over copyright. Therefore, authors must remember to honor those forms that a repository of manuscripts presents for signature at the door. The tenured cohort will line up against a colleague who breaks such a vow because the research library is their temple. Third, a covering letter should fit the particular addressee rather than revealing that it perhaps serves for a variety of journals.

Waiting for a Response

There's a relief when the article flies off in the mail along with, ominously, a stamped, self-addressed envelope. But after a well-run journal acknowledges safe arrival, the next problem sprouts: how to behave while the jury is out. Usually its verdict will take at least three months. After six months a simple inquiry, undisguised as a concern for the editor's happiness, is forgivable, although, ordinarily, some referee is the bottleneck. Phone calls can be annoying unless the editor happens to live inside the filing cabinet and has everything within reach. However long the delay, editors seldom bawl out a referee, who is by definition a busy scholar, and they cannot withhold a salary adjusted at zero.

But all sides deserve empathy. The author suffers with no assured date of relief and perhaps with a decision on tenure grinding toward its deadline. What about trying to withdraw the article and resubmit it elsewhere? I say "trying" because it is probably out in the pipeline and the editor can't recover it quickly. Another dilemma: to withdraw is to waste months of waiting, perhaps just a week short of a verdict. With most journals the sufferer will do best simply to meditate upon the relativity of emotional time. Or the action-oriented mind should draft another article. But what if the author tinkers meanwhile with the one creeping through the mail and discovers major flaws or just improvements? Should these be rushed off to the editor? Theoretically, perhaps. In practice, however, the ongoing round may as well finish up. The editor will feel delight, not chagrin, at learning that an article just accepted will upgrade itself. In the gloomy case, the author should feel that the particular journal has devoted as much effort as one article has a right to ask. In other words, if rejected the rebuilt manuscript should go elsewhere without an appeal.

Responding to the Response

To take the darker but more likely result, a familiar envelope comes back eventually. Then, as Hyman Rodman asks, "What shall I do if my excellent article is (foolishly, mistakenly) rejected?" First, I remind myself that the odds were against me. Second, I remember that eminent scholars have confessed to having tried two or three or more journals before an acceptance. Editors presume that now and then an article has rebounded from another journal, and they have had many chances to marvel at conflicting judgments, even as they may believe the real blunders occur elsewhere. Because they trust the collective judgment of their own referees, they don't try to discover the previous travels of a manuscript. On the other hand, the author, who has no obligation to describe those travels, can consider it courteous rather than shrewd to remove any signs of a world tour, if only by running off the first page to match the next journal's format for titles and the name of a contributor.

The author who believes in an article (and therefore feels ethical in burdening unpaid referees) will keep resubmitting it elsewhere with deliberated speed until the criticism grows convincing. A cleverly sardonic letter of protest will change not a rendered verdict but the writer's reputation with the addressee. Anybody who asked to hear any and all criticism has implicitly promised to take it without a whimper. Likewise, demanding to know the identity of the mistaken referees is pointless. If the editor did not include that fact routinely, it's because they have been promised or have requested anonymity to avoid a time-consuming and mostly futile debate. Another unwritten principle bars resubmitting even a basically improved article to the same journal. The absence of a specific invitation is in fact a genteel version of "Don't call us; we'll call you." Nevertheless, editors remain sincerely open to a different submission from any author who has behaved with at least minimal courtesy. I repeat: editors want good articles to accept. At their desk they don't see any humor in the gag: "Who won the beauty contest? Nobody."

So the author reenters the process of choosing a target, quicker this time perhaps. But not too quick! First, those causes for rejection must be considered—not supinely adopted, yet pondered, pondered. But perhaps not even that quick! One veteran challenges the author to achieve the discipline of rereading the article before taking in the letter of rejection.[9] Less heroically, I warn against assuming that the editor's report covered all the flaws. Now that time has distanced the article mentally, the author should struggle to judge it impersonally. If the criticisms still look wrong, then a qualified colleague could break the tie. But the votes must be counted honestly, not by a beginner who daydreams about proving to be the scholars' Billy Arnold or Francis Coppola. And the voters must be honest—not a Willie Loman desperate to be well liked nor a tweedy Boss Tweed.

Although that manila envelope eventually returns, sometimes it carries an acceptance. If it only breathes come-hitherness, how often did all the judges award a ten during the 1984 Olympics? A bill of revisions is an omen of eventual acceptance, especially if the author takes them up reflectively—not conforming humbly but not turning pigheaded either. Four more *don'ts*. First, a gullible author should not listen to the dopester's wisdom that suggestions for changes are just wordplay because editors want to flaunt their authority and will accept whatever comes back. Second, a weary author should not sag into simply correcting the article to mollify a superteacher. As I said, editors are delighted to let an article rise to greater excellence than they asked for. Third, the anxious author must not hurry just because the journal might fold or the editor might have a change of mind or scholarship might go out of fashion. So far only the first disaster has happened, rarely. Fourth, the triumphant author must not skimp when the call for rechecking of fact and style brings back the superbly crafted article too. Surprisingly many authors turn careless after the precision and effort needed to get that far. Errors have inevitably crept in between taking notes and polishing a typescript, and, fairly or not, readers will blame even the flagrant typos more on the author than on the editor.

Not all journals now incur the expenses of sending out a set of proofs. Authors lucky enough to get it should assume that it will contain typographical errors to be hunted down. They must prepare to hunt stoically also because some phrasings will cry out for improvement. But a subsidized journal cannot run up its bills to indulge the writer who didn't take the rechecking stage seriously. Any tinkerings with the proofs cost money. I'll always remember the request for very late changes if they "are not too much trouble for the printer." It visualizes an editor strolling to a ramshackle shop where an old-timer ("Doc" or "Pop") wearing a green eyeshade picks type out of a case and makes changes free of charge while chatting laconically. To steal from Mark Twain, I wish the world could be that young again. Changing "just one word" in a plate done through a computer may cost still more than casting and inserting a slug of linotype: an expert has to instruct a very expensive machine how to search its circuits while the savings promised by technology keep slipping away like a balanced federal budget. More generally it is helpful to remember that every journal has to stay within its income-plus-subsidy.

Breaking into Print

But we do achieve some of our dreams. A copy of the glorious issue will turn up followed months later by offprints, either free of charge or else at cost. If at cost, how many to buy? or how many to photocopy? The answer could dodge behind another, embarrassing question: How many friends do you have? I have never managed to send out many more than thirty offprints to friends and fellow specialists. The proud author who waits for requests will save handsomely on postage.

Having joined the side of editors and publishing scholars, the author may even start thinking in terms of solidarity. In positive terms that includes urging overly modest colleagues or students to aim for the pleasures of breaking into print. However, true solidarity also forbids encouraging the unready as a way of building a local image for kindness. Every journal gets submissions that don't rate so high as amateurish. Whoever encouraged them should pray that the covering letter did not identify him or her. Only the rarest undergraduate paper deserves to travel beyond the campus. A teacher can lavish enough praise, greedy as we all are for it, without causing work and expense for a subsidized journal. Another path toward solidarity with the profession leads to giving a frank and prompt critique if a colleague asks—and seems able to accept it.

Book Reviewing

My biggest surprise as managing editor of a quarterly has been the flow of offers to review books. Do journals welcome an unsolicited review? Categorically, no. Besides, because they receive their copies early they have already lined up a reviewer. Is it worthwhile applying for a specific review? Though the answer should again be "no," editors are always looking for qualified recruits and may gamble on having allowed press agentry or having seconded a vendetta. Before applying, check to see whether the journal designates an editor especially for book reviews; also, consider that the few journals that give all their space to reviewing are more likely to need volunteers. More specifically, is it worthwhile to submit a curriculum vitae or a statement on areas of strength? That can often bring results. But—the most important question by far—is it worthwhile for an untenured academic to do any reviewing at all? That answer depends on the home department, which can range from beaming proudly at any sign of print to deducting points for popping small corn. Finally, doing a review just to get a free copy of a book really means working far below the minimum wage.

The scholar who publishes several good articles will probably be offered more than enough reviewing. Even when moved solely by altruism, anybody who accepts a book should meet the deadline, if simply out of pity for the author, who hasn't been so impatient since childhood over how slowly time can pass. The reviewer should also honor the limit on words set by editors, who agonize over the deserving books that the journal can't make room for and who will bristle at excuses that the assigned length was unfair to the author, the subject, the large field, or—most deplorably of all—the reviewer.[10] While editors dislike having all the reviews wallow in kindness, they realize that usually more effort pours into a book than a gaggle of articles. Therefore, they welcome only the severity that is clearly deserved, and they know that the acrid reviewer will suffer through keeping poised to stroll the other way while scanning nametags at a convention.

Thinking Positively About Editors

I hope that nobody will avoid or else snub editors. There's no benefit in feeling resentful toward them. As publishing scholars they have learned that rejections hurt and that revising can feel like swimming in army boots. Editors who enjoy sadism soon get run out of the office. Those who last will commit errors of kindness, inconsistencies, oversights, and stupid mistakes, all of which are inevitably pointed out because they are so public. Editors have to apologize for any bloopers they helped to cause while silently digging out perhaps worse and certainly more frequent errors. They have to console themselves privately that they also helped an author to add effectiveness as well as missed sources.

A former adviser on scholarly publication to the American Council of Learned Societies has philosophized:

> Scholarly editors seem not infrequently to be harassed by the very people who should be their pride and joy, the apples of their editorial eyes—their contributors. And this is strange, because, much as the editor needs his contributors, the more do the contributors need him.
>
> For this reason, the maintenance of an editor in good health and humor is not only a worthy but a very practicable pursuit. He is a man who gives up to this work a good deal because he has probably long neglected his own research because of it; who is often unpaid or underpaid for his editorial services; who is assisted, if assisted at all, by colleagues half a country away; who is continually forced to argue with his treasurer or his university press or provost over his printing bills; and who on top of all this quite rarely receives manuscripts in really top condition, written with the style of his journal in mind, in good English, clear, clean and succinct.[11]

I am trying to fan not sympathy but empathy, to humanize editors in the mind of the author, who should see them as allies and who should recognize that they will respond to candid sincerity. They are particularly eager to hear what the profession is thinking and saying about their journal.

To finish where I began, I apologize for any dampening effect. Still, I don't intend to persuade the cynics to enlist. If they are not moved to publish for idealistic reasons, in good part anyway, then they won't write much that's worthwhile. Rather, I mean to assure the willing beginner that in spite of the pains there's much pleasure in conducting research and then promoting it into print. Hang gliding may carry sharper thrills, but scholarship can anchor a lifetime.

Notes

1 Terence Martin, "Meditations on Writing an Article," *American Literature* 55 (March 1983): 74. Hershel Parker's *Flawed Texts & Verbal Icons*: Literary Authority in American Fiction (Evanston, Ill.: Northwestern University Press, 1984) recurringly makes this point among much more substantial reasons.

2 From "Form and Matter in the Publication of Research"; published first in *Review of English Studies* in 1940, it gained semiofficial status by being reprinted in *PMLA* (April 1950) and then as part of a pamphlet from the Modern Language Association; it now is best available in John Philip Immroth, *Ronald Brunlees McKerrow: A Selection of his Essays* (Metuchen, N.J.: Scarecrow Press, 1974), pp. 195–202.

3 Martin, "Meditations," p. 76. Barbara R. Reitt, "An Academic Author's Checklist," *Scholarly Publishing* 16 (October 1984): 65–72, gives an excellently practical and compact set of guidelines; she also recommends other sources of advice.

4 "Editor's Column," *PMLA* (October 1984).

5 Henry M. Silver, "Putting It on Paper," *PMLA* 65 (April 1950): 14.

6 This and other pointers appear in Hyman Rodman, "Some Practical Advice for Journal Contributors," *Scholarly Publishing* 9 (April 1978), 235–41.

7 In *College English* (April 1980) Michael West rated journals mostly in the field of British and American literature; the December 1980 issue carried a storm of responses.

8 In the field of literature and languages, many journals have adopted the latest *MLA* manual for style. But surely those journals keeping an older form will not insist on it before a first reading.

9 Murray F. Markland, "Taking Criticism—and Using It," *Scholarly Publishing* 14 (February 1983): 139–47.

10 I amplify this point in "Bootcamp for Book Reviewers," *American Literature* 54 (May 1982): 277–83. More generally useful is Roy S. Wolper, "On Academic Reviewing: Ten Common Errors," *Scholarly Publishing* 16 (April 1985): 269–75; Wolper contains references to other sources, furthermore.

11 Silver, "Putting It on Paper," p. 11.

19   Publishing in Science

Boyd R. Strain

T his essay addresses the problems ex-
perienced by young scientists in publishing the results of their work. Why
publish and how does one go about it?

Several handbooks and manuals have been published on the subject. The
most useful is *How to Write and Publish a Scientific Paper.* The second
edition of this little book by Robert A. Day appeared in 1983. It is up-to-date,
even including a chapter on the electronic manuscript, and contains sound
advice from an experienced managing editor of a major scientific journal.
The bibliography of this handbook lists several other publications that provide additional information on the issues presented below.

Purpose of Scientific Publishing

The purpose of publishing scientific papers is to complete the task of
doing research. A scientific experiment, no matter how spectacular the
results, is not completed until the results are published. Knowledge gained
by the scientific method but not passed on to society by scientific writing is
of no more value and is no more reliable than the folk stories of prehistoric
tribes.

Why Publish Scientific Papers

There are primary motivating forces that encourage scientists to complete their research efforts. One of these is the scientific establishment. In
1974 the official government policy of the Federal Council of Science and
Technology stated: "The publication of research results is an essential part
of the research process. This has been recognized in part through authoriza-

tion to pay publication costs from federal research grant and contract funds." The scientific establishment demands that research results be published. The investigator who does not publish will not be retained within that establishment. The nonpublisher will be barred from normal vehicles of scientific interaction, that is, meetings, invited oral and letter symposia, and cooperative book-writing projects. The nonpublisher will not continue to receive external grant or contract funds awarded through the peer review process. The scientific establishment soon excludes those who fail to complete research by writing scientific papers.

A second force that encourages individuals to publish scientific papers is the simple fact that people like to be recognized. Individuals become known to the scientific community by publishing the results of their research. It is a great feeling to see your work in print; it is even more pleasing to have others contact you to discuss your research results after a paper has appeared in print. Thus, for some people, a personal sense of gratification is obtained from seeing their name and their research results and ideas in print.

In contemporary academia, there is a third reason for publishing. The investigator who does not believe it is necessary to publish to complete research, who neither expects nor desires personal attention, or who feels that his/her research is not yet ready to appear in print, frequently learns firsthand of the dictum *publish or perish*.

Universities and research institutes expect employees to do research and to carry it through to publication. Basically the employers believe that research unpublished is research not completed. Investigators are expected to organize their research so that it can be completed in units with some reasonable time scale. The average number of research papers your chairman expects you to publish per year varies with discipline and with institution. The "wise" young professor at a major research university, however, will strive to have six to nine senior-authored titles by the end of the third year of his or her initial appointment.

The Form of Scientific Papers

Writers of papers to be published in scientific journals do not have the freedom to arrange their papers in unique ways. By three hundred years of tradition, enforced by the need to communicate precisely and concisely, scientific writing has become rigidly stylized. Every scientific paper will have a title, an author with address, an abstract, an introduction, a section on methods and materials, a section on results, a discussion of those results, and a list of references cited in the paper. Lengthy papers may have additional sections or appendixes, but these too must fall within traditional guidelines. Very short research papers may be published without all of these section headings, but the information must be arranged in the above order. Some scientific journals have adopted modifications of this order, and the final authority to determine the actual form to be published is the editior-in-chief of the respective publication. Therefore an author may partially control the form of the paper by selecting a journal that uses an acceptable style. Rarely, however, can an author diverge from the traditional style of a given periodical and rarely do journals differ significantly from the historical norm.

How to Write Scientific Papers

Since the objective of publishing a scientific paper is to complete a given study by communicating the new discoveries, a paper should be direct, concise, and uncluttered with extraneous information. If a paper reports new and original results, it will be necessary to completely introduce the subject, state the objective, clearly describe the methods and materials used, and state the results in sufficient detail to allow others to judge the adequacy of the discussion and the accuracy of the conclusions. A paper may be much shorter if it is reporting results of a study conducted to repeat or test a previously published observation.

All scientists develop their own procedures for the preparation of papers. Many people prefer to write the results section first, but I begin with the section on methods and materials. This serves to get the easiest part on paper and to get me motivated. Then I write the section on results. The discussion flows naturally from writing the details of the results. Then the major conclusions can be stated in an itemized summary or in narrative form. Preparing the reference list is a purely technical operation and must follow the requirement of the journal to which the paper is to be submitted. This step should be postponed until the journal selection has been made. Experienced scientists may be able to select a journal style before preparing the first draft, but the beginner will need a draft in hand before advice can be sought on an appropriate journal.

After completing these sections, an introduction can be written that specifically addresses the paper as it will go out for review. If you attempt to write the introduction first, you may have difficulty staying on track. If your project is complex, it will be difficult to know how to introduce the paper until the content sections are finished.

Now, one has only to write a concise abstract and finally to select an informative and specific title. Titles and abstracts are the most read sections of all scientific papers. Consequently, both should be prepared very carefully. A good title contains the fewest possible words that adequately describe the content of the paper. Its purpose is to inform readers that something was done in a specific research area. If the reader is interested in that area, he or she will take the time to read the abstract. A good abstract will inform the reader of the basic content of the paper and will enable the reader to decide if the paper should be studied in more detail.

How to Complete a Paper and to Prepare It for Submission to a Specific Scientific Journal

Once a paper has been completed as explained above, it should be circulated among your colleagues and students for help in revisions. All papers will benefit from revision, revision, and more revision. You need assistance in clarifying sentences, finding redundancies, and discovering missing critical information. Ask your reviewers to consider the paper as if they had received it for an anonymous review from a journal editor. Take their suggestions seriously and improve the manuscript as much as possible. Avoid spelling, grammatical, and typographical errors. If you have figures, draw them neatly and carefully to insure that the manuscript "looks" professional. A reviewer with confidence in style will tend to have confidence in content.

It is now time to make the final decision on the journal to which the manuscript will be submitted. Several factors must be considered in making a journal selection. List the journals that have been publishing papers in your subject area. Scanning recent issues of *Current Contents* may help if you are not certain.

To determine if the editor of a given journal may be interested in your material, read the masthead statement in a current issue, review the table of contents of several recent issues, and read the "Instructions to Authors" usually provided inside the front or back cover of each issue. It is also appropriate to ask the editor if your material is suitable for the journal in question.

Of those journals that publish in your field, what is the average time from the date of first receipt by the editor to the date that the paper appears in print? Some scientific journals now have a two-year lag-time while the total elapsed time in others is less than six months. A young professor cannot afford to submit to a journal that takes a year or more to decide on publishability.

From those journals that you deem to be appropriate for your paper, select the journal that has the best prestige factor. Generally the highest prestige occurs in the journal of the major society in your discipline. Unfortunately, journals of the major societies are frequently the slowest in review and publishing. Another unfortunate fact is the high rejection rate of prestige journals. Some major journals must reject 60 percent or more of the manuscripts received for review. You will have to weigh prestige against lag-time and the probability of acceptance to make your final selection.

Once you have determined the journal, obtain a copy of the "Instructions to Authors" for that journal. Usually instructions are printed in at least one issue of each volume. Also instructions may be obtained by writing to the printer or the editor following instructions printed in the journals. Follow these instructions as closely as possible. Study papers similar to yours published in recent issues of the journal. Carefully prepare your paper following instructions on length and style, graphs, tables and illustrations, and citation style. As stated above, most prestige journals receive more good manuscripts than can be accepted. Reviewers and editors do not have time or patience for authors who do not follow instructions. Do not forget that your manuscript can be rejected for any reason. Do not give the editor the opportunity to reject your manuscript on the basis of style alone.

Submitting the Manuscript

Follow the instructions to the letter. Send the number of copies with all materials in the exact form and size required. If instructions call for all graphs to be submitted in three copies on glossy photographic paper in a size to be reduced 50 percent for printing, do just that!

Provide a covering letter addressed to the editor or as instructed by the journal. Include the title of your paper and any information that you think the editor may need to manage the review. I recently advised a student to include in his paper a lengthy and detailed review of the assumptions required to utilize his methods but to tell the editor in the covering letter that the material could be deleted if the editor considered it to be unnecessary for the average reader of the journal. If you will be at a different address from the one given on the manuscript when the editor will have to communicate with you, give complete mailing and telephone information with appropriate dates in the covering letter.

Response to the Review

A frequent response from scientific editors these days is that the material is appropriate for the journal but that the paper will have to be revised and shortened before it can be published. My advice is to make every change required and to return the corrected manuscript within two weeks. Delays in resubmitting the manuscript will increase the probability that the editor will send it back to the reviewers or even send it out to additional reviewers. It is sometimes possible to argue a point of disagreement on a required revision, but unless the change introduces an error you should not pursue the issue. If you disagree with an editor's decisions on revisions to the point that you cannot change the manuscript as suggested, my advice is to retype the paper in the form required by another journal and send it there. Unless you can conclusively prove your point, the editor will not change the decision. Remember, most top journals are rejecting good manuscripts on the subjective decisions of the editors. You seldom will win in a disagreement on style or emphasis.

If your paper is rejected, revise it to correct problems detected by the reviewers, clarify material where necessary, and prepare it for submission to another good journal. Even though science is supposedly an objective enterprise, decisions on approach and significance are subjective matters. Material that seems mundane and boring to one scientist may seem critically important and carefully done to another. You are an expert in your field, and your subjective opinions are as good and as justifiable as those of other experts. Rather than enter into a frustrating and sometimes lengthy dialogue with dissident reviewers and editors, it is advisable to simply try another journal and keep trying. If necessary select a journal of less prestige, especially if the tenure decision is coming up. A publication in any journal may be preferable at this stage to no publication.

Reading Proof

After your manuscript has been accepted it will be sent to a printer to be typeset. At some point you will receive page proofs or galley proofs with instructions on how to read and correct the proofs. You will also usually receive instructions to change only those items that are incorrect. Printers' errors in typesetting will be corrected and minor changes made by the author will be made at no charge to the author.

Significant changes required after the type has been set will only be made if the text is in error. If the error was on the manuscript sent to the printer, the author may be required to pay a charge for resetting the type.

Most printers send detailed instructions on how to mark the proofs. Follow these instructions as closely as possible. The *CBE Style Manual* (1978) has extensive instructions for editing proof copy. If specific instructions are not provided by the printer, find a style manual appropriate for your field and follow it to the best of your ability.

Many errors can creep into a manuscript in the typesetting process. You must read proofs with all of the care that you can muster. My technique is to have a coauthor or other knowledgeable person read the manuscript to me while I follow along studying every word and symbol on the proof. Another technique is to compare the proof to the manuscript reading the entire paper backwards one word at a time. I have never had the patience for that procedure, but some people use it. One of my colleagues swears that he gives the proofs to a graduate student along with the threat that the student will never graduate if that paper contains a printing error when it appears!

Remember, your published papers are the permanent record of your contributions to your discipline. A mistake that appears in print in a scientific paper will be there forever. You are the final authority for your published work, and the ultimate responsibility for its quality is yours. Reading, correcting, and approving proofs is your final opportunity to get it right.

Proofs should be corrected and returned to the printer by return mail. Some journals allow only forty-eight hours to correct and return proofs. If you cannot meet the designated time, write or call the person to whom proofs are to be returned and give them the date that the proofs will be returned.

Ordering Reprints and Paying Page Charges

You will be offered the opportunity to purchase reprints of your article when the proofs are returned to you. Payment will be due when the reprint order is submitted or a university purchase order must be supplied. Currently a six- to ten-page paper will cost about $100 per 100 reprints. The number of reprints to be ordered depends on the popularity of your subject and on the availability of funds. Some journals provide 25 or 50 free reprints. I usually order 300 reprints. Your published papers are the best advertisement of your work. Order many reprints and distribute them liberally. Young professors should send unsolicited reprints to well-known scientists in their field.

Page charges have been levied by most societies for publishing in the societal journals. Some societies allow five to ten free pages per member per year and then charge $40 to $60 per page beyond the free limit. Most societies also provide the option to apply for a page charge waiver if no research funds are available to pay the charges.

Not all journals make page charges. This is usually a factor to be considered when journals are being compared. Therefore, if funds are limited and paying page charges will be a problem, this factor may affect your choice of journal for the submission of your manuscript.

Authorship of Scientific Papers

Multiple-authored papers have become commonplace in science. Modern research is often complex and may require two or more experts to design and conduct the experiments. Laboratory heads sometimes add their names to every paper originating in their laboratory. Professors frequently expect to join their students as coauthors because of their conceptual and financial inputs into the work. As a professor, you should explain your policies to each of your students.

In multiple-authored papers, the order of listing the authors should be determined and agreed upon at the beginning of each series of experiments leading to a publication. The first listed author should be the person who actually did most of the work and writing. Second or third authors should be listed in decreasing order of time and effort put into the study. The last named author is traditionally the laboratory director or the major professor who may have been instrumental in framing the overall research direction and capabilities of the group. Paid technicians normally should not be listed as authors unless they have made significant contribution to the conceptualization, interpretation, and writing of the research.

Acknowledgments

You should acknowledge colleagues, associates, or students who loan equipment, collect material for the experiment, help integrate the results, or review the manuscript. Acknowledgments of financial support from grants or contracts are also appropriately made in scientific papers. Institutional service people (e.g., technicians, typists, draftsmen) are paid to perform their services. Normally it is not necessary to acknowledge routine technical contributions to the preparation of research papers. Each journal has its own style for the inclusion of acknowledgments in the manuscript.

Other Considerations in Scientific Publishing

REVIEWING MANUSCRIPTS

Most journals utilize unpaid peer reviewers to read and comment on the publishability of scientific manuscripts. Reviewers are usually anonymous. As a beginning scientist you will occasionally be asked to review manuscripts. If you do a good job and do it quickly, your name will soon move into the "good reviewers" card file of several editors. Before you know it you will be receiving more manuscripts than you care to read. If you begin to receive more invitations to review than you can comfortably manage, decline them. Do not delay manuscripts because of lack of time to complete good reviews.

Conceptually, all manuscripts should be reviewed from a completely objective viewpoint. Practically, however, there are two primary approaches to the review of scientific manuscripts. One approach assumes that every paper is weak, contains errors, and should be rejected. Your responsibility as an anonymous reviewer is to find the problems and explain them to the editor so that the manuscript can be rejected. A second approach assumes that every manuscript reports good research, properly done, that should be published as quickly as possible. Your job is to identify the strengths of a paper and to make suggestions for improvement where possible. Only those manuscripts that cannot be salvaged by detailed revision are recommended for rejection.

The former class of reviewers exists in a subsection of the card file of editors entitled "hatchet reviewers." If the editor is predisposed to reject your manuscript for any reason it will be sent to "hatchet reviewers." This is a primary reason for you to submit the most perfectly prepared manuscript possible. Carefully follow the "Instructions to Authors" for the particular journal to be used.

My advice is to be the second class of reviewer but to not accept manuscripts outside of your area of expertise and do not accept more than you can comfortably handle. We all must do our part to keep the peer review process working in scientific publication. Do not go overboard with this community service, however. Your primary obligation as a young professor is to your own work. Help the system where you can but remember your priorities and guard your time well to ensure that your own work gets done.

BOOK REVIEWS

Writing book reviews does not count in the credit column of your publish or perish ledger. A book review is not a scientific publication. If you are going to study a new book in detail for some other reason, summarizing your findings in a published book review may be a desirable by-product. But do not fall for the temptation to write book reviews in order to obtain free books. Writing a good book review requires many hours. When you divide the $60 to $80 price of a new reference book by the ten to fifteen hours that a worthwhile book review requires, your time was worth $4 to $8 per hour. You are better off to buy the book and use the time for jogging.

ETHICS IN PUBLISHING AND REVIEWING

An original scientific paper can be published only once in a scientific journal. If the same material is to be published in another journal it must be clearly marked and the original source cited. A copyright release must be obtained. Dual publication in primary research journals is basically unethical. If it can be justified, it must be done with the full awareness of all editors, publishers, and coauthors involved. Most scientific journals carry a statement that informs the authors that submission of a paper to that journal implies that the information is original and that it is not being submitted for publication to any other scientific journal. Previously published information can be republished in scientific reviews, but here also complete citation must be given and copyright laws must be honored.

Scientific writers must exert every effort to cite prior publication of concepts or results. Individuals who may have contributed ideas to a given original study should be acknowledged in the paper. It is not always possible to remember all of the stimuli leading to a scientific breakthrough, however. We must always be aware that our understanding is cumulative and is built from all of the experiences we have had. The individual components that lead to a new idea on your part may not all be remembered or identifiable. Don't forget they are there, however, and acknowledge or cite as many as possible.

PROPRIETARY INFORMATION

As a peer reviewer of manuscripts and proposals you will become aware of data and concepts before they are published. The use of this information before it is printed or without the consent of the original author is unethical.

I can only hope these few remarks on publishing will be helpful to those scientists (and nonscientists) about to embark on their publishing careers. If they are, of course, I will be doubly rewarded: in the knowledge that I have provided for you and in the knowledge your own work will shortly provide for me.

20 The Scholar and the Art of Publishing

Richard C. Rowson

To paraphrase a thought expressed by Stanley Hauerwas elsewhere in this volume, good publishing scholars are not those who know how to interest readers, but who write what is interesting because it is crucial to their disciplines. Publishing is the art of helping a scholar say something new and important that changes the way people think about a given problem or subject. As another author in this volume, Frank Lentricchia, said in commenting on the "central activist conception of the intellectual" in the United States, "it is not enough to interpret the world: one must try to change it as well." Good books do just that.

So, in introducing the subject of publishing to the budding scholar, it is not the "techniques" nor even the skill of communicating, but the quality of scholarship that is the controlling factor. Just what is the "quality of scholarship" that a publisher looks for in an offering from a prospective author? In a marvelously well-informed article entitled, "Scholarship: A Sacred Vocation," Professor Jaroslav Pelikan, an eminent Medieval and Renaissance scholar at Yale and formerly chair of the Yale University Press Publications Committee, offers these salient points.

First, Pelikan speaks of the need to bring the perspective of history to scholarly writing so that the reader not only learns *who* his "intellectual ancestors are," but *why* they merit such a distinction and *how* their ideas evolved. He writes: "It is one of our obligations, both as scholars and publishers, to introduce each succeeding generation of scholars to their intellectual ancestors"—rather than learning the "latest trendy jargon" or newest hypotheses—"so as to instill scientific and scholarly discipline as an intellectual virtue, without which scholarship would be only a job, not a sacred vocation."

Second, Pelikan speaks of the need for "imagination" in the interpretation of data and in determining the meaning of findings across and among disciplines; imagination, he argues, is the essential difference between "significant and trivial research." He admonishes the publisher to seek out and encourage the scholar whose work goes beyond the normal standards of good research and brings to his findings a new vision of his subject and of its true importance.

He adds an important corollary to this point: "Scholars and presses need to become themselves the communicators of the outcome of research . . . don't leave this task to the authors of textbooks, to trade publishers, and to the *New York Times Magazine*." In other words, a scholarly author, as any other author, should "keep it simple," and lend his ideas and findings the importance they deserve by utilizing language comprehensible to the widest possible readership. As a former member of an editorial review board for a university press, Pelikan confesses to being "distressed [over] how many manuscripts are written more with the reviewer than with the reader in mind." As any good scholarly publisher knows, and as all scholarly authors must remember, a work that speaks to a broader audience in understandable language always will be selected over one that treats the same subject with the same level of scholarship, but limits its readership by the use of unnecessarily complex means of presentation.

Third, he links this need for "imagination" and clarity to the responsibility of the scholar to *teach* and argues thereby that the need to publish does not conflict with the need to teach. "The difference between bad scholarship and good scholarship is the result of what we do in graduate school, but the difference between good scholarship and great scholarship is the result of what we do in college." For this reason, he suggests, it is the responsibility of the accomplished, senior scholar to teach the freshman survey course and to bring to the undergraduate the fruits of his extensive research and publication.

Finally, Pelikan places the injunction to "publish or perish" in the context of the university's overall mission and properly, I believe, divorces it from the pejorative connotations of "tenure-track" attainment and advancement. "Publish or perish!" he writes, "is a fundamental, psychological, indeed physiological, imperative that is rooted in the very metabolism of scholarship as a vocation." It is what keeps researchers honest by exposing their processes and findings to the criticism of other scholars. To Pelikan, a community of scholars in critical dialogue with one another is the sine qua non of any university. And to that extent, it can be argued that publishing is not only integral to the scholarly activities of the university, but constitutes an essential part of its organic wholeness.

Types of Publishers and Kinds of Books

Thus far, I have addressed scholarly publishing, but the partnership of scholar and publisher need not be limited to university press publication nor to other nonprofit enterprises. I began my publishing career with a commercial publisher whose house motto was "Books that Matter." We published scores of scholarly works each year and did so quite profitably—so profitably, in fact, that another publisher bought us out. There exist many specialized publishing houses that operate commercially and that offer special advantages to the scholar in terms of prompt, effective, and respected publication.

In addition, the scholar should not ignore the much larger number of commercial publishers who will seek his work if it has the potential of reaching a large market. For example, a scholar who seeks to reach a straight textbook market with major course adoptions in prospect will want to consult *Literary Market Place*, published by R. R. Bowker. This work categorizes publishers by "function" and subject matter interests. Or, should a scholar have written, or contemplate writing, a major work on an important public issue or about a significant scientific subject of interest to a large readership or should he be a fiction writer, then seeking out an appropriate commercial publisher may serve his interests better than would a scholarly press.

Before turning to the nuts and bolts of publishing with these various types of enterprises, it is important to sort out the kinds of books that a scholar may choose to write. A summary of these types and an evaluation of their relative importance to a scholar's career follows:

Scholarly monographs. These are the "stock in trade" of university presses and represent the majority of studies undertaken by scholars. They contribute to the mainstream of scholarship and as such command the serious attention of other scholars and tenure committees. They normally have very low print-runs of one thousand or fewer copies and are relatively high-priced, cloth editions. Illustrative subjects: Euripidean criticism, new musical interpretations, normal aging, a biographical study on statecraft.

Scholarly studies with textbook or general readership potential. The nature of the subject matter, or its topicality or design for student use, makes these books appeal to a larger readership, although the research base and analytical approach found in scholarly monographs also pertain here.

These studies range from fifteen hundred copies printed to a few thousand, often in simultaneous paperback and cloth editions. The "recognition" factor is greater for this type of book, but given their nature and intended use, the scholarly kudos are not apt to be so great. Books in this category might cover: NATO, the First Amendment, world politics and international law, economic thought, Afghanistan and the Soviet Union, or psychology and the arts.

Series. In an incisive but humorous article in *The American Scholar*, Robert Darnton, former member of the editorial board of Princeton University Press, in addressing the question, "how to get published?" says: "Don't submit a book. Submit a series . . . as far as I know we have never turned down a series, and we took on a half dozen during my four years on the board. Propose a series and slip in as its first volume your monograph on Jane Austen or urban politics in the Midwest." Examples: a series on the ecology of the U.S. coastline, or one analyzing literary trends and ideas, or an annual survey of the USSR and Eastern Europe. To serve as the editor of a series establishes one as a leading expert in the field covered. However, the responsibility tends to dissipate a scholar's creative energies on the arduous and time-consuming task of editing the material of others into publishable form.

Bibliographic. This is a field by itself and vital to scholars. Examples might include a bibliographic literature guide or an annotated review of autobiographical studies.

Trade. Scholars are perfectly capable of writing books that appeal to the general readership and sell, therefore, in bookstores as "trade" books. Such titles can merit print-runs of several thousand (in cloth only or with a follow-on or simultaneous paperback). However, unless you are a fiction writer in the English department or have the ability to popularize your subject area as in a book such as *The Lives of a Cell: Notes of a Biology Watcher* by Lewis Thomas (Viking Press, 1974), this is a very risky use of a young scholar's time.

Submitting a Manuscript

Turning to the business of submitting a manuscript and getting it published, Robert Darnton's article, "A Survival Strategy for Academic Authors," cited above, is instructive:

> First, dear author, you should know that the odds are stacked against you. I figure them at nine to one, or ten to one, calculating the number of manuscripts submitted against the number accepted (at Princeton Press, which may be on the high side, in 1981, 1129 submissions and 120 books published) . . . [your manuscript] must clear a series of

hurdles. It must catch the eye of an editor, win the favor of two or sometimes three readers, make a preliminary cut at a pre-editorial board meeting, and survive the final selection at a monthly meeting of the editorial board, when four professors will choose a dozen manuscripts from a field of fifteen to nineteen.

An important aside is in order here regarding the publication of your dissertation. A very good article on this subject appeared in the 5 February 1986 issue of the *Chronicle of Higher Education* (*CHE*). My own advice, based on the review of hundreds of recently minted scholars' *magna opera*, is to wait, contemplate, and reexamine your work. Stand back from it and consider how further research in more specific (or broader) areas of the subject matter could enhance its value to the scholarly world.

If you do decide on publication, keep these points in mind:

1. Revise your manuscript for the wider readership a "book" for scholars in your field may expect to reach by taking out extensive documentation and your "review of the literature," whose eruditeness may have impressed your dissertation committee but will be considered a "bore" by your other readers. Keep in mind the key question: "Does it tell the informed scholar something he doesn't know?"

2. Evaluate which scholarly presses specialize in your area and go straight to those, avoiding broadside submissions.

3. You may wish to seek out former university press editors who specialize in assisting untenured faculty members with the publication of their work (see *CHE* article cited above).

4. Consider rewriting or parceling out your dissertation in article form for various journals.

5. Keep these styling points in mind:

–write for a specific reader, including information that person needs to know, omitting the rest.

–avoid chronological organization; rather, seek out the key points and build around those.

–keep the book as short as possible, avoiding reiteration of materials already familiar to your readers.

–avoid buzz words or in-words in your field; use plain English.

–prepare your manuscript carefully, including your notes, and double-space *everything* using wide margins.

–prepare your presentation to a publisher as outlined elsewhere in this chapter; go, personally, to see the editor at the press if you can do so, as a "face" tied to the manuscript tends to tilt consideration in your favor.

Now, returning to the original point, submitting your manuscript, how should you decide which publisher to approach? *First*, get the facts straight regarding your book and be clear as to the type of book you are offering (see some of the possible categories above) and which publishers handle the kind of book you have written. Check publishers' catalogs in your library, take a look at their books in your subject area, speak with other scholars, check out publishers' exhibits at scholarly meetings, and consult *Literary Market Place*, which, in addition to categorizing publishers, lists names of editors, addresses, and phone numbers. *Second*, choose the best press for your needs, judging list orientation, marketing capabilities, financial terms, and reputation in your field. Consider your own university press, if you have one, and be rigorous in applying to it the same criteria you do to other presses. In weighing the pros and cons of publishing at home or away, keep in mind these additional considerations: (a) the convenience of firsthand consultation with your own press on editorial, production, marketing, and other matters; (b) the value of supporting your own university's academic publishing effort; and (c) that you may expect from the press of your own university a full peer review and not simply a peremptory or superficial consideration of your manuscript. Incidentally, the same oftentimes applies to the press of the institution from which you have recently graduated. Your choice of your own or another university press must also be considered in light of its possible impact on tenure review. I have known of situations where tenure was denied ostensibly because of some doubt as to the rigor one's own university brings to its examination of the work of one of its own scholars. On the other hand, I have also observed situations where the publication of a scholar's first book by his own university press was considered so advantageous that a second book was sought for home publication and as evidence of qualification for tenure, even though the author had changed his academic affiliation to another institution in the interim. *Finally*, your choice may be significantly affected by whether this is your first book, second, or third, and by whether it is the first press with which you have published, the second, or third.

Once you have selected a prospective publisher, follow these general guidelines. [Note: It is usually wise and considered fairer play to approach one publisher at a time unless you consider yourself author of a competitive work and you let those being approached know of your multiple submission]:

(1) Write to a person, not to a title. *Literary Market Place, Writer's Market*, and other directories (noted in the Selected Further Readings) list the

editors of all major university and commercial publishers. Keep in mind that in many presses the director is also an editor. Gather what information you can from your colleagues who have published with a particular press as to the subject area specializations of various editors and/or of the director. It is not wise to telephone, as publishers are readers and prefer to have something in front of them when considering a proposal.

(2) Do not send a manuscript unsolicited. Instead, send a short, explanatory letter with your book's title clearly indicated. Enclose a preface explaining the origin of your work, a table of contents or outline, your manuscript completion date (if the manuscript is not complete), its length, and your biographical sketch or curriculum vitae. Never submit a book without a preface; it or an introduction should summarize the argument so that the reader knows where you are going. Editors (and librarians and others) read prefaces. If the publisher responds by requesting completion of the now fairly standardized Author's Questionnaire, reply promptly and take special care in describing your book's contents (but be brief), its unique contribution to the literature, and its potential readership.

(3) If the manuscript, or sample material, is requested, be sure you send a clear, neat, readable (this means also typed on only one side), double-spaced copy that is paginated and includes a table of contents, also paginated. It is amazing how many authors paginate by chapter only, or fail to indicate chapter pages in the contents. This is very aggravating to the editor or reviewer, who must know the manuscript's length and be able to locate particular chapters easily. Volunteer to prepare an index; this is especially important for university presses, which are generally short on funds and indexing resources. Remember that most books require an index and your failure to provide one works against fair consideration of your work.

(4) It is perfectly proper to suggest some potential reviewers from whom the publisher can select, anonymously. If you can, include addresses and phone numbers. Do not send the publisher reviews from your friends or from colleagues from whom you have solicited comments, as they count for little in the publishing decision.

(5) It is unlikely that a press will make a publishing decision, that is, offer a contract in advance of the final manuscript submission to a new, untried author or even to a previously published author, if only a prospectus or partial manuscript is offered, except under special conditions, such as: you are editing a work based on a major grant or research project in which many experts are involved and/or are contributors and an advance contract is the sine qua non for creation of a manuscript; the publisher believes the only way

to acquire the book against competing publishers is to offer a contract in advance; the evidence of quality and potential publishability is so strong that the risk of nondelivery of an acceptable, final manuscript is reduced to near zero. Of course, even in such a case, your manuscript will still be subjected to final review when completed. Keep in mind that any reputable scholarly publisher must review your final manuscript before acceptance, even if you have been offered a contract up front, so you must go through the peer review process sooner or later anyway, with all of its by-products and consequences: rewriting, cutting or adding material, and reorganizing. Also, remember that rarely will a reviewer make a firm recommendation to a publisher on the basis of a partial manuscript; hence, this precludes an editor from recommending a partial manuscript to the press's editorial board for final approval.

(6) Your reaction to the reviewers' reports is most important. Keep in mind that this is an important part of the publisher's service to you as an author, as well as a means of judging the publishability of your work. Take very seriously all suggestions and criticisms, replying to each with clear indications of the action you propose to take or giving sound reasons for rejecting reviewers' criticisms. Defend against specious criticisms, as you view them, with concrete arguments based on well-informed positions— reviewers can be wrong, too. When resubmitting your revised manuscript (if that is called for), send along a letter explaining what you have revised and why, in direct response to the reviewers' specific points of criticism. This assists the re-review process and is most important to the editorial board, which will make the final decision.

The Press Decision

So, the decision on your proposal finally comes through. How do you handle the various options you may face then? First, the difficult one, *rejection*! If this comes prior to review, depending on the nature and tone of the rejection letter, you may wish to challenge it. However, if the letter says "not suited to our list," "we're overbooked in this area," "the work is too specialized," or some such comment, accept the decision and go to your next choice. If the publisher is a good one, you probably will receive advice on other avenues of publication, especially if your work has been favorably reviewed by at least one reviewer. A subsequent publisher may request reviews from your first publisher, but that publisher must first obtain permission from the reviewers, and can never reveal reviewers' names without permission. Usually, it is preferable to start over with a second publisher with a clean slate, but depending on the reasons given for the initial rejection, you may choose to reveal it.

Second, the long-awaited response *approving* your proposal and offering a contract. At this point, you may expect to receive an actual contract from your publisher which, when signed by you, transfers to the publisher your rights to your work. That is, the copyright that is vested in you by law because of your act of creating the work is, by contract, transferred to your publisher. So read your contract carefully. Most of the stipulations in it are standard, but check for these points: (a) the title (usually tentative) of your book and the order of authorship or editorship; (b) your manuscript due date; (c) the number of complimentary copies given upon publication (the norm is ten to the author) and the discount you are allowed on the purchase of additional copies (usually 40–50 percent); (d) your responsibility for preparation of an index; (e) your responsibility for paying for author's alterations (usually you are allowed 5 percent changes before you need pay the publisher); (f) whether you are required to submit any illustrative material (e.g., charts, graphs, figures) in camera-ready form or have to pay the publisher to do this for you; (g) royalties; *note*: oftentimes in the case of a scholarly work, particularly if very specialized, no royalties will be offered on the first printing or until production costs are earned back by the publisher (this is usually after the sale of five hundred copies or so). A book with a larger prospective sale might carry say, 10 percent royalties on net receipts (what the publisher receives from sales after discounts he offers purchasers) and 5 percent on any paperback editions. Foreign sales carry lower royalties (usually one-half of domestic) because of higher sales costs. On a "large" sale book, graduated royalties rising as high as 15 percent, as sales rise, may be expected.

It is important to remember that all publishers' contracts are contingent upon *acceptance* of your final manuscript by the publisher. This means that you must accomplish all revisions called for by your reviewer and publisher to the latter's satisfaction and that your final manuscript is complete in every respect (except for the index, normally prepared and submitted at the point you receive the composed pages of your book from the publisher), again as judged by your publisher. Not until acceptance is the publisher bound by your contract to publish your manuscript, so be sure you receive this final word from the publisher as it triggers the actual book production process.

So that acceptance of your manuscript for publication is ensured, be certain that *all* material is double-spaced (especially footnotes, references, and the like); that an "about the author(s) or editor(s)" statement and one "about contributors" if it is an edited work is included; that you obtain a transfer of copyright release from each contributor if yours is an edited book (publisher can supply the appropriate forms), and forward these with your manuscript, as otherwise your book cannot properly be published; that all permissions for quotations are cleared for use; that the title page, dedication page, table of contents, list of illustrations, appendixes, and notes are all in the proper sequence with page numbers in the upper right-hand corner, consecutively numbered from beginning to end, and that all these elements of the book are included in the table of contents. If you have to insert pages, designate them 84a, 84b, etc. Footnotes should be numbered consecutively within each chapter. Consult your editor on proper handling and/or inclusion of illustrative materials; all graphics should be numbered consecutively and their suggested placement, by number, indicated in the text. Be sure to provide sources for all illustrations and graphics, including tables. Consult a manual of style on any questions you may have and the style sheet for preparation of manuscripts, available from your publisher. Be prepared to have the publisher request two copies of your manuscript. It is important to comply with this request because a "checking" copy is useful at the copyediting stage or should one copy be lost or destroyed.

Upon acceptance of your final manuscript for publication, you should be so notified as stated above by your editor, and subsequently (usually by the production department) a production schedule will be sent, giving you information on when to expect a copyedited manuscript, page proofs, and the finished, bound book. It is most important that you hold up your end of the schedule so that your book will be published on time and as projected.

During the production process, expect to receive from the marketing department a "Marketing Questionnaire." The information you provide is very important to the success of your book, especially with regard to "marketing opportunities" known only to you, for example, key organizations and meetings, special mailing lists, special review journals, etc.

After your book is published, your publisher should maintain contact by mailing advertisements in which your book appears, catalogs and brochures, copies of reviews, and special promotion plans. If he does not, remind him. You should receive annual or semiannual royalty and sales reports. Send your publisher reviews, items of interest mentioning your book, and always alert your publisher to any special marketing opportunities of which he may not be aware.

If your book sells well or if there is a recognizable need and continuing demand for your work, your publisher may propose updating and issuing a revised edition. Or, volunteer this, if warranted, as oftentimes the publisher will not approach you. Should a paperback edition be indicated, let your publisher know why you believe this to be so. Should any other publishers wish to purchase rights, such as translation rights or prepublication rights to a chapter for a journal, advise your publisher. If your book goes out of print (OP), consult your contract as to your rights. These normally include due notice of this fact by the publisher, with reversion of rights to you at a given point. But oftentimes you will have to request such a reversion of rights, which is your due, if the publisher refuses to keep your book in print. You are also entitled to purchase, at cost, remaining copies of your book and the book plates when it goes OP. At that point, it is wise to inquire as to its continuing availability through microfilm or microfiche services such as University Microfilms International.

The Author-Publisher Relationship

In your dealings with your publisher, keep in mind that you have entered a form of partnership in which each party is very important to the other. This is not the place to discuss in detail the business side of publishing but keep in mind that you are working with a professional who is, in his/her line of business, just as expert as you are in your chosen field of scholarship. So while it is your responsibility to place in your publisher's hands all relevant information regarding the potential readership (the market) for your book, it is the publisher's responsibility to translate this into a suitable book price, an economically sound print-run, a decision as to cloth and/or paperback editions, a marketing budget, the book design, and the like. You place your life's work in his hands, he places at risk his financial resources, his professional time (and that of your peer reviewers), as well as his publishing reputation, when placing the name of his press on your work.

So, the old adage pertains: "A rising tide lifts all boats." In short, publishing is a teamwork process. Consider your publisher your partner, not your protagonist.

Also keep in mind that you (and all authors) are your publisher's most important asset; how your publisher handles your work is obviously of crucial importance to you personally and to your career. Through the medium of scholarship and your publisher's appreciation of its significance, you may even become close friends. Many times I have met authors years after our initial association by mail and have felt an instant rapport despite the absence of any previous personal contact.

A final word is in order concerning the responsibility of the scholar for peer review of other scholars' work on behalf of a publisher. Publishers, as well as potential authors, must rely on the expertise and the goodwill of scholarly colleagues for the execution of this useful, sometimes satisfying, but often difficult task. As suggested in the introductory portions of this paper, the peer review process lies at the heart of the "sacred vocation" of the scholar. Hence, it is as important for you as a scholar to be responsive to a reasonable request from a publisher for review of a work relevant to your field or discipline, as it is for you to have your own work reviewed for prospective publication. When you are next approached with the request for a review and accept, keep in mind how important it would be to your own work to have that review completed promptly by the deadline indicated by the publisher. Consider also how valuable a careful, intelligent, and constructively critical review will be to the author. You will not find yourself enriched financially by your reviewing tasks, but you deserve and should expect a reasonable reader's fee. Most presses today offer an option: either a nominal cash fee or a selection of twice that amount from books on the publisher's list. Most important of all, your effort in reviewing the work of your peers will have made a vital contribution to scholarship and to the all-important process of its dissemination.

SIX

Academic Administrations

It will no doubt seem odd that we have devoted a chapter of this volume to describing governance at the modern university. After all, most of our readers have already spent at least ten years in such an institution and ought, therefore, to know what it is. And yet it is clear that most new academics have experienced only a small fraction of the university as such, and that even here, within a single program or department, they do not really understand how decisions are made or how business actually gets done. Perhaps, in short, the new academic has never thought of the university as a corporation, with all the problems of diversity, governance, and structural hierarchies that affect any business.

In the papers to follow, therefore, we have tried to offer two different views of the system of higher education in America today. The first may be called the macrocosmic view: what are the range of types of schools, kinds of administrative structures, and general problems of university governance. The second is a more microcosmic view: what is a department and how is it run, what responsibilities do boards of trustees have, what does the provost do. For the new academic, negotiating his or her way between the urgent daily demands of teaching and the equally urgent demands of research and publication, the structural politics of the university or college may not seem as pressing. But this is the community the new academic has chosen to call home, and it is essential, therefore, that he or she discover as quickly as possible the basic laws by which it operates. In any community, the well-being of the whole depends upon the wise and committed service of each individual and the university is no exception to that rule.

A. Kenneth Pye has recently been appointed as President of Southern Methodist University after a distinguished career at Duke University. At Duke, he served as University Counsel, twice as Dean of the Law School, twice as Chancellor of the University, and as Samuel Fox Mordecai Professor of Law. President Pye has written widely on criminal procedure, as well as on issues of administrative structures in higher education in America.

Joel Colton is Professor and former Chairman of the History Department at Duke University, as well as past Chairman of the University's Academic Council. A specialist in European history, Professor Colton's many books have been widely acclaimed and frequently reissued. In addition to having received several of Academe's most distinguished fellowships, including election to the American Academy of Arts and Sciences, Professor Colton served as Director for Humanities at the Rockefeller Foundation.

21 University Governance and Autonomy—Who Decides What in the University

A. Kenneth Pye

A recurring issue in academic life is that of governance—who, trustees, administrators, faculty, students, or others, should decide or participate in the decision on matters that arise in the conduct of university affairs. An equally important issue is that of autonomy—which matters directly affecting university life should be decided on campus and which should be decided elsewhere, by state boards, legislatures, courts, or other public or private persons or bodies.[1]

A young professor may understandably inquire why he or she should be concerned or involved with matters of governance or autonomy. Two reasons should be obvious. Participation in significant matters affecting a community are components of good citizenship and faculty are citizens of an academic community. Effective participation requires knowledge of issues and processes by which they are resolved. A second reason is more self-serving. University communities are not composed solely of scholars. Faculty participation in governance is necessary to assure that academic priorities receive appropriate status in university planning and that scarce resources are used most effectively. The purpose of this paper is to provide a general description of the processes and problems involved in governance and the impact upon the role of faculty in governance posed by recent threats to university autonomy.

Governance

Patterns of university governance vary widely in higher education between liberal arts colleges and universities, research universities and universities whose primary mission is teaching, larger and smaller institutions, private and public institutions. There are significant differences among institutions that are similar in purpose, size, and primary source of support. Such diversity makes it difficult to generalize. This paper attempts to describe processes that are common in private and public research universities of the first rank. Many of the observations also apply to other institutions of higher learning.

Many young professors approach the mysteries of university governance with an institutional model that Robert Paul Wolff once described as "a sanctuary of scholarship"[2]: a self-governing community in which experienced and apprentice scholars engage in a mutual search for truth with relatively little concern about factors other than admission of newcomers and quality of the scholarship being undertaken. Faculty make all important decisions because the mission of the intellectual community is research and teaching, and these functions are performed by faculty. The faculty is not *a* constituency; it is *the* constituency.

This perception offers a generally accurate description of European universities prior to World War II, with the caveat that authority rested almost exclusively in the senior professoriate, but it does not describe European universities today nor American universities at any time in their history. The increased size and complexity of universities, impact of the "egalitarian ethic," democratization of all societal institutions, increased dependence upon funding from governments for medical and scientific research and financial support to students, and more intense regulation of all institutions in society for health, safety, equality, security, and other social objectives have combined to make the process of governance much more complex.

University governance today is a process in which trustees, administrators, faculty, students, and sometimes others, share responsibility for making important decisions required for an institution to perform its missions of teaching, research, and public service. The crucial issues are who participates at what times in what decisions in what ways.[3]

Board of Trustees

The hallmark of the American governance process in private, and in many public institutions, has been the independent campus governed by laymen, usually called trustees or regents, who are neither state officials nor professional educators. Most early American colleges were private institutions, but even the early publicly controlled colleges had their own lay boards of trustees. The great thrust forward in public higher education occurred in the mid-nineteenth century when Congress, through the Morrill Act, stimulated development of land-grant universities aimed primarily at providing instruction in the mechanical and agricultural arts. These institutions were also conceived of primarily as autonomous units, more closely akin to publicly supported, chartered, independent private colleges than to a coherent integrated state system of higher education.[4] Despite a recent trend toward consolidation in state systems, the single campus lay board of trustees continues to be the most prevalent form of governance and almost the only form in the private sector.

Boards of trustees differ in size. Some have fewer than ten members; some more than fifty. Frequency of meetings also differs, although most, if not all, meet at least quarterly. Larger boards that commonly meet less frequently have executive committees that transact business during intervals between board meetings.

The source of board authority also differs. Some boards receive powers from state constitutions; others were created as corporate bodies and given certain powers by virtue of their incorporation. Some were created through special enactments of state legislatures. Most public universities derive their authority from state statutes or the state constitution. The legal source of authority in private colleges is sometimes ambiguous: some claim authority by charter; others through incorporation; many have had no reason to face the question.[5]

Boards are also selected in different ways: external election, external appointment, self-selection, or ex officio selection. Some public officials may be ex officio members of boards by statute. Most members of boards of trustees of public universities are appointed by state officials, usually by governors. Trustees are elected by the public in a few states. The most common method of choosing new trustees in private institutions is self-selection; members of an existing board elect their successors. Boards in some private institutions are selected by religious organizations or other groups that originally created the university, but a board may be de facto self-perpetuating because of willingness of a group to accept nominations proffered by an existing board. Alumni of an institution may elect some members.[6]

Composition of boards frequently reflects the history and purposes of an institution and current societal concepts of the need for representation of different segments of society. Approximately one-third of board members are from the business community.[7] Women and minorities are still underrepresented in many universities.

A board of trustees is entrusted with responsibility for administering the institution in accordance with its stated purposes, which are frequently expressed in broad language. It has an obligation to plan the development of the institution, select and determine the tenure of its chief executive, hold assets of the institution in trust, act as a court of last resort, and play an important role in public relations.[8] It may be called upon to interpret the institution to society or serve as a barrier to protect the academic community from that society.[9] In theory, trustees have power to make almost all decisions affecting the institution: appointment, promotion, and conferral of tenure of faculty; commencement, modification, and termination of academic programs; establishment of standards for admission of students and requirements for degrees; approval of curricula; authorization of construction or renovation of buildings; approval of annual budgets; decisions concerning whether to borrow money and how to invest endowment; and long-range planning.

The extent to which a board delegates its responsibilities, and to whom, varies, depending in large part on historical factors, its confidence in its officers or faculty, and sometimes the political reality that delegating power to decide certain matters is advisable in order to assure tranquility on the campus. Boards in many universities delegate power broadly to the president and accept his decisions concerning what powers should be entrusted to faculty, students, or other groups.

Central Administration

The "central administration" of a university is the chief executive (usually denominated "president") and his principal subordinate officers (usually denominated "vice presidents"), and their staffs.

Responsibilities of a central administration in one university may differ significantly from those in another. Some universities resemble a confederacy of schools. Power is highly centralized in others. In general, however, central administration is responsible for executing, implementing, and monitoring the policies of the board, proposing new ones, supervising investments, raising external support (other than grants to individual professors), relating to the community, providing support services, maintaining the physical plant, and developing an academic strategy for the institution as a whole.

President

The president is responsible for academic quality, athletic success, fund-raising, public relations, financial management, and institutional integrity.[10] What he actually does personally depends upon the nature of the institution and the personality of the incumbent. Some spend much of their time culti-vating legislators, foundations, and private donors. All must represent the university in educational associations, before public bodies, and with alumni and other external constituencies. Some are personally involved in recruit-ment and promotion of senior faculty; others delegate such duties to their provosts. Some are intimately involved in business and investment issues; others leave such issues primarily to their boards and vice presidents for business affairs. Most have particular academic areas that they wish to emphasize and do so through control of the university budget.

A president's concept of the kind of leadership he should provide is of crucial importance to the nature of the participation he will expect from faculty. Presidential styles reflect different conditions, traditions, and per-sonalities. Some presidents permit programs to develop and then administer them as ably as possible, regardless of the directions of such programs. Some take a more active role, serving first as a catalyst for development of a consensus concerning appropriate directions and then leading the university toward achievement of the goals so determined. Others are not content with administering consensus policies. They consult with appropriate constituen-cies, determine personally the wisest directions, and lead the university toward their accomplishment. A few presidents act decisively with little prior faculty involvement.

Faculty have considerable power when a president sees his primary role as one of serving as a catalyst for developing a consensus. By definition, a consensus cannot be reached in the face of significant disagreement. In reality, such an approach may give the faculty a veto over fundamental initiatives for change.

Faculty obviously have a less dynamic role where the president is pre-pared to sponsor initiatives after consultation, even if no consensus emerges. The quality of the consultative process may be the key to the reality of faculty participation.

Few universities are committed to any single approach. Frequently, the issue under consideration will determine the relationship between a presi-dent and faculty if processes have not been formalized to the degree that flexibility is no longer possible.

The real issue in many major institutions is the ethos of the presidential-faculty relationship and perceptions of the degree to which dynamic leadership is needed. Some universities, faced with inadequate resources, a significant legacy of deferred maintenance, inadequate salaries, noncompetitive financial aid, a need to reallocate funds and reorganize academic units to be on the "cutting edge" of newly emerging fields of knowledge, aging and overtenured faculty, and resistance to change, may conclude that a consensus on most significant issues is impossible, except on basic values that cannot be translated into effective initiatives. Faculty and presidents in some universities with such problems may be prepared to sacrifice faculty participation to permit presidents to deal with such issues decisively. Faculty and presidents in other institutions may conclude that no long-range progress is possible without faculty consensus in university initiatives, even if the price of faculty acquiescence may be action less responsive to perceived needs than some would desire.

Figure 21.1

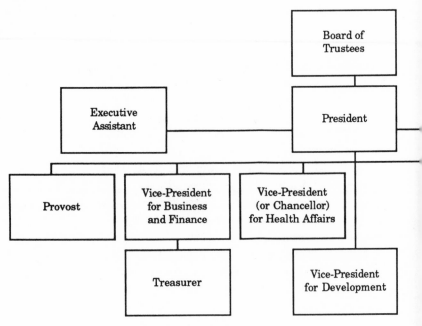

Other University Officers

Universities usually have at least two senior officers directly under the president, a provost or vice president for academic affairs and a vice president for business and financial affairs. A university with an academic medical center normally has a vice president or chancellor for health affairs as well. Several other officers may exist, depending upon the complexity of the institution. A vice president for external relations or development is common, as are a vice president for student affairs, vice president for computer services, university counsel, secretary, and a treasurer. The duties are suggested by their titles. (See figure 21.1.)

The exact authority of different vice presidents may be perplexing to them as well as to the faculty. For instance, the extent to which the vice president for business and finance has responsibility for business operations of hospitals or grant administration within a medical center, the extent to which a provost has responsibility for academic promotions within a school of medi-

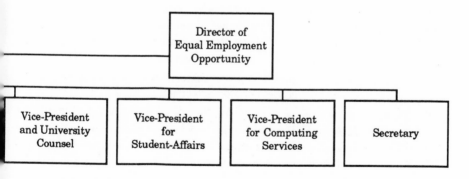

cine, or the division of responsibility between a provost and a vice president for business and finance on budgetary matters may not always be clear.

Such issues obviously may have considerable importance for a junior faculty member who has a problem and doesn't understand to which officer he should turn for advice or decision. Sometimes, the answer can be determined by reference to a faculty manual, available in most institutions. A chairman can often provide the answer, and, if not, usually the dean will be available to provide guidance.

Schools

Deans, appointed by the president, provost, or a board of trustees, have general responsibility for operation of schools within a university. In some settings, deans function as chairmen, a "first among equals" with faculty colleagues. In others they function more as an executive officer directly subordinate to the provost. Institutional history may determine which areas are appropriate for a decanal decision and which are appropriate for decision by a school faculty. For instance, allocation of financial aid may be a decanal prerogative in one school and may be determined by a faculty in another.

Usually a school develops its own academic programs within the framework of the university's overall academic plan. It determines its program of instruction and research, approves courses proposed by departments, establishes rules governing academic requirements, determines its priorities, and allocates revenue made available by central administration to carry out its programs. But universities differ concerning which matters a school decides for itself and which will be determined by a provost. An individual provost's conception of his job may be the decisive determinant. Some provosts see their job as one of strategic management of the overall academic programs of a university, delegating individual decisions to schools. Others feel the need to decide any issue that they consider important and do not hesitate to intervene in school decisions within the province of deans and schools elsewhere. Common techniques are enforcement of tight budgetary controls and active participation in faculty selection, promotion, and tenure.

Medical schools exercise much greater independence than other schools. Several factors contribute to their special status: size of sponsored research programs, broader base of federal support, mixture of research, patient care, and instruction, historic primacy of clinical departments, complexity of operating a university hospital, differences in sources of faculty salaries, and lengthy tenure of departmental chairmen. Other professional schools occupy a lesser degree of independence but tend to be more independent than arts and sciences. Most operate their own admissions, placement, and alumni affairs offices and maintain separate libraries. A higher degree of independence is most likely where a professional school generates income sufficient to cover most or all of its expenditures ("each tub on its own bottom") and has a reputation superior to that of most other schools within the university.

Departments

Departments presided over by chairmen are common in large schools. The department has been the key academic unit over most of the past century.[11] Departments determine their curricula subject to school approval; they also make the initial recommendations for promotion and tenure; they admit and award financial aid to graduate students within rules and resources made available by a school; and they determine the requirements for their majors, subject to school approval.

The role of departmental chairmen (or sometimes called head) also differs widely. The chairman of a department within the arts and sciences commonly serves for a term of three to five years and may be reappointed. Frequently, his tenure and limited powers require reliance upon persuasion to lead.[12] Chairmen of departments in a school of medicine sometimes serve indefinitely, basically at the pleasure of the vice president for health affairs or dean. Decisions made by such chairmen tend to encompass areas that would be reserved to faculty in an arts and sciences department.

Faculty Participation

Faculty participate in governance in different ways. They participate directly in departments. Junior faculty serve on committees and normally vote on all matters entrusted to a department other than promotion and tenure. Faculty also participate personally in the governance of some schools. Other schools function through a representative body, frequently denominated a senate or council, that normally conducts much of its business through committees. Faculty from different schools may meet annually or semiannually in general faculty meetings, but university governance is usually entrusted to a faculty senate or council representing all faculties of the university and sometimes different ranks. Much of its business is also conducted through committees, and it may select faculty to represent it on a host of other committees that report to the board of trustees, the president, the provost, or others.

Powers of faculty bodies are normally the product of a long history of negotiation between faculty and administrators and boards. In general, most major universities entrust a significant role, if not virtually complete authority, to faculty to make decisions in three of the "key areas" of academic autonomy:[13] (1) admission and examination of students; (2) curriculum and courses studied; (3) appointment, promotion, and tenuring of faculty. Central administration or a board may reserve a right to intervene in exceptional cases when it appears that a faculty is not proceeding along lines that best serve the purposes of the institution. Intervention occurs most often when (l) a faculty decision has been made without adequate consideration of long-range financial implications or (2) where there is a fundamental disagreement concerning appropriate priorities.

Generally, however, administrators and boards acquiesce in faculty judgments of an academic nature. Differences concerning an appropriate faculty role occur more frequently when a faculty claims a right to influence decisions on other subjects.

Many faculty believe that faculty should be involved in *all* important decisions. Administrators and boards are sometimes reluctant to accept the need for faculty consultation on some matters that are not academic in nature. The following arguments are among those advanced for acting without submitting all matters to the faculty:

(1) The faculty may have no special competence in many areas such as labor relations, investment policy, hiring and firing of coaches and senior administrators, tax policy, or whether the university should build a hotel or a student union.

(2) Some faculty are preoccupied with the impact of decisions upon their own immediate work and welfare and are relatively uninformed or unconcerned with the "big picture." Many issues in which faculty have an interest also affect students, alumni, nonacademic workers, and the public. Consulting with faculty alone may produce a distorted view of the best interests of the university. What is good for the faculty is not necessarily good for the university.

(3) Involvement of faculty may cause delay that precludes administrators from meeting time schedules imposed by a board; issues raised by faculty may divert administrative resources from matters that administrators or boards think more important.

(4) Relatively few of the most distinguished faculty participate in university senates or faculty committees outside their departments in many institutions. As a consequence, despite notable exceptions, faculty political lead-

ership tends to fall more to people who devote more of their time to academic politics than to scholarship. The faculty participation process is also sometimes gerrymandered in such a way that faculty participation involves disproportionately high representation of the arts and sciences.

(5) The faculty concept of "participation" often includes the notion that administrators should not take action without approval of representatives of the faculty. "Participation" is transformed into a veto power. Chief executives, who serve at the pleasure of boards that hold them personally responsible, may not be prepared to defer to faculty, most of whom will not occupy chairs or preside over a department or school and some of whom will not receive tenure or promotion.

(6) Issues may arise at any time. Many faculty are not available during almost one third of the year. Delay may result in loss of opportunity. Attempts to consult with individual faculty members who are available may result in recriminations that administrators by-passed appropriate channels of faculty participation.

Faculty, on their part, sometimes are understandably distrustful of administrative motives when issues of importance are not submitted for their advice. They offer the following arguments, among others, for greater participation:

(1) Faculty are better qualified to reflect important educational values that may be shortchanged by administrators in the interest of expediency. Administrators may be too prone to react to more vocal or politically powerful constituencies that are less interested in research and teaching. They may tend to view the campus as a "multiversity," an indifferent amalgam of ideologies, constituencies, and pressures that require compromises "as an imperative rather than a reasoned choice among elegant alternatives,"[14] compromises that sacrifice principle and are inconsistent with faculty values. Administrators may be more concerned with balancing the budget than with how revenue is used.

(2) Faculty are usually committed to the educational enterprise for life and have the most to lose from unwise decisions. Some administrators move freely among academia, business, and government and may have less commitment to the university and academic ideals.

(3) A university faculty has broader areas of expertise than administrators admit, capabilities that could be directly of use in resolving issues a university must face.

(4) Faculty councils or senates are rarely driven by parochial concerns. Historically, they have shown at least as great a concern for broad social issues and the public interest as administrators.

(5) Faculty must be regarded either as colleagues in policymaking or as employees. If faculty are treated as employees, trade unions and confrontation rather than cooperation will likely result.

(6) Any categorical separation of academic and nonacademic matters is necessarily artificial. Every important nonacademic matter has some impact on academic affairs.

These differences can easily be overestimated. Faculty and administrators share an essential community of interest in furthering the welfare of the institution they serve, although they may differ concerning which measures will best serve the common purpose. Furthermore, many, if not most, university administrators are tenured faculty who have devoted much of their academic lives to teaching and research and usually intend to return to those pursuits when they leave their administrative posts.

Faculty involvement tends to be less in institutions whose primary mission is teaching than in major research universities. Administrators, including departmental chairmen, serve for longer periods in many such institutions. Boards, religious denominations, and local communities may exert greater influence on routine decisions. The perimeters within which policy is made may be greatly narrowed by economic realities.

Autonomy

There has been a consistent trend toward increased faculty participation in governance in major universities in recent years. Simultaneously, other trends have tended to reduce the real influence of faculty on decisionmaking. Faculty gains in participation in governance have been offset in part by: (1) greater participation by others in the decisionmaking process on the campus and (2) a trend toward overall loss of campus autonomy.

Participation by Others

Faculty now share participation in governance on the campus with students and nonacademic staff. Student participation is a product of the late 1960s when students acquired the right to consult, usually in the form of service on joint committees, in most areas where faculty participate. Students sometimes sit on boards of trustees where there is no faculty representation.

The advent of collective bargaining on campus has provided a more significant role to nonacademic workers. Collective bargaining contracts often affect academic priorities. Funds made available to improve salaries and working conditions for staff are unavailable for faculty salaries, books, or financial assistance. A library may be required to close when the temperature-humidity ratio reaches a certain point; certain holidays may be required without regard to impact on academic operations.

Academic senates have been replaced by university senates in some universities. Such bodies may include faculty, administrators, nonacademic staff, students, and alumni, and frequently possess broader jurisdiction, but less power, than the faculty senates they supplanted. Creation of such an institution relegates the faculty to only one of many constituencies sharing in governance.

Loss of Autonomy

Little is gained by increased participation in decisionmaking if important issues are decided outside the university. "Autonomy" in the sense of full self-governance—the ability of a university to govern itself without any outside control—does not now exist nor has it existed for a very long time, if ever.[15] Indeed, few in higher education would want autonomy if it involved full financial autonomy, that is, freedom from external support in any form. The real issue is not total freedom, but a high degree of freedom from public or private control, particularly in certain areas. The major concern is that government, state and federal, and private bodies are imposing too many controls over the manner in which universities function. As Sir Zelman Cowen has noted, universities are "in danger of becoming utilities subject to general regulation in the public interest."[16]

Many once independent state university campuses are now part of state systems governed by a "superboard." Others have been made subject to "coordinating boards" charged with responsibility to plan, budget, and program but without authority to "manage" or "govern" individual institutions within the system. Powers of a faculty to admit students, determine curriculum, or appoint professors or of a president or board to allocate income among various categories of expenditures are much less important if a "superboard" or "coordinating board" has the authority to determine what programs will be offered on a campus; faculty size and student enrollment on a campus; funds that will be allocated to a campus; faculty salary scales, where buildings will be built, tuition rates, and similar matters.

Private universities likewise face significant external controls arising out of use of public funds. State boards sometimes attempt to exert control over them. Federal programs providing financial assistance to students and funding research in science, engineering, and medicine bring with them a host of regulations limiting university discretion.

General legislation also limits university autonomy. A national trend to regulate almost all forms of private activity to achieve important social goals is reflected in legislation not aimed specifically at universities, but which does not exclude them from its scope. Such legislation often causes significant unintended problems because of essential differences between universities and private profit-making organizations. Laws regulating minimum wages, health and safety, health insurance and retirement programs are examples. Laws and regulations in the field of civil rights have special consequences for universities in hiring, promotion, firing, and compensation of personnel.

There is nothing exceptional in these requirements. Problems, nonetheless, result from the manner in which statutes are interpreted by federal agencies, from the presence of trained bureaucracy within the university to assure compliance, and from costs in terms of formality and collegiality, as well as money, in proving compliance.

Faculty decisions on promotion or tenure and salary determinations are examples. Certainly universities should not discriminate, but a decision today must be reached in such a way that a faculty will be able to prove that it has not discriminated, as well as honestly deciding each case on its merits. A decision to pay one faculty member a different salary than another involves judgments of quality of mind, promise of productivity, uniqueness of contributions to knowledge, and salaries paid by competitors. They are rarely quantifiable, but a decision of an administrator must be defensible in a court of law.

A different type of influence on university decisionmaking is posed by legislation and administrative rules specifically aimed at universities. The federal government's experiments requiring medical schools to admit American students studying abroad as a condition to receipt of capitation grants, regulating in detail privacy and access to student records, and requiring universities to equalize per capita expenditures for men and women in intercollegiate athletics are examples.

Usually, extreme action is promptly modified. A year after the congressional intrusion into medical education, Congress restored at least the appearance of institutional autonomy. It amended the Privacy Act of 1974 within a year. Federal regulators ultimately retreated from their broad interpretation of what constitutes equality in intercollegiate athletics. All three examples, however, reflect areas that in an earlier era would have been a matter for unilateral university decision.

Similar direct intervention occurs at the state level, particularly when state legislatures or governors become upset about something happening on a public campus. "Speaker bans," efforts by legislatures to preclude speakers of certain political persuasions from speaking on a public campus, or dispatch of the National Guard to a campus to maintain order without request by a university president are examples.

Courts also limit university autonomy. Court decisions now recognize and enforce statutory and constitutional rights that either did not exist or previously had gone unnoticed. Issues of "academic due process," academic freedom, and tenure are now frequently determined in courts rather than on campuses.

Governmental regulation obviously has justification. Governments have the right to determine whether public funds are being used for intended purposes and have a legitimate interest in efficient use of those funds. The size and influence of higher education is such that it cannot be permitted to ignore issues of importance to society as a whole because of more parochial interests. Constitutional and statutory rights are sometimes invaded by men and institutions of goodwill, and victims should not be without redress because an infraction occurred on a university campus. Occasionally, universities do make serious policy mistakes, and the people have a right in extreme cases to expect their elected public officials to act if the university is unresponsive to public concerns. Together, these limitations on autonomy reflect the reality that all institutions in a modern democratic society are accountable to the public.

Accrediting associations, particularly professional associations, also limit autonomy by imposing requirements as a condition of accreditation. A university may be forced to transfer resources from one school to another to assure continued accreditation of one of its components.

Often forgotten is the influence of donors and grantors. A private individual, a foundation, or a corporation may be prepared to provide a gift, grant, or enter into a contract for a purpose that is low on a faculty priority list. Faculty may want money for faculty salaries, graduate student aid, or libraries; donors may wish to give it for organs, football, or an academic program in which they see great promise. A university may be forced to choose whether to forgo a gift or engage in an activity that it views skeptically. Whether to accept a gift or enter into a contract may produce acrimony when priorities differ within the university, particularly where the gift or contract in dispute would benefit one segment of the university at a potential long-range cost to another.

Many thoughtful observers are increasingly concerned that institutional autonomy is being endangered to a degree that values implicit in such autonomy are in serious jeopardy. The battleground in the future may well not be the extent to which faculty participate in decisionmaking within the university but what issues will be decided there.

Advice to the Young Scholar

The foregoing observations pose obvious issues for a young professor. Participation in governance will not only benefit a university, it often will benefit a participant. Nevertheless, participation may require a significant expenditure of time, perhaps a scholar's most precious resource. Involvement may also involve conflict with persons who have the power to affect promotion, salary, and tenure.

Opportunities for service are almost endless. University standing committees, boards, or councils, such as academic affairs, student life, building and grounds, business and finance, the university press, long-range planning, faculty compensation and fringe benefits, interdisciplinary programs, faculty development, the library, university computing, alumni relations and fundraising, government sponsored research, university-corporate relationships, intercollegiate athletics, social implications of investment policies, affirmative action, experimentation on human subjects, administrative oversight, research incentives, community relations, etc., abound. School opportunities, normally in the form of membership on a governing council or committee, or participation in the work of subcommittees dealing with subjects such as admissions, financial aid, curriculum, scheduling, undergraduate or graduate student life (housing, cocurricular activities, placement, etc.) need able people. Professional schools have additional committees that relate to particular professions and their concerns. A host of responsibilities, ranging from undergraduate and graduate studies to faculty appointments, require faculty involvement at the departmental level.

Some areas of possible participation are more likely to be rewarding than others. No firm rules can be laid down, but, on balance, work on committees or boards dealing with student life, building and grounds, financial or business issues, athletics, or the kind of committee that is likely to strain mightily and produce an ambiguous statement of philosophy to govern yet unknown problems is likely to be less valuable to a young scholar than service on committees that permits him or her to learn and contribute to solution of a concrete problem involving teaching or research. Service within a department where a young scholar's contribution may relate more directly to improvement of academic quality, and may be better appreciated by senior colleagues, may be especially desirable.

There are, of course, exceptions. It may be imprudent to decline an appointment by a provost or president. Service on a committee dealing with community relations may advance the young professor's professional career and benefit his institution in a small college where a tenure decision is less likely to depend upon research. In a professional school, service on a committee relating to the profession may not only serve the cause of the university, but fulfill a professional obligation, open up contacts, and suggest areas for useful research.

Some committees deal with issues that some regard as political and others as moral. Some faculty have deep beliefs that some things should or should not be done by or within a university—ROTC, government-supported "Star Wars" research, affirmative action, investment in companies doing business in South Africa, DNA research, research financed exclusively by private companies that retain patent rights, experiments upon animals, etc. Obviously, a faculty member with a deep conviction should act according to the dictates of conscience and his or her concept of the purposes of the university.

A reasonable compromise may involve commitment of service in one important capacity during untenured years and budgeting time in a way to permit such service without detracting substantially from research and teaching. Simultaneously, a young faculty member can treat other areas as appropriate subjects of study during early years in a university. Valuable experience for future leadership can be gained vicariously without expenditure of time that can endanger a promising career.

Resolution of the issue of how much time should be devoted to participation in governance and the form such participation should take may be crucial to a young scholar. Conflict exists between values to which universities pay lip service and the reward system that is operative. Universities speak of the importance of teaching, research, public service, and service in university affairs, as if all were of equal value. Such statements may be believed by the public, trustees, legislators, alumni, and students but not by those who administer the rewards system. Promotion and tenure are conferred only upon those who conduct research and publish work of high quality in many institutions.

There is frequently a wide gap between such professed values and reality. Many senior faculty who assert the right to participate in governance, and the importance of such participation, neither wish to be involved personally nor place a high value upon contributions by those who are involved. Participation in governance is not discouraged, but is given little weight in assessing a junior colleague's worth or promise. It may be even less significant than quality of teaching or public service, which are also regarded as inadequate substitutes for research. Furthermore, senior faculty may be unaware of governance participation outside a department.

The young professor who participates in governance extensively may do so at his peril. If he can do so without prejudice to his research, it will not be held against him. But every minute diverted from research is time not devoted to achievement of the primary requirement for advancement. A junior professor who participates excessively in university governance may find that he or she is an unemployed faculty leader.

Notes

1   The literature on university governance and autonomy, the nature of universities, and relationships between universities and society is voluminous. A classic, although dated, is J. Barzun, *The American University* (1968). A thoughtful recent study is W. H. Cowley, *Presidents, Professors and Trustees: The Evolution of American Academic Government* (1980). Expressions of the theme that universities are controlled by a business/professional elite who use them to serve their own parochial purposes have appeared periodically from Upton Sinclair, *The Goose Step* (1922), to D. A. Smith, *Who Rules the Universities* (1974), and B. A. Scott, *Crisis Management in Higher Education* (1983).

   The thirteen-year period between 1967 and 1980 was an especially fertile period for studies of universities, only some of which related directly to governance or autonomy. The Carnegie Commission on Higher Education published twenty-two official policy reports and eighty commissioned research studies between 1967 and 1973, culminating in its final report, *Priorities for Action* (1973). Its successor, the Carnegie Council on Policy Studies in Higher Education, published fifteen official policy studies, including its final report, *Three Thousand Futures: The Next Twenty Years in Education* (1980). The Sloan Commission on Government and Higher Education published fifty-five policy studies between 1977 and 1980, ending with *A Program for Renewed Partnership* (1980). The Carnegie Foundation for the Advancement of Teaching has more recently published *The Control of the Campus: A Report on The Governance of Higher Education* (1982). Several other commission committees and task forces supported by government or foundation funding also made major contributions. Some of the major activities are summarized in Scott supra. References will be made only to a few of the many recent books in the field.

2   Wolff listed four common concepts:

   The university as a sanctuary of scholarship; the university as a training camp for the professions; the university as a social services station; the university as an assembly line for the establishment of man, before proposing his own ideas of what a university should be. R. P. Wolff, *The Ideal of the University* (1969).

3 The Carnegie Commission on Higher Education noted five special features of governance of American educational institutions:

1. Absence of centralized control by the national government—essential authority has rested with state governments and with boards of trustees.

2. Concurrent existence of strong public and private segments.

3. Trustee responsibility—basic responsibilities to provide for governance of individual institutions has been in the hands of lay boards in both public and private institutions.

4. Presidential authority—the president has had substantial authority delegated to him by the lay board.

5. Department authority—within the faculty the department has been the key unit of academic organization over most of the past century.

These characteristics contrast with the systems of some other nations in which "(1) the central government has had more control, (2) the private sector has not been as strong, (3) a council of deans or senior faculty members has performed many of the functions of the lay board in the United States, (4) the role of the president has been carried out more largely on a ceremonial level by a rector either elected for a short term by the senior faculty or appointed by the central government, and (5) faculty authority has rested with the chair 'professors who are arranged into central faculty groupings'." *The Carnegie Commission on Higher Education, Governance of Higher Education* 5, 6 (1973).

4 S. V. Martorana, *College Boards of Trustees* 8 (1963).

5 Ibid. at 22–23.

6 Ibid. at 40–47.

7 F. J. Atelsek and I. L. Gomberg, *Composition of College and University Governing Boards* (1977).

8 M.A. Rauh, *The Trusteeship of Colleges and Universities* 5–9 (1969).

9 Perkins, *Conflicting Responsibilities of Governing Boards*, n. 7, at 203–214 (1973).

10 J. L. Fisher, *Power of the Presidency* (1984); *Presidents Make a Difference, A Report of the Commission on Strengthening Presidential Leadership* (Clark Kerr, director, 1984).

11 See note 3 supra.

12 See A. Tucker, *Chairing the Academic Department: Leadership Among Peers* (1984).

13 The "key areas" are those so denominated by Sir Eric Ashby. E. Ashby, *Any Person, Any Study: An Essay on Higher Education in the United States* (1971), summarized in L. B. Mayhew, *The Carnegie Commission on Higher Education* 278 (1974).

14 The concept of multiversity is that of Dr. Clark Kerr.

15 *The Carnegie Commission on Higher Education, Governance of Higher Education*, n. 3 at 17.

16 Cowen, "The Governance of Universities," in *Universities in the Western World* 59, 62 (P. Seabury, ed., 1975).

22   The Role of the Department in the Groves of Academe

Joel Colton

The department—the living embodiment of the scholarly discipline in which one receives one's professional training—remains at the core of every academic's life and career. "History speaking," the young teacher in *Lucky Jim*, Kingsley Amis's academic novel, announces on the office telephone, and we know at once that he does not mean the voice of the past but his department. "Who are those two?" someone asks. "One is Political Science, the other is Sociology," comes the reply, and everyone understands perfectly. In an academic novel entitled *The Department*, the hero, a professor of English about to retire, looks back over the many years in which his personal and professional life has been intertwined with those of his colleagues. Or, in a real-life episode, a popular scholar-teacher delivers a talk to a group of students extolling at length the virtues of an academic career: the lifelong opportunity for intellectual growth, the chance to participate in the world of scholarship and learning through research and publishing, the continuing invitation to assist in the expansion of young minds, a more often than not stimulating cultural and intellectual environment in which to live, the flexibility of the day-to-day and year-round work calendar, job security (compensating for lower material rewards in other professions and business), sabbaticals and additional leaves for travel and research, and other tangible and intangible benefits. When queried about any disadvantages, our speaker hesitates momentarily and replies: "Yes—the colleagues in one's department!" The reply, intentionally facetious and good-humored, brings a smile but makes a point.

What is the department? What are its origins, functions, responsibilities, authority, and power, the limits to its jurisdiction and autonomy? How does it affect academic lives and careers? How does it administer its affairs? What is its internal governance like? What tensions and frictions lie beneath the surface? How does it attempt to administer individualistic scholar-teachers, all highly trained professionals with an adamant resistance to being managed? What tensions exist between it and something called the central administration? The young academic may not learn here everything that he or she has wished to know about the department from undergraduate days on and has been afraid to ask, but some information and enlightenment may be forthcoming.

The Department and Specialization

The departments are at the heart of the teaching and research enterprise of the college and university precisely because they represent the disciplines, the specialized contributions to the perpetuation, dissemination, and advancement of knowledge that higher education is all about. These academic disciplines took shape in the last century. The liberal arts colleges, founded for the most part in the nineteenth century, believed that the goals of a liberal or general education were best accomplished through the teaching of specialized subjects. But even more so, the founders of the modern university at the end of the nineteenth century, borrowing from European prototypes, believed firmly in specialization in teaching and research. Specialization called for craftsmanship and expertise, to be perfected by young apprentices in the graduate programs and seminars offered in the departments of the major universities. From the 1870s to the present, graduate schools have demanded an "original contribution to knowledge," embodied in the doctoral dissertation, as part of one's research training and as a requirement for the Ph.D. degree, which, in turn, certifies and licenses the young scholar to become a full-fledged practitioner in the discipline, to "join" a department, and to embark on a career in teaching and research at a college or university. Specialization took on added reinforcement in this century, and especially after the Second World War, when science assumed so large a role in society and when all disciplines sought to emulate the prestige of the sciences.

It is because of the specialized disciplines that colleges and universities are divided into departments—not unlike, dare we say, Macy's or the Galeries Lafayette, where furniture, clothing, home accessories, garden equipment, and the like are all found on different floors. An institution on the average will run to about twenty-five departments, ranging alphabetically from art to zoology. In colleges, the traditional well-known arts and sciences disciplines are taught; in the universities (which by definition also have graduate M.A.

and Ph.D. programs, as well as professional schools in engineering, law, medicine, theology, and other areas) there are more exotic units; there may be, for example, a Department of Altaic and Uralic Languages. At times, loose groupings of departments, or divisions, are formed to correspond to the broader fields of scholarly inquiry, such as the humanities, the social sciences, the natural sciences. But these divisions are often employed for limited curricular and administrative purposes only and seldom impinge on the authority of the individual departments.

Specialization leads to its own problems. The discipline or department can become an end in itself. There is always the danger of lack of communication and cooperation at the expense of the broader institutional goals set by the administration and the faculty as a whole. At the very least, as a Darwinian fact of life, the departments will compete strenuously for what they consider their proper share of the college's or university's budgetary resources—and often for students because budgetary allocations (especially in public institutions) are often made in direct correlation with "full-time enrollments." Storm clouds gather when a department senses encroachment on its discipline, whether in the form of course offerings, joint faculty appointments, interdisciplinary programs, or budgetary allocations to new academic enterprises.

The picture does not end with simple specialization. Many disciplines, and hence the departments, break down further into subspecialties, so that it becomes difficult to define a faculty member simply as a professor of economics, or history, or physics; one is in economic theory or labor economics, medieval or Latin American history, low-temperature or high-energy physics. Geographical, topical, chronological, and methodological subspecialties have evolved, each with its own learned societies, annual conferences, publications. Within some larger departments these subdivisions can lead to internal competition for resources, and on occasion even to disagreement on the proper training of graduate students. The subspecialties often seek a critical mass of faculty appointments to guarantee their viability; non-Western components in history departments, always outnumbered by older areas of specialization, will often press for such appointments. In some departments, psychology as an example, experimental, clinical and social psychology components often amount to three separate departments with separate outside grants, budgets, and administrative personnel for each.

If young academics do not know much about the external relations of departments, they already know a good deal about the internal workings of an academic department even before joining one. They have "majored" in a subject, and hence in a department, as undergraduates (and perhaps have had a "second major" or "minor" as well). Moreover, their graduate training has taken place almost exclusively within a department (with perhaps a few courses in a second discipline). Subject to overall institutional regulations (e.g., length of residency, number of courses, language requirements), the department exercises virtual autonomy in determining the curriculum for the M.A. or Ph.D. degree in the discipline—the distribution of courses, the breadth and depth of knowledge to be examined in the Ph.D. general orals, the nature and quality of the dissertation. Once the new Ph.D.s go job-hunting, moreover, they quickly learn how large a role the department plays in the appointment process, from advertising the vacancy to final selection; even the letter of appointment often comes from the department chair. Less visibly to the new faculty member, an administrative officer of the college or university (the dean—generally the dean of arts and sciences or dean of faculty, but sometimes the provost or president) has invariably authorized the appointment and approved or set the salary. Although the administrative officer, along with other administrative colleagues, may meet the candidate during the campus visit, the major contacts—interviews with individual faculty or groups of faculty, the seminar presentation, social gatherings —will be with the department and its members. For a junior appointment, the administration will generally accept the department's recommendation.

For all searches and appointments these days, however, the department may be reminded that it is no longer the independent agent that it once was. The dean may ask the department: How carefully did it search? Did it advertise the position adequately? Did it take care to track down minority candidates? Were there women candidates? Despite growing self-consciousness over the past several decades and conscious efforts to change matters, academic departments have remained notoriously male and white—before the Second World War they were overwhelmingly male, white, and Protestant —and the reminders are necessary. The former "old-boy" network of recruitment—the quick personal phone call by a department chair to a favored graduate department asking for a suitable newly trained Ph.D. to fill a vacant slot—is less the practice and at least in theory no longer permissible. Moreover, since the 1960s, because of the expanded need for faculty at the time and the simultaneous emergence of many additional graduate departments offering the Ph.D. degree, colleges and universities now recruit more broadly geographically than ever in the past.

Subject to overall administrative controls—a phrase that inevitably appears frequently in these remarks—the department continues to play a major role in one's career after appointment: in the renewal of the appointment, the promotion from assistant to associate professor, the award of tenure (generally at the end of six or seven years), the promotion to full professor. (The old rank of instructor, incidentally, once the initial rank of appointment for the new Ph.D., went by the boards in the 1960s, although it is still retained for part-time or for non-tenure-track positions.)

Although new assistant professors become members of the faculty of the college or university to which they are appointed, and have a vague feeling of such faculty solidarity, they are immeasurably more closely identified with their department from the moment of their arrival on campus. In many career patterns they may remain members of that department for their entire career, with close professional and personal attachments to department colleagues, and even if one moves off to another institution, those bonds may last. Despite the jesting remarks cited about "colleagues" at the opening of this essay, some of one's closest friends will be members of the department that one has joined; common professional interests and personal attachments, despite frictions and tensions, bind members of a department with strong and lasting ties.

Departmental Responsibilities

Not until one is a member of a department does one fully appreciate how much of a beehive of activity it is. Its responsibilities are many, whether it is small (two to six members, say in a college) or large (thirty to sixty or more, in a university). Heading the department in all instances is the chair, whose special functions merit separate consideration below. The budget is central to the department's operations—and the most important limit on its autonomy. Annually, the chair submits a budget on behalf of the department with a supporting report and detailed documentation to the appropriate dean. Typically, the budget request seeks funding for new appointments, salary increments, secretarial support, office and laboratory space, supplies and equipment; a graduate department will also seek funds for graduate fellowships and assistantships. The dean and other central administrative officers must assess the competing budgetary requests that arrive from all departments, each couched in equally persuasive rhetoric and buttressed with equally convincing arguments and statistics. At the administrative level, decisions have to be made on the basis of the institution's goals, resources, and short- and long-term commitments, all of which are debated and set by the highest administrative echelons on up to the president and eventually by the trustees, who have the special responsibility to oversee the long-range welfare of the institution as they understand it. At that point, sometimes, one is far removed from the day-to-day frontline activities of departments and faculties. Among the faculty, especially in their role as members of departments, there is an inherent suspicion, half-jesting, half-earnest, about something called "the administration," and a tacit (or voiced) concern that it will subordinate educational goals and faculty needs to other objectives—buildings and grounds, athletics, public relations, additional administrative appointments, and the like. Tensions, in varying degrees and forms, between central administrations and departments are never absent from academic life; nothing unites a divided department like griping about the administration.

As to the budget, the departments bargain competitively, sometimes feverishly, for their share of the budgetary pie in a *bellum omnium contra omnes*. Without adequate resources, they argue, how does an ambitious department recruit and retain first-rate faculty? carry out its teaching responsibilities? encourage research? or, if a graduate department, attract the most promising graduate students? Some departments press their claims with self-confidence and aplomb; others follow the precept that the squeaky wheel gets the lubrication. But bargain competitively they all do, conceding only grudgingly the need for administrative allocation of limited institutional resources. In the natural sciences, more so than in other areas, it must be added, large outside grants from government and private funding sources are often available to supplement college or university allocations.

No matter what their research concerns, a primary responsibility of the departments is to satisfy teaching demands. The department advises its majors and other students, disseminates information about courses and faculty, and responds to inquiries. Each semester the chair, with the help of selected associates, determines teaching schedules, remembering (or being reminded of) each faculty member's foibles and other relevant factors: the owl who is of no use in the morning, the lark who chirps cheerfully only in the morning, the colleague who is willing to teach a section of introductory courses, the colleague who is not, the colleague willing to teach freshmen, and the colleague from whom freshmen must be protected. The department arranges coverage for faculty members on sabbatical or other leaves, often not knowing the details of these leaves until the late spring, when many outside fellowships and grants are announced. Within the framework of the overall curriculum established by the faculty as a whole and the administration (and perennially reviewed), the department shapes the requirements for the major, deciding on the number and sequence of courses to be taken, distribution among subdivisions within the department (organic, inorganic chemistry; English, American literature, etc.) It reviews and reorganizes the introductory courses. It tries not only to provide coverage of the subject matter but to offer also a variety of forms of instruction—lectures, discussion groups, seminars, colloquia, preceptorials, tutorials, honors programs, independent study. (Similarly, with variations, if a graduate department, it makes arrangements for its graduate program.) It also decides, on the basis of changes in faculty personnel or changing faculty interests, on courses to be introduced, modified, or dropped. The faculty as a whole will exercise some jurisdiction over these courses—largely to avoid duplication and proliferation—but the principal initiative for course offerings and listings rests with the individual departments. The department, moreover, will gather statistics on course enrollments, students taught, full- and part-time instructional personnel, and other data, all of which are useful for historical reasons, for forecasting—and justifying—budgetary requests.

The department, principally through the chair, also carries on extensive day-to-day correspondence. As a communications link it represents the department to the profession as a whole; many of the professional organizations publish a directory of the larger departments in the discipline. It circulates to members of the department information about fellowships and grants and about conferences to be held. In graduate departments it circulates information to the graduate professors of vacancies in other institutions which might be filled by the department's new Ph.D.s. It replies to letters from the public, or is called upon to assist in such replies by undergraduate and graduate admissions officers. The chair is in constant touch with officers of the central administration—the deans and the associate and assistant deans, the bursar's office, the registrar—and with other academic departments. All correspondence of individual faculty members with the administration, such as requests for leaves, is funneled through the department. The chair's mailbox is never empty.

The Day-to-Day Operations

How, then, are these extensive operations carried out? Obviously the magnitude of the operation varies with the size of the department and the number of students taught, and whether it is also a graduate program; but not surprisingly, many of the same functions are carried out even by small departments. Departments organize themselves to carry out these functions in a variety of ways but follow many common patterns. At the top of the structure, needless to say, is the chair. In larger departments, the chair may ask two or three faculty members to accept appointment for a period of time to assist in the administrative chores, say to supervise graduate studies or undergraduate studies or freshman instruction or to act as overall assistant chairpersons. In that way some of the duties are divided up, although the chair is never relieved of primary responsibility.

For its daily tasks a department almost invariably comes to depend upon the sine qua non of a well-run department—a long-term, experienced department secretary (or administrative assistant) who has lived through many incumbencies of the chair, and from experience knows the administrative ropes about a multitude of matters—the budget, the mail, the never-ending paperwork, the files, statistics, and requisitioning of supplies. The department secretary keeps in constant touch with faculty members, undergraduates, graduate students, department alumni, the staff in other department and administrative offices, and with everyone else at the college or university in ways that are indispensable to the chair. Like a first sergeant in the army or a chief petty officer in the navy, the department secretary facilitates the work of the commanding officer in immeasurable ways. Woe to the young newly commissioned second lieutenant or ensign (read: newly commissioned Ph.D. –assistant professor) who fails to respect the authority of the office or does not quickly learn that courtesy and deference will accomplish more than pulling rank or throwing one's (not very substantial) weight around. In a good-sized department a core of at least three or four additional secretaries will form part of the staff—and department family—and be available to provide secretarial assistance to the individual members of the faculty. No department, let it be noted, has ever been able to meet the secretarial needs of its faculty, especially when the demands converge, as they invariably do, at the same time, and in this, as in other matters, the chair is called upon to use consummate skill in mediating such conflicts and in sorting out priorities.

Democracy, in Winston Churchill's formula, is the worst form of government until one considers the alternatives. And democracy, in a department, works through committees. The chair will need and appoint faculty committees, standing (or continuing) and ad hoc. An executive committee, about which more will be said, is also often appointed or elected. The department may have among its standing committees a committee on courses (and a committee on the introductory course or courses), a library committee (to coordinate acquisitions and purchases), a committee on audiovisual materials or laboratory equipment, a committee on outside lecturers, and many others. Ad hoc committees will be periodically appointed, such as a long-range planning committee to review the department's strengths and weaknesses at any given time and to help plan future development. A similar committee may prepare materials for outside evaluations requested by the administration or required by a state board or commission of higher education or in connection with a site visit by an accrediting or funding agency. Many ad hoc committees will be appointed for personnel matters. A search committee may help seek out candidates for an authorized vacancy (at any level) and do much of the preliminary sifting of credentials and interviewing before candidates are invited to the campus. An ad hoc committee may evaluate the file of a member of the department coming up for contract renewal or tenure or for promotion to associate or full professor and make a preliminary assessment for the department's consideration.

Although no alternative to committees has ever been invented, the consequence can be many committees, much committee work, and endless deliberations. Add in the college or university committees (again, standing and ad hoc) on which a faculty member is asked to serve (curriculum, courses, admissions, academic standards, the library, athletic policies, parking facilities, student publications, the United Way and other charities, the university press, personnel evaluations, etc.), and the burden visibly mounts. As time goes by, faculty members may expect more and more committee responsibilities, not less, both in the department and in the institution—with the exception of some colleagues who succeed in demonstrating or dramatizing their ineptitude for such assignments. Nor should one forget the time consumed (but not begrudged) when one is elected by department colleagues or by the faculty as a whole to such representative governing bodies as faculty senates and undergraduate or graduate faculty councils. Everyone is expected to play a role in "secondary management" in higher education.

The young faculty member may mercifully be spared many of these committee assignments, or a thoughtful chair may intervene to "protect" the young colleague if excessive requests are made from outside the department. On the other hand, the junior faculty member can learn a good deal and gain valuable perspectives from working with faculty colleagues within the department and even more across the disciplines. The danger (for younger and older faculty alike) is that they may be distracted (or consciously or unconsciously seek distraction) from research responsibilities. When the times for tenure and promotion and other personnel decisions arrive, attention will be paid, to be sure, to institutional and departmental committee work, but no amount of "service" (or for that matter—in universities at least—even evidence of outstanding teaching) is likely to compensate for the absence of publications that signify a continuing commitment to research and scholarship. There are few exceptions to this rule at major universities, where the faculty enjoy reduced teaching loads (two or three courses per semester, as against four or even more elsewhere) specifically to have time for research and writing. At the stronger liberal arts colleges, teaching and service components may be given significant weight in personnel decisions, but the research and publication record will not be ignored. On the other hand, in many small colleges where the faculty is small and the teaching load is heavy, and a diversity of courses remote from one's specialty are to be taught, teaching is often given the highest priority, and it is recognized that the kind of research that leads to publication is difficult to carry on. At some small colleges, one hears, publication and research may even be viewed negatively, interpreted as a neglect of one's teaching responsibilities; one dean is reputed to have remarked: "If my faculty published, my college would perish."[1] The tensions between teaching and research are omnipresent, in every institution and every department, even if on a different scale and in different ways. Few departments or institutions, however, no matter how eager they are to earn reputations for research and publication, will be sanguine about professors who cut corners on their teaching responsibilities and minimize the time and attention given to students in order to rush off to the library, laboratory, typewriter, word processor, test tube, computer, or nuclear accelerator.

The Functions of the Chair

All this detail is by way of explaining how much goes on in a department. There is, however, another intriguing set of questions. How are decisions made? What forms of governance have evolved? What authority does the department possess?

For a long time, at least until the 1950s, the administration of academic departments remained an anachronism in a democratic society. The chair, either alone or with a small group of senior professors, ran the department's affairs under an authoritarian or at best an oligarchical regime. With the expansion of faculties after the Second World War, the pattern underwent initial change, and with further expansion and the campus upheavals of the late 1960s and early 1970s, it evolved in even more striking ways. From "prehistoric" times to this relatively recent past, the chair of the department, often called the "head," was generally appointed by the dean or other central administrative officer for an indefinite period of time and held office until retirement. It was tacitly understood that he or she—generally in those days, it was "she" only in women's colleges—represented the administration to the department. It is still possible to find a department head (and still called that) appointed by an administration in this same way for an indefinite period of time, but the practice is disappearing. This older pattern somewhat resembles the European and British model, where a single professor (Professor, capital p) often heads a large department, presiding over numerous senior lecturers, lecturers, readers, assistants, fellows, and tutors. It remains the pattern in American schools of medicine where many departments are still run under long-term continuing appointments, with the chair exerting the predominant authority.

Under the newer scheme, in liberal arts and sciences departments at least, it has become increasingly common for the chair to be rotated, the term of office limited (two, three, or five years, with renewals possible), and the appointment based on close consultation with the department through nominations to the administration or even election. Although debate may still continue about the primary allegiance of the chair, it is fair to say that with a strong department voice in the selection the incumbent tends to view the office as representing the department to the administration rather than vice versa—even though an astute department chair will quickly understand the need to reconcile department goals with those of the administration as skillfully as possible.

In the majority of cases, the chair is chosen from within the department (and administrations are generally relieved when this is possible). A 1984 survey of 323 history departments revealed that 94 percent of the chairs acquired the position from within the department.[2] An appointment from the outside, however, is not to be ruled out. If a department is perceived (sometimes by the department faculty members themselves) as weak or not living up to its potential, rent by factionalism (not unknown in departments), or thought to be in need of a major reorientation, the administration may select a head or chair from outside the institution. Even then, these days, the department generally participates in the search and meets with candidates before an appointment is made.

That the chair is now rotational and less powerful than previously, and departments more democratically run, does not mean that the office of the chair is unimportant. The incumbent is not likely any longer to be an autocrat, or even a benevolent despot; word of autocracy or despotism would quickly get around in the profession and make faculty recruitment (and retention) impossible. Under the new model, however, the chair need not be merely a presiding officer or convener. Even if decisionmaking is shared with the department, much latitude remains for leadership, initiative, resourcefulness, and imagination on the part of an able incumbent.

About the office, past and present, few have written more perceptively or picturesquely than a seasoned former chair of a major university department of history. "There are many kinds of chairmen," he writes and proceeds to describe the most objectionable or least desirable:

> There is the enlightened despot. There is the unenlightened despot. There is the enlightened despot whose enlightenment is fading. There is the dean's viceroy, a Levantine opportunist who by deception and guile carries out the dean's intentions, which he can never disclose. There is the conscientious presiding officer, who rigorously executes the will of the majority, even when it is destructive or unjust. There is the party chieftain, ruling in the name of the dominant faction. There is the Phanariot hospodar [*sic!*], a Balkan carpetbagger who plunders the travel and entertainment funds and has his courses taught by the serfs of the junior faculty. There is the native son, custodian of those fashions called tradition, who tries to keep the future continuous with the fabled past. Finally, there is the manager, champion of accountability and productivity, who works under enrollment-driven budgets and labors to produce a healthy bottom line.[3]

The list, be it noted, is far from complete and does not rule out an overlapping of the categories. The usual disclaimers about resemblance to former or present holders of the office, living or dead, might be in order, but few incumbents these days would resemble any of these disagreeable portraits. A wise chair, in contemporary times, knows that authority must be exercised but also shared, a pattern that has increasingly become the rule.

The governance of departments varies with the history and traditions of departments. Generally, each department determines its own "constitution" and rules of procedure, sometimes as a matter of custom and tradition, sometimes in written bylaws. Many departments will have an executive committee to help in the governance of the department, consisting of two or three ex officio members (those assisting in the administrative chores of the department) and the remaining members elected by the department, with specific provision sometimes made for representation of junior, nontenured faculty. Like a presidential cabinet, an executive committee is generally advisory to the chair. It meets regularly, relieving the department of the need for overly frequent meetings—often a source of complaint and contention in a large department. The chair keeps the executive committee informed of negotiations with the administration and calls attention to pending or emerging issues, personnel and otherwise. The executive committee in turn keeps the chair enlightened on the tides of opinion within the department—in all ranks—on a variety of matters, nominates colleagues for committees, shares in preliminary discussions on personnel and other matters, and helps keep the lines of communication open between chair and department.

The chair's tasks remain formidable. It is a continuing challenge to administer a group of professionals, all of whom are rugged individualists, not readily amenable to direction or management and eager only to be left alone to carry out their professional and personal pursuits. Yet, if these individualists are not consulted or brought into the decisionmaking process when major departmental interests or concerns are involved, the reverberations will be consequential. Democracy or not, the senior professors remain self-consciously important, and a major problem for any chair is to keep the department's "prima donnas" happy—even if, as one chair noted testily, some of them cannot even carry a tune. The judicious chair, even if the office is construed as primus inter pares, can still be more primus than pares and can exercise genuine leadership, but only through consultation and consensus.

The everyday pressures on the chair itself are many. An industrious and efficient chair must foresee needs, keep ahead of deadlines, keep cool in the midst of friction, and head off gathering resentments and grievances. As part of the duties of the office the chair guards the department's confidential records and correspondence, manages and evaluates the nonacademic secretarial and laboratory staff as well as academic colleagues, meets with students and student committees, listens to complaints of faculty and students, keeps colleagues informed about vital statistics in the department —marriages, births, illnesses, deaths, etc.—and keeps up with news of emeriti and alumni. The chair may preside over social gatherings of the department at his or her home or elsewhere or may organize dinners or receptions to welcome visiting lecturers or to honor retiring colleagues. (An alert chair keeps a ready list of the birth dates of members of the department to remind the department and the dean of retirement vacancies and replacements.) The chair may organize an all-day "retreat" to assess the strengths and weaknesses of the department and plan for the future. There are hospital or home visits to stricken colleagues and on an even more somber note, memorial services to preside over or participate in for those who have died in retirement or in active service; at such services the department sits in a body in a final gesture of guildlike fraternity. (From Ph.D. sheepskin to terminal shroud the department will ever be with ye!) A proper chair will also preserve the traditions and memories of the department, keep confidential any skeletons in the departmental closet, and make every effort to see to it that humane relations are maintained in the department regardless of the deep political, intellectual, professional disagreements, and even factionalism that may exist.

The duties and responsibilities are many and tell something about the qualities called for in the ideal chair. A partial job description would read: mediator, negotiator, and arbitrator; budget, personnel, and recruiting officer; advisor on community housing and schooling, and on career opportunities for spouses; chief justice; pastor; parliamentarian; social director; lecture bureau director; team coach; Dutch uncle (or aunt); statistician; housekeeper; general office manager; and personal counselor and mentor. One could easily add to or amend the list; one former chair has included "jungle fighter" in his description. The seasoned observer quoted earlier, reinforcing the personal counseling duties mentioned above, reminds us that a chair must be concerned with many personal situations that may undermine the effectiveness of colleagues: "If Tacitus freezes at the sight of his typewriter, or Livy abuses the students, or Suetonius becomes enslaved to Bacchus, then the [chair] must consider how best to help them." And he concludes: "A department realizes its full potential when all its faculty members are achieving the highest quality of scholarship, teaching and service of which they are capable."[4]

This latter statement—to help a department realize its "full potential" —may explain why anyone accepts appointment to the chair. Why else would anyone be willing to take on the responsibilities and headaches? "I have no more taste for housekeeping than does my wife," said one chair.[5] The material rewards and perquisites are small—a reduction in teaching load, a modest stipend (described by one dispensing dean as "aspirin money"), some small travel and entertainment funds, a more commodious office (at least during the incumbency). One answer, of course, is that not many are asked—or chosen. Many (including some excellent scholars) are ruled out from consideration—by their colleagues or by administrators—for reasons of temperament or other personality factors. Many take the job precisely because it is on a rotational limited-time basis and their "turn" has arrived or they look to it as a change of pace; others may take it to head off a rival candidate considered undesirable. The time for choosing a chair, incidentally, can raise anxieties to a feverish pitch. One faculty member has remarked that it is more important to know who the next chair of one's department will be than to know who is to be the next president of the college or university.

Most frequently, those who accept the post see it as an opportunity to be of service in advancing the growth and development of the department by influencing appointments and other personnel decisions and by competing actively and successfully in the institution's budgetary politics. In larger departments in universities many believe that they can enhance the department's national stature and visibility, as mirrored in various professional ratings of departments (e.g., those of the American Council on Education). To be rated among the top five (or even top ten or twenty) departments in one's discipline is a goal many departments believe worth striving for. These peer ratings are based on the reputation of the departments as measured by faculty publications, fellowships, grants, prizes, appointments to the boards of editors of professional journals, and election to national academies or to presidencies and other offices in leading professional associations. Although the ratings are sometimes subjective—they may reflect reputations from bygone days like the light from distant stars—there is generally a correlation between the ratings and achievement. The chair with ambitions for the department, like an athletic coach, brings the record of accomplishments to the attention of the department, boasts of or bemoans its national standing, and exhorts it to mightier efforts. The chair will also employ prestigious ratings as a bargaining chip with the administration.

One unenviable responsibility of the chair is to evaluate annually, in connection with the annual budget report and salary increases, each faculty member in the department, from the senior ranks to the most recent junior appointee, on the basis of their teaching, research, and service. No one has ever evaluated professional colleagues easily. What to do about the slow-publishing scholar who at the end of many years will produce a volume of lasting distinction or a few seminal articles, as against the colleague who publishes many articles or even books of lesser distinction? How to take into account a strong teaching record based on enthusiastic student teacher-course evaluations if unaccompanied by scholarly accomplishment? (How to evaluate student teacher-course evaluations in general?) What of the faithful committee member, and the faithful department servant, with minimal tangible evidence of research and publication? What of the faculty member who is sought elsewhere and must be given additional remuneration and other blandishments to be retained? What of deserving colleagues, solid and responsible scholar-teachers, whose real salary has become seriously eroded by inflation and in need of a major adjustment? The chair's judgments go forward to the administration which then translates them into annual "merit" increases (over and above any minimum "cost-of-living" increases). Be it noted that the departments (and the faculty as a whole) have little or no voice in the total sums set aside by the administration for salary increases. The departments, through their respective chairs, can only help the administration allocate the merit increases by assessing the professional contributions of the faculty in their departments. Although minimum and median salaries for faculty at all ranks are available through the cooperation of college and university administrations in the annual reports published by the AAUP (American Association of University Professors), individual salaries are another matter. They are often public knowledge at state and municipal institutions, or at least available to those who seek them out; in private colleges and universities they are, traditionally, closely guarded state secrets, kept confidential and locked away in the files of the department and administration. The secretiveness and confidentiality take on ironic dimensions when one realizes the limited range of all academic salaries; in the liberal arts and sciences, at least, from beginning assistant professor to retiring full professor, the spread is something like a factor of three, small indeed compared to other professions and occupations. But that does not make salaries, annual increments, and the modest differentials any less important nor the department chair's annual task any easier. With confidentiality the rule, one has to trust in the equity, fair-mindedness, professionalism, and sober judgment of the chair, and indeed of the administration.

Younger faculty members soon learn that another key responsibility of the conscientious chair is to serve as their chief mentor. By exercising the proper influence and leadership in the recruitment process, the chair can see to it from the beginning that only young persons of the highest promise are chosen. Then, by constant vigilance, tactful supervision, and frequent consultation the chair, on behalf of the department, can make sure that the newly appointed faculty members understand the rules of the game, sharing with them any written or unwritten bylaws and procedures. The chair assists or should assist them in all ways possible to meet the teaching, research, and service criteria set up by the institution and the department for promotion and tenure. The chair may find it necessary to help them overcome problems of initial adjustment to teaching and should promptly share any adverse criticisms that may surface, perhaps in student evaluations of classroom performance. If necessary, the chair should protect the young faculty from excessive committee assignments or other administrative chores that might interfere with their research, and even seek released duties for them at critical junctures in their research and writing. In universities at least, the young faculty must be periodically reminded, if reminders are called for, that of the teaching, research, and service trinity, the most important remains research, as reflected in publication. In short, the chair should encourage, counsel, scold if necessary, and take all conceivable measures to nurture the young faculty—and help weed out the less promising candidates for permanent appointments. Finally, the painful duty also devolves on the chair to break the news to the young colleague if the decision of the department or the administration on renewal or tenure is negative and share the reasons why, aware that such a decision in times of job scarcity can mean termination of an academic career in many disciplines. "Termination—always horrible," tersely commented one chair.[6]

A proper chair will oversee the department's personnel procedures and deliberations equitably and judiciously, appoint balanced and fair-minded ad hoc personnel committees, and present departmental recommendations to the administrative authorities effectively and persuasively. All personnel decisions, but especially tenure decisions, occasion soul-searching difficulties in a department (and in an institution). It falls to the responsibilities of the chair to oversee the entire, often tumultuous, process, and to communicate its results—to the administration, to the university's tenure and promotion committee, and to the candidate (see Professor Goodwin's essay earlier in this volume). Some of these are pleasant chores; others are among any chair's most painful obligations.

Limits on Departmental Autonomy

We have said much about the authority and autonomy of the department, and something of the limitations imposed upon it, but more needs to be said about the waning of departmental authority in recent years. College- and university-wide appointment, promotion, and tenure committees operate to curb the department's traditional power in personnel matters. On another front administrations have tended to encourage interdisciplinary programs and interdepartmental coordination, partly for sound intellectual reasons, partly in times of inflation and slow faculty growth to maximize existing resources and effect necessary economies. Programs, institutes, and joint appointments have come into administrative favor, transcending the authority of the single department. Since the 1960s a number of inter- or codisciplinary fields of study have developed. These programs often represent cooperative endeavors arising out of the combined initiatives of several departments, in which case there is no problem. But at other times programs, centers, and entire institutes emerge from student pressure or from administrative initiative or because they are part of the national academic scene. In other instances administrators (with the support of many faculty) will encourage curricular changes that the departments perceive as weakening their hold on courses that once met requirements for the degree and hence meant large student enrollments. Interdisciplinary courses in a "core curriculum" may replace older departmental offerings, or a writing program may be instituted quite separate from an English department. Many of these new academic activities run counter to the disciplinary specialization embodied in the traditional departments and are viewed as threatening their autonomy or at least as diverting funds from them. Where opposition is impossible, departments will press, with varying success, to retain control over the faculty associated with these programs in order to have a voice in personnel decisions.

On still another front differences emerge between departments and administrations over vacancies to be filled within departments. For budgetary or other institutional reasons administrations sometimes resist departmental requests for replacements when faculty retire or resign to go elsewhere, or at least replacements in the very same narrow specialty being vacated. (The art of the French baroque must be taught, the Art Department will argue; the specialist in Kant must be replaced, Philosophy will contend.) For some vacancies administrators will approve replacements at a lower rank than the department seeks. At the other end of the spectrum some ambitious and energetic administrations will cajole or pressure departments into accepting high-priced luminary or "star" appointments in a search for "instant visibility." Departments are sometimes reluctant to turn down such appointments but are often apprehensive about the financial implications or the promotion opportunities for the present faculty or do not see the appointments as fitting the priorities they have themselves set.

Aware of the tender sensitivities of the departments, administrators impinge upon departmental autonomy as diplomatically as possible, but they do so nevertheless. When these administrative forays are made, many a department will forget its sharp internal divisions and draw together in a siege mentality to protect its territorial boundaries against the perceived threat. No matter what the philosophical and educational justification for the administrative initiatives, the departments will often adamantly resist them or accept them reluctantly when they are introduced. In the tensions that arise between departments and administrators it is not always the administrators who play the conservative role. The departments, it cannot be denied, represent a form of vested interest that it is difficult to dislodge. Although the conclusion may be contested by some, a scholar in his recent "biography" of a major university bluntly sums up the tug of war in a conclusion not flattering to the departments: "In a modern university the reformers, the idealists, even the would-be utopians, are most often administrators. . . . The resistance to change comes from the academic provinces, from the tough oligarchs that run departments, those who often are brilliant and innovative in their own scholarship, possibly leftist in their political leanings."[7] They are willing, he is saying, to challenge received truths in their scholarship and combat vested interests in society—but not in their universities.

The latent tensions between departments and central administrations can at times result in conflicted loyalties. Yet the tension should not be exaggerated. The faculty as a whole, through its representative bodies, and even departments, will often subordinate disciplinary and departmental interests to broader educational objectives in establishing or revising the curriculum and in other matters or will demonstrate a sensitivity to budgetary stringencies that demand economies and limitations on expenditures. Moreover, there is tacit recognition that only through mutual cooperation of the department and the administration can the welfare of the institution be sustained. Administrators also recognize that the prestige and stature of the institution rest in the final analysis on the faculty, trained in specialized disciplines, and organized into departments, stubborn obstacles though they may be at times to the administrators' own agenda. Lastly, administrators know that their most productive faculty, despite institutional loyalties, can always be lured away by better opportunities elsewhere—to another department in another institution. In times of expansion and mobility such movements happen frequently, but even in times of reduced mobility "raiding" takes place and invitations to join other institutions are forthcoming to top scholars. Such invitations are based almost wholly on professional achievements and reputation within the discipline. It is a sign of a department's and institution's strength and prestige when its faculty are sought elsewhere. With the support of the administration, the department may seek to counter such "outside offers," negotiating special salary increases or other emoluments, sometimes with success, sometimes without. At the same time, alert departments and supportive administrations will be out "raiding" other institutions and recruiting for their own faculty.

Throughout an academic career one remains as much a member of a department as of one's professional discipline. One is, to be sure a professor at X College or Y University, but one is also a biologist, classicist, economist, geologist, mathematician, political scientist, sociologist, philologist, physicist, etc. (Presumably, at least in theory, one could earn a living by practicing that profession—but try hanging out a shingle as Middle English scholar or French Revolution specialist.) Academics, whether they teach at small colleges or large universities, are also reminded of their discipline when each year they attend their professional meetings, or "conventions," organized by the many alphabet-soup national learned societies (AEA, AHA, APA, MLA, PSA, etc.) or the even more subspecialized organizations. They meet at these annual meetings, discuss current research, read and debate each other's papers, participate in panel discussions, and listen to presidential and other addresses, but they also renew personal and professional ties—with old friends of graduate school days, with the older scholars under whom they once studied, and with the younger scholars whom they themselves have "trained" (perhaps as dissertation advisor, or *Doktorvater*, in the quaint German term). Invariably, conversation turns at some point to the departments in which they all teach and carry on their professional lives. The department, a corporate entity with its collective ego, represents on each campus the guild into which one is initiated for life upon receiving one's Ph.D. in a given branch of knowledge that we call a discipline.

If we learn anything from this essay, it is that the department remains at the center of one's academic life and career. We learn also that life within a department as a junior or senior faculty member bears little resemblance to the fabled ivory tower. The department, if it is ambitious, vigorous, aggressive, and competitive, is necessarily a focal point for continuing intellectual and political tensions and conflicts—within itself, with other departments, with administrations. Within the department, the clash of mind and will frequently matches the bitter battles of corporate boardrooms even if, ironically, the financial stakes are hardly comparable. Both in colleges and universities, in good times or bad, under able central administrative leadership or weak, with serious-minded students or frivolous, with more rigorous or more permissive curricula, in periods of growth or contraction, one's academic life and career are more closely linked to one's department (capital D) than to any other segment of the college or university campus.

Notes

1   William Heywood, "Administering the History Department." *AHA [American Historical Association] Newsletter* 17, no. 4 (April 1979): 12.

2   John M. McGuire, "History Department Chairs: Characteristics, Influence and Role," *Perspectives* [American Historical Association Newsletter] 23, no. 4 (April 1985): 13.

3   George P. Taylor, "Administration of Large Departments," *AHA Newsletter* 17, no. 5 (May 1979): 13.

4   Ibid., p. 15.
5   Samuel P. Hays, "On Having Been a Departmental Chairman," *AHA Newsletter* 17, no. 3 (March 1979): 12.
6   McGuire, "History Department Chairs," p. 14.
7   Paul K. Conkin, *Gone With the Ivy: A Biography of Vanderbilt University* (Knoxville, University of Tennessee Press, 1985), p. 395. The quotation first came to my attention in a review of the volume by Thomas G. Dwyer in the *Journal of Southern History* 53 (August 1986): 499.

Selected Further Readings

Adams, Hazard. *The Academic Tribes*. New York: Liveright, 1976.

Behling, J. H. *Guidelines for Preparing the Research Proposal*. Lanham: University Press of America, 1984.

Bower, Howard R., and Jack H. Schuster. *American Professors*. New York: McGraw-Hill, 1986.

Cahn, Steven M. *Saints and Scamps: Ethics in Academia*. Totowa, N.J.: Rowman and Littlefield, 1986.

Caplan, Theodore, and Reece McGee. *The Academic Marketplace*. New York: Ayer, 1972.

The Chicago Manual of Style. 13th ed. Chicago: University of Chicago Press, 1982.

Conrad, D. L. *The Quick Proposal Workbook*. San Francisco: Public Management Institute, 1980.

Cook, Claire Kehrwald. *Line by Line: How to Edit Your Own Writing*. Boston: Houghton Mifflin, 1985.

Council of Biology Editors Style Manual. 4th ed. Washington, D.C.: Council of Biology Editors, 1978.

Day, R. A. *How to Write and Publish a Scientific Paper*. 2d ed. Philadelphia: ISI Press, 1983.

DeSole, Gloria, and Leonore Hoffmann, eds. *Rocking the Boat: Academic Women and Academic Processes*. New York: Modern Language Association, 1981.

Dowell, Walter W. *Getting Into Print: The Decision Making Process in Scholarly Publishing*. Chicago: University of Chicago Press, 1985.

Dudovitz, Resa L., ed. *Women in Academe*. New York: Pergamon Press, 1984.

Gullett, Margaret M., ed. *The Art and Craft of Teaching*. Cambridge: Harvard University Press, Harvard-Danforth Center for Teaching, 1984.

Hall, Roberta M., and Bernice R. Sandler. *The Classroom Climate: A Chilly One for Women?* Washington, D.C.: Project on the Status and Education of Women, 1982.

Higham, Robin. *The Compleat Academic*. New York: St. Martin's, 1974.

Ikenberry, Stanley O., and Renee C. Friedman. *Beyond Academic Departments*. San Francisco: Jossey-Bass, 1972.

Pelikan, Jaroslav, et al. *The Teaching of Values in Higher Education: A Seminar*. Washington, D.C.: Woodrow Wilson International Center for Scholars, 1986.

Schuster, Marilyn R., and Susan R. Van Dyne. *Women's Place in the Academy*. Totowa, N.J.: Rowman and Allanheld, 1985.

Seldin, Peter. *Changing Practices in Faculty Evaluation.* San Francisco: Jossey-Bass, 1984.

Shils, Edward. *The Academic Ethic.* Chicago: University of Chicago Press, 1983.

Smelser, Neil J., and Robin Content. *The Changing Academic Market.* Berkeley: University of California Press, 1980.

Strunk, W., Jr., and E. B. White. *The Elements of Style.* 3d ed. New York: Macmillan, 1979.

Theodore, Athena. *The Campus Troublemakers: Academic Women in Protest.* Houston: Cap and Gown Press, 1986.

Touraine, Alain. *The Academic System in American Society.* New York: McGraw-Hill, 1974.

Ulich, Robert. *Three Thousand Years of Educational Wisdom.* Cambridge: Harvard University Press, 1954.

Veysey, Lawrence R. *The Emergence of the American University.* Chicago: University of Chicago Press, 1965.

Whitehead, Alfred North. *Aims of Education and Other Essays.* New York: Macmillan, 1929.

Index

Library of Congress Cataloging-in-Publication Data
The Academic's handbook / edited by A. Leigh DeNeef, Craufurd D.
Goodwin, and Ellen Stern McCrate.
p.   cm.
Bibliography: p.
Includes index.
ISBN 0-8223-0742-1.   ISBN 0-8223-0807-X (pbk.) : $12.95
1. College teachers—United States.   2. Universities and colleges—
United States.   I. DeNeef, A. Leigh.   II. Goodwin, Craufurd D. W.
III. McCrate, Ellen Stern.
LB1778.A24 1988
378'.12—dc19   87-32958